2014 | World Development Indicators

THE WORLD BANK

Preface

In 2013 the World Bank Group announced that it would focus on two overarching measurable goals: ending extreme poverty by 2030 and promoting shared prosperity. The chance to end poverty in a generation is an unprecedented opportunity—and one that requires data to monitor progress, to understand the complexities of development, and to manage the effective delivery of programs and services.

World Development Indicators 2014 provides a compilation of relevant, high-quality, and internationally comparable statistics about global development and the fight against poverty. It is intended to help users of all kinds—policymakers, students, analysts, professors, program managers, and citizens—find and use data related to all aspects of development, including those that help monitor and understand progress toward the two goals.

Six themes are used to organize indicators—world view, people, environment, economy, states and markets, and global links. As in past editions, *World view* reviews global progress toward the Millennium Development Goals (MDGs) and provides key indicators related to poverty. A complementary online data analysis tool is available this year to allow readers to further investigate global, regional, and country progress on the MDGs: http://data.worldbank.org/mdgs. Each of the remaining sections includes an introduction; six stories highlighting specific global, regional, or country trends; and a table of the most relevant and popular indicators for that theme, together with a discussion of indicator compilation methodology.

This printed edition, and its companion *The Little Data Book 2014*, presents a subset of the data collected in World Development Indicators; an index to the full list of available indicators is at the end of each section. Many additional relevant indicators are available online, in database and tabular formats, and through applications for web and mobile devices, at http://data.worldbank.org/wdi. Online applications also provide the indicator description and footnotes in several languages, including Arabic, Chinese, French, and Spanish.

World Development Indicators is the result of a collaborative effort of many partners, including the United Nations family, the International Monetary Fund, the International Telecommunication Union, the Organisation for Economic Co-operation and Development, the statistical offices of more than 200 economies, and countless others. I am extremely grateful to them all—and especially to government statisticians around the world. Without their hard work, professionalism, and dedication, measuring and monitoring trends in global development, and advancing toward the new World Bank goals, would not be possible.

I welcome your suggestions to improve the usefulness of *World Development Indicators*.

Haishan Fu
Director
Development Economics Data Group

Acknowledgments

This book was prepared by a team led by William Prince under the management of Neil Fantom and comprising Azita Amjadi, Maja Bresslauer, Liu Cui, Federico Escaler, Mahyar Eshragh-Tabary, Juan Feng, Masako Hiraga, Wendy Ven-dee Huang, Bala Bhaskar Naidu Kalimili, Haruna Kashiwase, Buyant Erdene Khaltarkhuu, Tariq Khokar, Elysee Kiti, Ibrahim Levent, Hiroko Maeda, Maurice Nsabimana, Leila Rafei, Evis Rucaj, Umar Serajuddin, Rubena Sukaj, Emi Suzuki, Jomo Tariku, and Rasiel Victor Vellos, working closely with other teams in the Development Economics Vice Presidency's Development Data Group.

World Development Indicators electronic products were prepared by a team led by Soong Sup Lee and comprising Ying Chi, Jean-Pierre Djomalieu, Ramgopal Erabelly, Shelley Fu, Omar Hadi, Gytis Kanchas, Siddhesh Kaushik, Ugendran Machakkalai, Nacer Megherbi, Shanmugam Natarajan, Parastoo Oloumi, Manish Rathore, Ashish Shah, Atsushi Shimo, and Malarvizhi Veerappan.

All work was carried out under the direction of Haishan Fu. Valuable advice was provided by Poonam Gupta, Zia M. Qureshi, and David Rosenblatt.

The choice of indicators and text content was shaped through close consultation with and substantial contributions from staff in the World Bank's four thematic networks—Sustainable Development, Human Development, Poverty Reduction and Economic Management, and Financial and Private Sector Development—and staff of the International Finance Corporation and the Multilateral Investment Guarantee Agency. Most important, the team received substantial help, guidance, and data from external partners. For individual acknowledgments of contributions to the book's content, see *Credits*. For a listing of our key partners, see *Partners*.

Communications Development Incorporated provided overall design direction, editing, and layout, led by Jack Harlow, Bruce Ross-Larson, and Christopher Trott. Elaine Wilson created the cover and graphics and typeset the book. Peter Grundy, of Peter Grundy Art & Design, and Diane Broadley, of Broadley Design, designed the report. Staff from The World Bank's Publishing and Knowledge Division oversaw printing and dissemination of the book.

Table of contents

Preface   iii

Acknowledgments   iv

Partners   vi

User guide   xii

1. **World view**   1

2. **People**   27

3. **Environment**   43

4. **Economy**   57

5. **States and markets**   71

6. **Global links**   85

Primary data documentation   99

Statistical methods   110

Credits   113

Introduction
MDG 1 Eradicate extreme poverty
MDG 2 Achieve universal primary education
MDG 3 Promote gender equality and
        empower women
MDG 4 Reduce child mortality
MDG 5 Improve maternal health
MDG 6 Combat HIV/AIDS, malaria, and
        other diseases
MDG 7 Ensure environmental sustainability
MDG 8 Develop a global partnership for
        development
Targets and indicators for each goal
World view indicators
About the data
Online tables and indicators
Poverty indicators
About the data

Introduction
Highlights
Table of indicators
About the data
Online tables and indicators

Partners

Defining, gathering, and disseminating international statistics is a collective effort of many people and organizations. The indicators presented in *World Development Indicators* are the fruit of decades of work at many levels, from the field workers who administer censuses and household surveys to the committees and working parties of the national and international statistical agencies that develop the nomenclature, classifications, and standards fundamental to an international statistical system. Nongovernmental organizations and the private sector have also made important contributions, both in gathering primary data and in organizing and publishing their results. And academic researchers have played a crucial role in developing statistical methods and carrying on a continuing dialogue about the quality and interpretation of statistical indicators. All these contributors have a strong belief that available, accurate data will improve the quality of public and private decisionmaking.

The organizations listed here have made *World Development Indicators* possible by sharing their data and their expertise with us. More important, their collaboration contributes to the World Bank's efforts, and to those of many others, to improve the quality of life of the world's people. We acknowledge our debt and gratitude to all who have helped to build a base of comprehensive, quantitative information about the world and its people.

For easy reference, web addresses are included for each listed organization. The addresses shown were active on March 1, 2014.

International and government agencies

Carbon Dioxide Information Analysis Center	**International Diabetes Federation**
http://cdiac.ornl.gov	www.idf.org
Centre for Research on the Epidemiology of Disasters	**International Energy Agency**
www.emdat.be	www.iea.org
Deutsche Gesellschaft für Internationale Zusammenarbeit giz	**International Labour Organization**
www.giz.de	www.ilo.org
Food and Agriculture Organization	**International Monetary Fund**
www.fao.org	www.imf.org
Internal Displacement Monitoring Centre	**International Telecommunication Union**
www.internal-displacement.org	www.itu.int
International Civil Aviation Organization	**Joint United Nations Programme on HIV/AIDS** 
www.icao.int	www.unaids.org

Partners

National Science
Foundation

www.nsf.gov

The Office of U.S. Foreign
Disaster Assistance

www.globalcorps.com/ofda.html

Organisation for Economic
Co-operation and
Development

www.oecd.org

Stockholm International
Peace Research Institute

www.sipri.org

Understanding
Children's Work

www.ucw-project.org

United Nations

www.un.org

United Nations Centre for
Human Settlements,
Global Urban Observatory

www.unhabitat.org

United Nations
Children's Fund

www.unicef.org

United Nations Conference on
Trade and Development

www.unctad.org

United Nations Department of
Economic and Social Affairs,
Population Division

www.un.org/esa/population

United Nations Department of
Peacekeeping Operations

www.un.org/en/peacekeeping

United Nations Educational,
Scientific, and Cultural Organization,
Institute for Statistics

www.uis.unesco.org

United Nations
Environment Programme

www.unep.org

United Nations Industrial
Development Organization

www.unido.org

United Nations
International Strategy
for Disaster Reduction

www.unisdr.org

United Nations Office on
Drugs and Crime

www.unodc.org

United Nations Office
of the High Commissioner
for Refugees

www.unhcr.org

United Nations
Population Fund

www.unfpa.org

Upsalla Conflict
Data Program

www.pcr.uu.se/research/UCDP

World Bank

http://data.worldbank.org

World Health Organization

www.who.int

World Intellectual
Property Organization

www.wipo.int

World Tourism
Organization

www.unwto.org

World Trade
Organization

www.wto.org

Partners

Private and nongovernmental organizations

Center for International Earth Science Information Network

www.ciesin.org

Containerisation International

Lloyd's List CONTAINERISATION

www.ci-online.co.uk

DHL

www.dhl.com

International Institute for Strategic Studies

IISS

www.iiss.org

International Road Federation

IRF

www.irfnet.ch

Netcraft

http://news.netcraft.com

PwC

www.pwc.com

Standard & Poor's

STANDARD
&POOR'S

www.standardandpoors.com

World Conservation Monitoring Centre

www.unep-wcmc.org

World Economic Forum

WORLD
ECONOMIC
FORUM

www.weforum.org

World Resources Institute

www.wri.org

User guide to tables

World Development Indicators is the World Bank's premier compilation of cross-country comparable data on development. The database contains more than 1,300 time series indicators for 214 economies and more than 30 country groups, with data for many indicators going back more than 50 years.

The 2014 edition of *World Development Indicators* offers a condensed presentation of the principal indicators, arranged in their traditional sections, along with regional and topical highlights.

World view   People   Environment

Economy   States and markets   Global links

Tables

The tables include all World Bank member countries (188), and all other economies with populations of more than 30,000 (214 total). Countries and economies are listed alphabetically (except for Hong Kong SAR, China and Macao SAR, China, which appear after China).

The term *country,* used interchangeably with *economy,* does not imply political independence but refers to any territory for which authorities report separate social or economic statistics. When available, aggregate measures for income and regional groups appear at the end of each table.

Aggregate measures for income groups

Aggregate measures for income groups include the 214 economies listed in the tables, plus Taiwan, China, whenever data are available. To maintain consistency in the aggregate measures over time and between tables, missing data are imputed where possible.

Aggregate measures for regions

The aggregate measures for regions cover only low- and middle-income economies.

The country composition of regions is based on the World Bank's analytical regions and may differ from common geographic usage. For regional classifications, see the map on the inside back cover and the list on the back cover flap. For further discussion of aggregation methods, see *Statistical methods.*

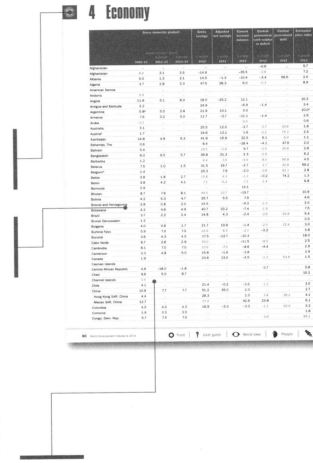

Data presentation conventions

- A blank means not applicable or, for an aggregate, not analytically meaningful.
- A billion is 1,000 million.
- A trillion is 1,000 billion.
- Figures in blue italics refer to years or periods other than those specified or to growth rates calculated for less than the full period specified.
- Data for years that are more than three years from the range shown are footnoted.
- The cutoff date for data is February 1, 2014.

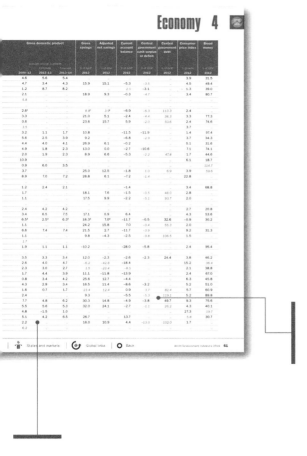

Classification of economies

For operational and analytical purposes the World Bank's main criterion for classifying economies is gross national income (GNI) per capita (calculated using the *World Bank Atlas* method). Because GNI per capita changes over time, the country composition of income groups may change from one edition of *World Development Indicators* to the next. Once the classification is fixed for an edition, based on GNI per capita in the most recent year for which data are available (2012 in this edition), all historical data presented are based on the same country grouping.

Low-income economies are those with a GNI per capita of $1,035 or less in 2012. Middle-income economies are those with a GNI per capita of more than $1,035 but less than $12,616. Lower middle-income and upper middle-income economies are separated at a GNI per capita of $4,085. High-income economies are those with a GNI per capita of $12,616 or more. The 18 participating member countries of the euro area are presented as a subgroup under high-income economies.

Statistics

Additional information about the data is provided in *Primary data documentation,* which summarizes national and international efforts to improve basic data collection and gives country-level information on primary sources, census years, fiscal years, statistical methods and concepts used, and other background information. *Statistical methods* provides technical information on some of the general calculations and formulas used throughout the book.

Symbols

..	means that data are not available or that aggregates cannot be calculated because of missing data in the years shown.
0 or 0.0	means zero or small enough that the number would round to zero at the displayed number of decimal places.
/	in dates, as in 2011/12, means that the period of time, usually 12 months, straddles two calendar years and refers to a crop year, a survey year, or a fiscal year.
$	means current U.S. dollars unless otherwise noted.
<	means less than.

Country notes

- Cabo Verde is the new name for the country previously listed as Cape Verde.
- Data for China do not include data for Hong Kong SAR, China; Macao SAR, China; or Taiwan, China.
- Data for Serbia do not include data for Kosovo or Montenegro.
- Data for Sudan include South Sudan unless otherwise noted.

User guide to WDI online tables

Statistical tables that were previously available in the *World Development Indicators* print edition are available online. Using an automated query process, these reference tables are consistently updated based on revisions to the World Development Indicators database.

How to access WDI online tables

To access the WDI online tables, visit http://wdi.worldbank.org/tables. To access a specific WDI online table directly, use the URL http://wdi.worldbank.org/table/ and the table number (for example, http://wdi.worldbank.org/table/1.1 to view the first table in the *World view* section). Each section of this book also lists the indicators included by table and by code. To view a specific indicator online, use the URL http://data.worldbank.org/indicator/ and the indicator code (for example, http://data.worldbank.org/indicator/SP.POP.TOTL to view a page for total population).

Breadcrumbs to show
where you've been

Click on an indicator
to view metadata

Click on a country
to view metadata

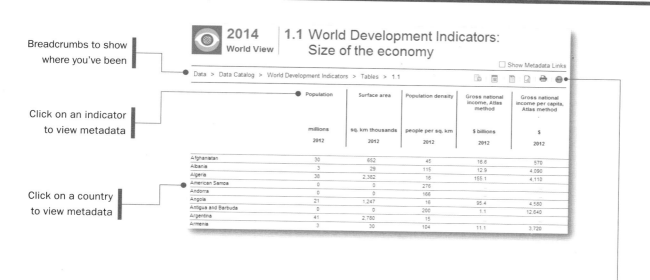

How to use DataBank

DataBank (http://databank.worldbank.org) is a web resource that provides simple and quick access to collections of time series data. It has advanced functions for selecting and displaying data, performing customized queries, downloading data, and creating charts and maps. Users can create dynamic custom reports based on their selection of countries, indicators, and years. All these reports can be easily edited, saved, shared, and embedded as widgets on websites or blogs. For more information, see http://databank.worldbank.org/help.

Actions

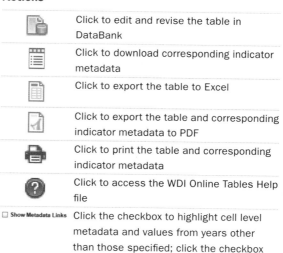

	Click to edit and revise the table in DataBank
	Click to download corresponding indicator metadata
	Click to export the table to Excel
	Click to export the table and corresponding indicator metadata to PDF
	Click to print the table and corresponding indicator metadata
	Click to access the WDI Online Tables Help file
☐ Show Metadata Links	Click the checkbox to highlight cell level metadata and values from years other than those specified; click the checkbox again to reset to the default display

User guide to DataFinder

DataFinder is a free mobile app that accesses the full set of data from the World Development Indicators database. Data can be displayed and saved in a table, chart, or map and shared via email, Facebook, and Twitter.

DataFinder works on mobile devices (smartphone or tablet computer) in both offline (no Internet connection) and online (Wi-Fi or 3G/4G connection to the Internet) modes.

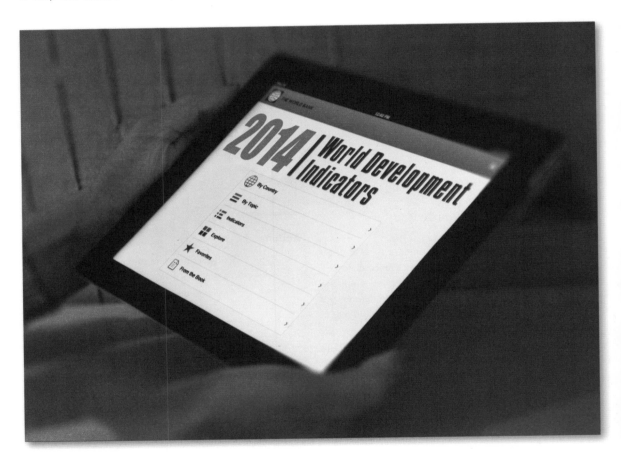

- Select a topic to display all related indicators.
- Compare data for multiple countries.
- Select predefined queries.
- Create a new query that can be saved and edited later.

- View reports in table, chart, and map formats.
- Send the data as a CSV file attachment to an email.
- Share comments and screenshots via Facebook, Twitter, or email.

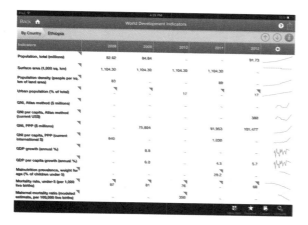

Table view provides time series data tables of key development indicators by country or topic. A compare option shows the most recent year's data for the selected country and another country.

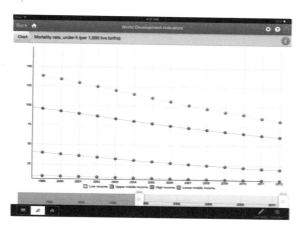

Chart view illustrates data trends and cross-country comparisons as line or bar charts.

Map view colors selected indicators on world and regional maps. A motion option animates the data changes from year to year.

Economy | States and markets | Global links | Back

User guide to MDG Data Dashboards

The World Development Indicators database provides data on trends in Millennium Development Goals (MDGs) indicators for developing countries and other country groups. Each year the World Bank's *Global Monitoring Report* uses these data to assess progress toward achieving the MDGs. Six online interactive MDG Data Dashboards, available at http://data.worldbank.org/mdgs, provide an opportunity to learn more about the assessments.

The MDG progress charts presented in the *World view* section of this book correspond to the *Global Monitoring Report* assessments (except MDG 6) and cannot be compared with those in previous editions of *World Development Indicators*. Sufficient progress indicates that the MDG will be attained by 2015 based on an extrapolation of the last observed data point using the growth rate over the last observable five-year period (or seven-year period, in the case of MDG 7). Insufficient progress indicates that the MDG will be met between 2016 and 2020. Moderately off track indicates that the MDG will be met between 2020 and 2030. Seriously off track indicates that the MDG will not be met by 2030. Insufficient data indicates an inadequate number of data points to estimate progress or that the MDG's starting value is missing.

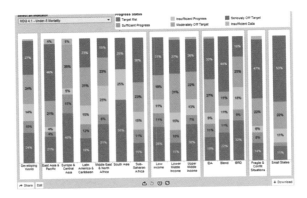

View progress status for regions, income classifications, and other groups by number or percentage of countries.

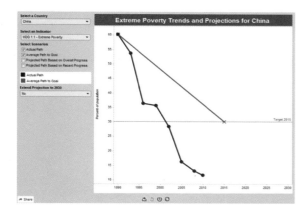

View details of a country's progress toward each MDG target, including trends from 1990 to the latest year of available data, and projected trends toward the 2015 target and 2030.

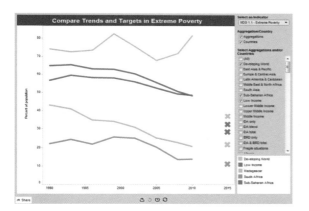

Compare trends and targets of each MDG indicator for selected groups and countries.

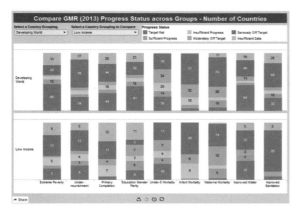

Compare the progress status of all MDG indicators across selected groups.

WORLD VIEW

World view presents progress toward the eight Millennium Development Goals (MDGs), drawing on the charts of progress in online interactive visualizations (http://data.worldbank.org/mdgs). It complements the detailed analysis in the World Bank Group's *Global Monitoring Report*, and it uses the same methodology to assess whether countries are on track or off track to meet the targets by 2015.

The new twin goals of the World Bank Group, announced in October 2013, are to end extreme poverty and to boost shared prosperity across the world. Progress will be closely monitored using two indicators: the proportion of the population living on less than $1.25 a day (in 2005 purchasing power parity terms) and the growth in the average real per capita income of the bottom 40 percent of the population in every country. While poverty rates have fallen across the world, progress has been uneven, and meeting the new targets will require a sustained effort. As Jim Yong Kim said in the World Bank's 2013 *Annual Report*, "We must halve poverty once, then halve it again, and then nearly halve it a third time—all in less than one generation."

Two tables in *World view* present the latest estimates of poverty rates at the international poverty line. The World Development Indicators online database and tabular presentations also present poverty rates at national poverty lines. Work is under way to develop a reliable database of growth in the per capita incomes of the bottom 40 percent of the population in most countries. We expect to publish it later in 2014 as part of World Development Indicators online.

The target year of 2015 for the MDGs is now just around the corner. One important aspect of the MDGs has been their focus on measuring and monitoring progress; this has presented a clear challenge in improving the quality, frequency, and availability of relevant statistics. In the last few years much has been done by both countries and international partners to invest in the national statistical systems where most data originate. But weaknesses remain in the coverage and quality of many indicators in the poorest countries, where resources are scarce and careful measurement of progress may matter the most. While the focus will continue to be on achieving the MDGs, especially in areas that have been lagging, the international community has started to discuss what comes next.

The 2013 report of the 27-member High-Level Panel on the Post-2015 Development Agenda, convened by the UN Secretary-General, recognizes the important role of data and the challenge of improving development data. It calls for a "data revolution for sustainable development, with a new international initiative to improve the quality of statistics and information available to citizens." This is timely and welcome, as is the panel's call to "take advantage of new technology, crowd sourcing, and improved connectivity to empower people with information on the progress toward the targets." Both governments and development partners should invest in national statistical systems, where much of the data will continue to originate.

MDG 1 Eradicate extreme poverty

Poverty rates continue to fall · 1a

People living on less than $1.25 a day (% of population)

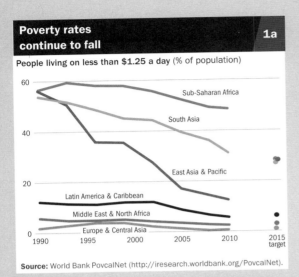

Source: World Bank PovcalNet (http://iresearch.worldbank.org/PovcalNet).

Progress in reaching the poverty target by region · 1b

Countries making progress toward reducing extreme poverty (% of countries in region)

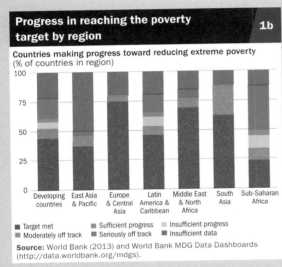

- ■ Target met
- ■ Moderately off track
- ■ Sufficient progress
- ■ Seriously off track
- □ Insufficient progress
- ■ Insufficient data

Source: World Bank (2013) and World Bank MDG Data Dashboards (http://data.worldbank.org/mdgs).

Progress by income and lending group · 1c

Countries making progress toward reducing extreme poverty (% of countries in group)

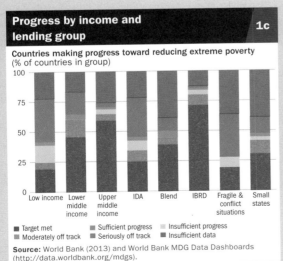

- ■ Target met
- ■ Moderately off track
- ■ Sufficient progress
- ■ Seriously off track
- □ Insufficient progress
- ■ Insufficient data

Source: World Bank (2013) and World Bank MDG Data Dashboards (http://data.worldbank.org/mdgs).

The world will not have eradicated extreme poverty in 2015, but it will have met the Millennium Development Goal target of halving world poverty. The proportion of people in developing countries (those classified as low and middle income in 1990) living on less than $1.25 a day fell from 43.1 percent in 1990 to 20.6 percent in 2010 and reached a new low in five of six developing country regions. Except in South Asia and Sub-Saharan Africa the target was met at the regional level by 2010 (figure 1a).

Further progress is possible—and likely—before the 2015 target date. Developing economies are expected to maintain GDP growth of 5.3–5.5 percent over the next two years, with GDP per capita growth around 4.2 percent. Growth will be fastest in East Asia and Pacific and in South Asia, which still have more than half the world's poorest people. Growth will be slower in Sub-Saharan Africa, the poorest region, but faster than in the preceding years, quickening the pace of poverty reduction. According to these forecasts, the proportion of people living in extreme poverty will fall to 16 percent by 2015.

Based on current trends, around 40 percent of developing countries have already achieved the first Millennium Development Goal, and only 17 percent are seriously off track, based on the methodology used in the 2013 *Global Monitoring Report* (World Bank 2013). However, in Sub-Saharan Africa up to a third of countries are seriously off track—meaning that they would be unable at current rates of progress to halve extreme poverty rates by 2030 (figure 1b). Progress is also sluggish among countries classified as fragile and conflict situations and small states (figure 1c).

Data gaps remain and hinder the monitoring of progress. About a fifth of developing countries have not conducted a survey since 1990, the minimum requirement for monitoring progress when using national accounts data to interpolate or extrapolate survey data. By number of countries the gaps are greatest in East Asia and Pacific and especially among small states and fragile and conflict situations (figures 1b and 1c).

Poverty estimates for 2010 are provisional; revised estimates will be published later in 2014, along with new estimates for 2011. Any revisions will affect estimated projections to 2015.

MDG 2 Achieve universal primary education

The commitment to provide primary education to every child is the oldest of the Millennium Development Goals, having been set at the first Education for All conference in Jomtien, Thailand, more than 20 years ago.

Primary completion rates—the proportion of new entrants in the last grade of primary school—reached nearly 90 percent for developing countries as a whole in 2009 but have since stalled, with no appreciable gains in any region. Three regions have attained or are close to attaining universal primary education: East Asia and Pacific, Europe and Central Asia, and Latin America and the Caribbean. Completion rates in the Middle East and North Africa have stayed at 90 percent since 2009. South Asia has reached 88 percent, but progress has been slow. And Sub-Saharan Africa lags behind at 70 percent (figure 2a).

Progress among the poorest countries has accelerated since 2000, particularly in South Asia and Sub-Saharan Africa, but full enrollment remains elusive. Fifty-three countries have achieved or are on track to achieve the Millennium Development Goal, while 38 countries remain seriously off track (figure 2b). Even if the schools in these countries were to now enroll every eligible child in the first grade, they would not be able to meet the 2015 deadline.

Another challenge is helping more children stay in school. Many children start school but drop out before completion, discouraged by cost, distance, physical danger, and failure to progress. Today, 55 million primary school–age children remain out of school in low- and middle-income countries—80 percent of them in Sub-Saharan and South Asia, where dropout rates are highest (figure 2c).

Even as countries approach the Millennium Development Goal target, the education demands of modern economies expand, and primary education will increasingly be of value only as a stepping stone toward secondary and higher education. In that context, demand is growing for measuring and monitoring education quality and learning achievement. The primary completion rate does not always ensure the quality of education, and some children complete basic education without acquiring adequate literacy and numeracy skills.

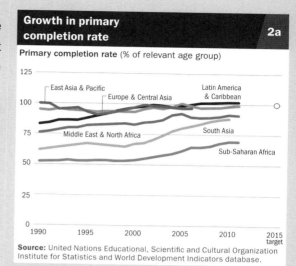

Growth in primary completion rate 2a

Primary completion rate (% of relevant age group)

Source: United Nations Educational, Scientific and Cultural Organization Institute for Statistics and World Development Indicators database.

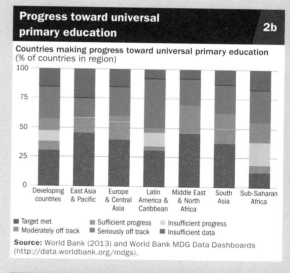

Progress toward universal primary education 2b

Countries making progress toward universal primary education (% of countries in region)

- Target met
- Sufficient progress
- Insufficient progress
- Moderately off track
- Seriously off track
- Insufficient data

Source: World Bank (2013) and World Bank MDG Data Dashboards (http://data.worldbank.org/mdgs).

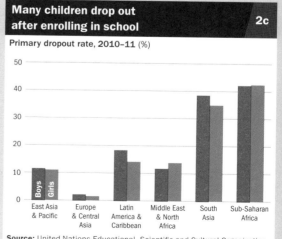

Many children drop out after enrolling in school 2c

Primary dropout rate, 2010–11 (%)

Source: United Nations Educational, Scientific and Cultural Organization Institute for Statistics and World Bank EdStats database.

MDG 3 Promote gender equality and empower women

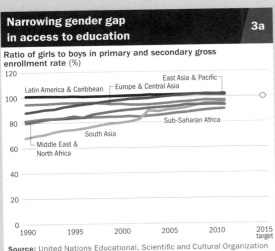

Narrowing gender gap in access to education — 3a

Ratio of girls to boys in primary and secondary gross enrollment rate (%)

Latin America & Caribbean
Europe & Central Asia
East Asia & Pacific
Sub-Saharan Africa
South Asia
Middle East & North Africa

1990 · 1995 · 2000 · 2005 · 2010 · 2015 target

Source: United Nations Educational, Scientific and Cultural Organization Institute for Statistics and World Development Indicators database.

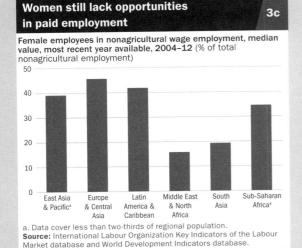

Progress toward gender equality in education — 3b

Countries making progress toward gender equality in education (% of countries in region)

Developing countries · East Asia & Pacific · Europe & Central Asia · Latin America & Caribbean · Middle East & North Africa · South Asia · Sub-Saharan Africa

■ Target met   ■ Sufficient progress   ■ Insufficient progress
■ Moderately off track   ■ Seriously off track   ■ Insufficient data

Source: World Bank (2013) and World Bank MDG Data Dashboards (http://data.worldbank.org/mdgs).

Women still lack opportunities in paid employment — 3c

Female employees in nonagricultural wage employment, median value, most recent year available, 2004–12 (% of total nonagricultural employment)

East Asia & Pacific[a] · Europe & Central Asia · Latin America & Caribbean · Middle East & North Africa · South Asia · Sub-Saharan Africa[a]

a. Data cover less than two-thirds of regional population.
Source: International Labour Organization Key Indicators of the Labour Market database and World Development Indicators database.

Women make important contributions to economic and social development. Expanding their opportunities in the public and private sectors is a core development strategy, and education is the starting point. By enrolling and staying in school, girls gain skills to enter the labor market, care for families, and make decisions for themselves.

Girls have made substantial gains in school enrollment. In 1990 girls' primary school enrollment rate in developing countries was only 86 percent of boys'. By 2011 it was 97 percent. Improvements in secondary schooling have also been made, with girls' enrollments having risen from 77 percent of boys' in 1990 to 96 percent in 2011. But the averages mask large differences across and within countries. Low-income countries lag far behind, and only 8 of 36 countries reached or exceeded equal education for girls in primary and secondary education. Poor households are less likely than wealthy households to keep their children in school, and girls from wealthier households are more likely to enroll in school and stay longer.

Women work long hours and contribute much to their families' welfare, but many are in the informal sector or are unpaid for their labor. The highest proportion of women in wage employment in the nonagricultural sector (median value) is in Europe and Central Asia (46 percent). The lowest is in Middle East and North Africa (16 percent) and South Asia (19 percent), where women's full economic empowerment remains a distant goal.

More women are taking part in public life at the highest levels. The share of parliamentary seats held by women continues to increase. The largest gains have been in the Middle East and North Africa, where the proportion more than quadrupled between 1990 and 2013, though it remains a mere 16 percent.

Lack of data hampers the ability to understand women's roles in the economy. Led by the Inter-agency and Experts Group on Gender Statistics, many new international initiatives—including the World Bank's gender statistics projects, Evidence and Data for Gender Equality, and Data2X—are tackling the paucity of data by mapping data gaps, providing technical assistance, and developing methods to produce statistics in emerging areas.

MDG 4 Reduce child mortality

In 1990, 13 million children died before their fifth birthday. By 1999 fewer than 10 million did. And in 2012, 7 million did. Over that time the under-five mortality rate in developing countries fell 46 percent, from an average of 99 per 1,000 live births in 1990 to 53 in 2012. The rates remain much higher in Sub-Saharan Africa and South Asia than in the other four developing country regions (figure 4a). All developing regions except for Sub-Saharan Africa have halved their under-five mortality rate since 1990. Overall, progress has been substantial, but globally the rate of decline is insufficient to achieve Millennium Development Goal 4 to reduce the under-five mortality rate by two-thirds between 1990 and 2015. However, the average annual rate of decline in under-five mortality accelerated, from 1.2 percent in 1990–95 to 3.9 percent in 2005–12. This recent progress is close to the average needed to be on track to achieve Millennium Development Goal 4 (figure 4b).

Most children die from causes readily preventable or curable with existing interventions, such as pneumonia (17 percent), diarrhea (9 percent), and malaria (7 percent). Roughly 70 percent of deaths of children under age 5 occur in the first year of life, and 60 percent of those in the first month. Preterm birth complications account for 15 percent of deaths, and complications during birth another 10 percent (UNICEF 2013). Reducing child mortality thus requires addressing the causes of neonatal and infant deaths: malnutrition, poor sanitation, inadequate care at and after birth, and exposure to acute and chronic disease.

Improving infant and child mortality are the largest contributors to higher life expectancy in most countries. Childhood vaccinations are a proven, cost-effective way of reducing childhood illness and death. But despite years of vaccination campaigns, many children in low- and lower middle-income economies remain unprotected, as with measles. To succeed, vaccination campaigns must reach all children and be sustained over time. That is why it is worrisome that measles vaccination rates in the two highest mortality regions, South Asia and Sub-Saharan Africa, have stagnated in the last three years, at less than 80 percent coverage (figure 4c).

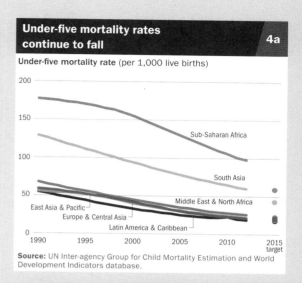

Under-five mortality rates continue to fall 4a

Under-five mortality rate (per 1,000 live births)

Source: UN Inter-agency Group for Child Mortality Estimation and World Development Indicators database.

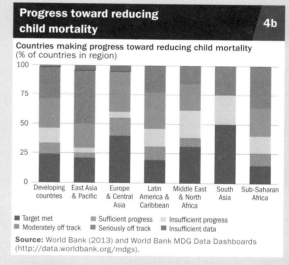

Progress toward reducing child mortality 4b

Countries making progress toward reducing child mortality (% of countries in region)

- Target met
- Moderately off track
- Sufficient progress
- Seriously off track
- Insufficient progress
- Insufficient data

Source: World Bank (2013) and World Bank MDG Data Dashboards (http://data.worldbank.org/mdgs).

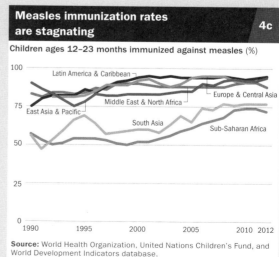

Measles immunization rates are stagnating 4c

Children ages 12–23 months immunized against measles (%)

Source: World Health Organization, United Nations Children's Fund, and World Development Indicators database.

MDG 5 Improve maternal health

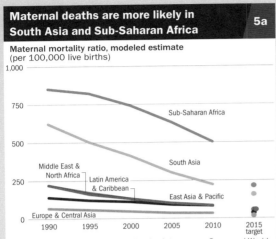

Maternal deaths are more likely in South Asia and Sub-Saharan Africa · 5a

Maternal mortality ratio, modeled estimate
(per 100,000 live births)

- Sub-Saharan Africa
- South Asia
- Middle East & North Africa
- Latin America & Caribbean
- East Asia & Pacific
- Europe & Central Asia

Source: UN Maternal Mortality Estimation Inter-agency Group and World Development Indicators database.

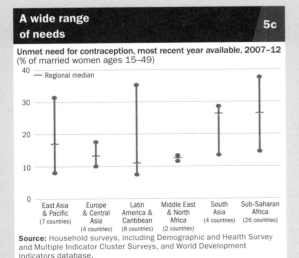

Progress toward reducing maternal mortality · 5b

Countries making progress toward reducing maternal mortality
(% of countries in region)

Developing countries · East Asia & Pacific · Europe & Central Asia · Latin America & Caribbean · Middle East & North Africa · South Asia · Sub-Saharan Africa

- Target met
- Moderately off track
- Sufficient progress
- Seriously off track
- Insufficient progress
- Insufficient data

Source: World Bank (2013) and World Bank MDG Data Dashboards (http://data.worldbank.org/mdgs).

A wide range of needs · 5c

Unmet need for contraception, most recent year available, 2007–12
(% of married women ages 15–49)

— Regional median

East Asia & Pacific (7 countries) · Europe & Central Asia (4 countries) · Latin America & Caribbean (8 countries) · Middle East & North Africa (2 countries) · South Asia (4 countries) · Sub-Saharan Africa (26 countries)

Source: Household surveys, including Demographic and Health Survey and Multiple Indicator Cluster Surveys, and World Development Indicators database.

An estimated 287,000 maternal deaths occurred worldwide in 2010, a 47 percent decline since 1990. All but 2,400 maternal deaths were in developing countries. In 2010 more than half the maternal deaths were in Sub-Saharan Africa and a quarter in South Asia. While the number of maternal deaths remains high in South Asia, the region has made the most progress toward the Millennium Development Goal target, reaching a maternal mortality ratio of 220 per 100,000 live births in 2010, down from 620 in 1990, a reduction of 65 percent. The Middle East and North Africa and East Asia and Pacific have also reduced their maternal mortality ratios more than 60 percent (figure 5a).

These achievements are impressive, but progress in reducing maternal mortality ratios has been slow, far slower than the 75 percent reduction between 1990 and 2015 imagined by the Millennium Development Goals. Few countries and no developing region on average will achieve this target. But the average annual rate of decline has accelerated, from 2.1 percent in 1990–95 to 4.3 percent in 2005–10. This recent progress is closer to the average rate needed to be on track to achieve Millennium Development Goal 5 (figure 5b).

Better maternal health care and lower fertility can reduce maternal deaths. Family planning and access to contraception can help avoid the large number of births that are unwanted or mistimed. At least 200 million women want to use safe and effective family planning methods but are unable to do so (figure 5c; UNFPA 2014).

Many health problems among pregnant women are preventable or treatable through visits with trained health workers before childbirth. Good nutrition, vaccinations, and treating infections can improve outcomes for mother and child. Skilled attendants at delivery and access to hospital treatments are essential for dealing with life-threatening emergencies such as severe bleeding and hypertensive disorders. In South Asia and Sub-Saharan Africa many births are not attended by doctors, nurses, or trained midwives.

Front | User guide | World view | People | Environment

MDG 6 Combat HIV/AIDS, malaria, and other diseases

Epidemic diseases exact a huge toll in human suffering and lost development opportunities. Poverty, armed conflict, and natural disasters contribute to the spread of disease and are made worse by it. In Africa the spread of HIV/AIDS has reversed decades of improvement in life expectancy and left millions of children orphaned. Malaria takes a large toll on young children and weakens adults at great cost to their productivity. Tuberculosis killed 900,000 people in 2012, most of them ages 15–45, and sickened millions more.

In 2012 35 million people were living with HIV/AIDS, and 2.3 million more acquired the disease. Sub-Saharan Africa remains the center of the epidemic, but the proportion of adults living with AIDS has begun to fall even as the survival rate of those with access to antiretroviral drugs has increased (figures 6a and 6b). At the end of 2012, 9.7 million people in developing countries were receiving antiretroviral drugs. The scale-up has been exponential in recent years (UNAIDS 2013) but still far short of universal access.

In 2012 8.6 million people were newly diagnosed with tuberculosis, but incidence, prevalence, and death rates are falling (figure 6c). If these trends are sustained, the world could achieve the target of halting and reversing the spread of tuberculosis by 2015. People living with HIV/AIDS, which reduces resistance to tuberculosis, are particularly vulnerable, as are refugees, displaced persons, and prisoners living in close quarters and unsanitary conditions. Well managed medical intervention using appropriate drug therapy is crucial to stopping the spread of tuberculosis.

There were an estimated 200 million cases of malaria in 2012, causing 600,000 deaths (WHO 2013). Malaria is a disease of poverty, but there has been progress. Although it occurs in all regions, Sub-Saharan Africa is where the most lethal malaria parasite is most abundant. Insecticide-treated nets have proved effective for prevention, and their use is growing.

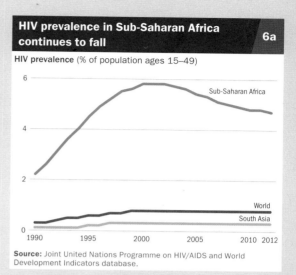

HIV prevalence in Sub-Saharan Africa continues to fall — 6a

HIV prevalence (% of population ages 15–49)

Source: Joint United Nations Programme on HIV/AIDS and World Development Indicators database.

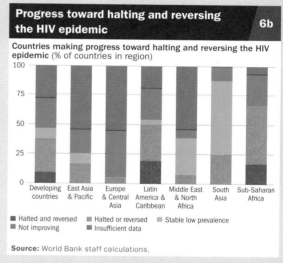

Progress toward halting and reversing the HIV epidemic — 6b

Countries making progress toward halting and reversing the HIV epidemic (% of countries in region)

- ■ Halted and reversed
- ■ Not improving
- ■ Halted or reversed
- ■ Insufficient data
- ■ Stable low prevalence

Source: World Bank staff calculations.

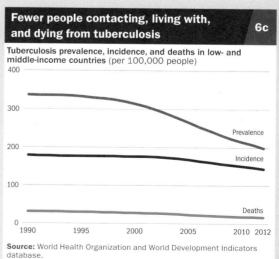

Fewer people contacting, living with, and dying from tuberculosis — 6c

Tuberculosis prevalence, incidence, and deaths in low- and middle-income countries (per 100,000 people)

Source: World Health Organization and World Development Indicators database.

MDG 7 Ensure environmental sustainability

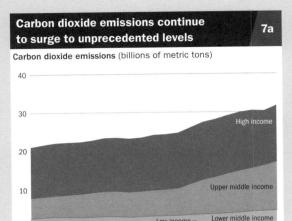

Carbon dioxide emissions continue to surge to unprecedented levels 7a

Carbon dioxide emissions (billions of metric tons)

High income
Upper middle income
Lower middle income
Low income

Source: Carbon Dioxide Information Analysis Center and World Development Indicators database.

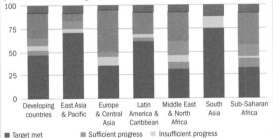

Progress toward halving the proportion of people without sustainable access to safe drinking water 7b

Countries making progress toward halving the proportion of people without sustainable access to safe drinking water (% of countries in region)

Developing countries · East Asia & Pacific · Europe & Central Asia · Latin America & Caribbean · Middle East & North Africa · South Asia · Sub-Saharan Africa

■ Target met ■ Sufficient progress ■ Insufficient progress
■ Moderately off track ■ Seriously off track ■ Insufficient data

Source: World Bank (2013) and World Bank MDG Data Dashboards (http://data.worldbank.org/mdgs).

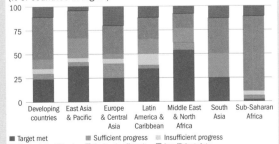

Progress toward halving the proportion of people without sustainable access to basic sanitation 7c

Countries making progress toward halving the proportion of people without sustainable access to basic sanitation (% of countries in region)

Developing countries · East Asia & Pacific · Europe & Central Asia · Latin America & Caribbean · Middle East & North Africa · South Asia · Sub-Saharan Africa

■ Target met ■ Sufficient progress ■ Insufficient progress
■ Moderately off track ■ Seriously off track ■ Insufficient data

Source: World Bank (2013) and World Bank MDG Data Dashboards (http://data.worldbank.org/mdgs).

Millennium Development Goal 7 is the most far-reaching, affecting each person now and in the future. It addresses the condition of the natural and built environments: reversing the loss of natural resources, preserving biodiversity, increasing access to safe water and sanitation, and improving living conditions of people in slums. The overall theme is sustainability, improving people's lives without depleting natural and humanmade capital stocks.

Failure to reach a comprehensive agreement on limiting greenhouse gas emissions leaves billions of people vulnerable to climate change, with the effects expected to hit hardest in developing countries. Higher temperatures, changes in precipitation patterns, rising sea levels, and more frequent weather-related disasters pose risks for agriculture, food, and water supplies. The world released 33.6 billion metric tons of carbon dioxide in 2010, up 5 percent over 2009 and a considerable rise of 51 percent since 1990—the baseline for Kyoto Protocol requirements (figure 7a). Global emissions in 2013 are estimated at an unprecedented 36 billion tons, with a growth rate of 2 percent, slightly lower than the historical average of 3 percent since 2000.

The Millennium Development Goals call for halving the proportion of people without access to an improved water source and sanitation facilities by 2015. In 1990 almost 1.3 billion people worldwide lacked access to drinking water from a convenient, protected source. By 2012 that had improved to 752 million people—a 41 percent reduction. In developing countries the proportion of people with access to an improved water source rose from 70 percent in 1990 to 87 percent in 2012. However, almost 27 percent of countries are seriously off track toward meeting the water target (figure 7b). In 1990 only 35 percent of the people living in low- and middle-income economies had access to a flush toilet or other form of improved sanitation. By 2012 the access rate had risen to 57 percent. But 2.5 billion people still lack access to improved sanitation. The situation is worse in rural areas, where 43 percent of the population has access to improved sanitation, compared with 73 percent in urban areas. This large disparity, especially in Sub-Saharan Africa and South Asia, is the main reason the sanitation target is unlikely to be met on time (figure 7c).

MDG 8 Develop a global partnership for development

The financial crisis that began in 2008 and the ensuing fiscal austerity in many high-income economies have undermined commitments to increase official development assistance (ODA) from members of the Organisation for Economic Co-operation and Development's Development Assistance Committee (DAC). Since 2010, the year of its peak, ODA has fallen 6 percent in real terms, after adjusting prices and exchange rates. Net disbursements of ODA by DAC members totaled $127 billion in 2012, a decrease of 4 percent in real terms. This decline has been accompanied by a noticeable shift in aid allocations away from the poorest countries and toward middle-income countries. Bilateral ODA from DAC members to Sub-Saharan Africa, $27.3 billion in 2012, fell 4.3 percent in real terms from 2011. As a share of gross national income, it fell to 0.29 percent in 2012, well below half the UN target of 0.7 percent (figure 8a).

Economic growth, improved debt management, debt restructuring, and outright debt relief have enabled developing countries to substantially reduce their debt burdens. This is in part due to 35 of the 39 countries being eligible for the Heavily Indebted Poor Country (HIPC) Debt Relief Initiative and Multilateral Debt Relief Initiative (MDRI) benefiting from substantial relief. The ratio of debt service to exports in low- and middle-income economies fell to 9.8 percent in 2012, well below half the 21.1 percent at the start of the decade. Sub-Saharan Africa, home to the majority of the HIPC and MDRI countries, has one of the lowest ratios of debt service to exports: 4.5 percent in 2012 (figure 8b).

Telecommunications is essential for development, and new technologies are creating new opportunities everywhere. By the end of 2012 there were 6.3 billion mobile phone subscriptions, and 2.5 billion people were using the Internet worldwide. As the global mobile-cellular penetration rate approaches market saturation, the growth rates for both developing and developed economies are slowing. Mobile phones are one of several ways of accessing the Internet. And like telephone use, Internet use is strongly correlated with income. Since 2000 Internet users per 100 people in developing economies has grown 28 percent a year, but the low-income economies of South Asia and Sub-Saharan Africa lag behind (figure 8c).

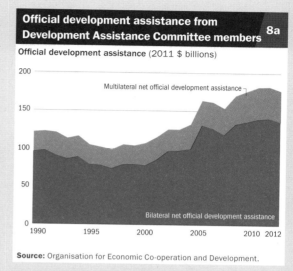

Official development assistance from Development Assistance Committee members 8a

Official development assistance (2011 $ billions)

Source: Organisation for Economic Co-operation and Development.

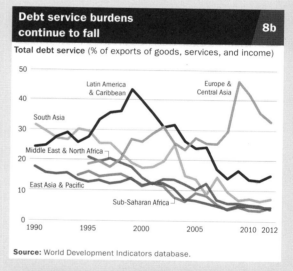

Debt service burdens continue to fall 8b

Total debt service (% of exports of goods, services, and income)

Source: World Development Indicators database.

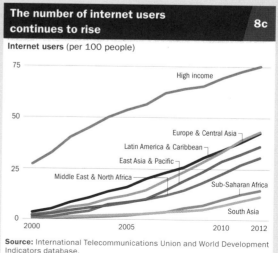

The number of internet users continues to rise 8c

Internet users (per 100 people)

Source: International Telecommunications Union and World Development Indicators database.

 Economy | States and markets | 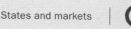 Global links | Back

Millennium Development Goals

Goals and targets from the Millennium Declaration	Indicators for monitoring progress

Goal 1   Eradicate extreme poverty and hunger

Target 1.A	Halve, between 1990 and 2015, the proportion of people whose income is less than $1 a day	1.1	Proportion of population below $1 purchasing power parity (PPP) a day[a]
		1.2	Poverty gap ratio [incidence × depth of poverty]
		1.3	Share of poorest quintile in national consumption
Target 1.B	Achieve full and productive employment and decent work for all, including women and young people	1.4	Growth rate of GDP per person employed
		1.5	Employment to population ratio
		1.6	Proportion of employed people living below $1 (PPP) a day
		1.7	Proportion of own-account and contributing family workers in total employment
Target 1.C	Halve, between 1990 and 2015, the proportion of people who suffer from hunger	1.8	Prevalence of underweight children under five years of age
		1.9	Proportion of population below minimum level of dietary energy consumption

Goal 2   Achieve universal primary education

Target 2.A	Ensure that by 2015 children everywhere, boys and girls alike, will be able to complete a full course of primary schooling	2.1	Net enrollment ratio in primary education
		2.2	Proportion of pupils starting grade 1 who reach last grade of primary education
		2.3	Literacy rate of 15- to 24-year-olds, women and men

Goal 3   Promote gender equality and empower women

Target 3.A	Eliminate gender disparity in primary and secondary education, preferably by 2005, and in all levels of education no later than 2015	3.1	Ratios of girls to boys in primary, secondary, and tertiary education
		3.2	Share of women in wage employment in the nonagricultural sector
		3.3	Proportion of seats held by women in national parliament

Goal 4   Reduce child mortality

Target 4.A	Reduce by two-thirds, between 1990 and 2015, the under-five mortality rate	4.1	Under-five mortality rate
		4.2	Infant mortality rate
		4.3	Proportion of one-year-old children immunized against measles

Goal 5   Improve maternal health

Target 5.A	Reduce by three-quarters, between 1990 and 2015, the maternal mortality ratio	5.1	Maternal mortality ratio
		5.2	Proportion of births attended by skilled health personnel
Target 5.B	Achieve by 2015 universal access to reproductive health	5.3	Contraceptive prevalence rate
		5.4	Adolescent birth rate
		5.5	Antenatal care coverage (at least one visit and at least four visits)
		5.6	Unmet need for family planning

Goal 6   Combat HIV/AIDS, malaria, and other diseases

Target 6.A	Have halted by 2015 and begun to reverse the spread of HIV/AIDS	6.1	HIV prevalence among population ages 15–24 years
		6.2	Condom use at last high-risk sex
		6.3	Proportion of population ages 15–24 years with comprehensive, correct knowledge of HIV/AIDS
		6.4	Ratio of school attendance of orphans to school attendance of nonorphans ages 10–14 years
Target 6.B	Achieve by 2010 universal access to treatment for HIV/AIDS for all those who need it	6.5	Proportion of population with advanced HIV infection with access to antiretroviral drugs
Target 6.C	Have halted by 2015 and begun to reverse the incidence of malaria and other major diseases	6.6	Incidence and death rates associated with malaria
		6.7	Proportion of children under age five sleeping under insecticide-treated bednets
		6.8	Proportion of children under age five with fever who are treated with appropriate antimalarial drugs
		6.9	Incidence, prevalence, and death rates associated with tuberculosis
		6.10	Proportion of tuberculosis cases detected and cured under directly observed treatment short course

Note: The Millennium Development Goals and targets come from the Millennium Declaration, signed by 189 countries, including 147 heads of state and government, in September 2000 (www.un.org/millennium/declaration/ares552e.htm) as updated by the 60th UN General Assembly in September 2005. The revised Millennium Development Goal (MDG) monitoring framework shown here, including new targets and indicators, was presented to the 62nd General Assembly, with new numbering as recommended by the Inter-agency and Expert Group on MDG Indicators at its 12th meeting on November 14, 2007. The goals and targets are interrelated and should be seen as a whole. They represent a partnership between the developed countries and the developing countries "to create an environment—at the national and global levels alike—which is conducive to development and the elimination of poverty." All indicators should be disaggregated by sex and urban-rural location as far as possible.

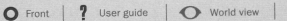 Front | ? User guide | World view | People | Environment

Goals and targets from the Millennium Declaration Indicators for monitoring progress

Goal 7	Ensure environmental sustainability		

Target 7.A	Integrate the principles of sustainable development into country policies and programs and reverse the loss of environmental resources	7.1	Proportion of land area covered by forest
		7.2	Carbon dioxide emissions, total, per capita and per $1 GDP (PPP)
		7.3	Consumption of ozone-depleting substances
Target 7.B	Reduce biodiversity loss, achieving, by 2010, a significant reduction in the rate of loss	7.4	Proportion of fish stocks within safe biological limits
		7.5	Proportion of total water resources used
		7.6	Proportion of terrestrial and marine areas protected
		7.7	Proportion of species threatened with extinction
Target 7.C	Halve by 2015 the proportion of people without sustainable access to safe drinking water and basic sanitation	7.8	Proportion of population using an improved drinking water source
		7.9	Proportion of population using an improved sanitation facility
Target 7.D	Achieve by 2020 a significant improvement in the lives of at least 100 million slum dwellers	7.10	Proportion of urban population living in slums[b]

Goal 8	Develop a global partnership for development		

Target 8.A	Develop further an open, rule-based, predictable, nondiscriminatory trading and financial system (Includes a commitment to good governance, development, and poverty reduction—both nationally and internationally.)	Some of the indicators listed below are monitored separately for the least developed countries (LDCs), Africa, landlocked developing countries, and small island developing states.
Target 8.B	Address the special needs of the least developed countries (Includes tariff and quota-free access for the least developed countries' exports; enhanced program of debt relief for heavily indebted poor countries (HIPC) and cancellation of official bilateral debt; and more generous ODA for countries committed to poverty reduction.)	**Official development assistance (ODA)** 8.1 Net ODA, total and to the least developed countries, as percentage of OECD/DAC donors' gross national income 8.2 Proportion of total bilateral, sector-allocable ODA of OECD/DAC donors to basic social services (basic education, primary health care, nutrition, safe water, and sanitation) 8.3 Proportion of bilateral official development assistance of OECD/DAC donors that is untied 8.4 ODA received in landlocked developing countries as a proportion of their gross national incomes 8.5 ODA received in small island developing states as a proportion of their gross national incomes
Target 8.C	Address the special needs of landlocked developing countries and small island developing states (through the Programme of Action for the Sustainable Development of Small Island Developing States and the outcome of the 22nd special session of the General Assembly)	**Market access** 8.6 Proportion of total developed country imports (by value and excluding arms) from developing countries and least developed countries, admitted free of duty 8.7 Average tariffs imposed by developed countries on agricultural products and textiles and clothing from developing countries 8.8 Agricultural support estimate for OECD countries as a percentage of their GDP 8.9 Proportion of ODA provided to help build trade capacity
Target 8.D	Deal comprehensively with the debt problems of developing countries through national and international measures in order to make debt sustainable in the long term	**Debt sustainability** 8.10 Total number of countries that have reached their HIPC decision points and number that have reached their HIPC completion points (cumulative) 8.11 Debt relief committed under HIPC Initiative and Multilateral Debt Relief Initiative (MDRI) 8.12 Debt service as a percentage of exports of goods and services
Target 8.E	In cooperation with pharmaceutical companies, provide access to affordable essential drugs in developing countries	8.13 Proportion of population with access to affordable essential drugs on a sustainable basis
Target 8.F	In cooperation with the private sector, make available the benefits of new technologies, especially information and communications	8.14 Fixed-line telephones per 100 population 8.15 Mobile cellular subscribers per 100 population 8.16 Internet users per 100 population

a. Where available, indicators based on national poverty lines should be used for monitoring country poverty trends.

b. The proportion of people living in slums is measured by a proxy, represented by the urban population living in households with at least one of these characteristics: lack of access to improved water supply, lack of access to improved sanitation, overcrowding (three or more people per room), and dwellings made of nondurable material.

	Population	Surface area	Population density	Urban population	Gross national income				Gross domestic product	
					Atlas method		Purchasing power parity			
	millions	thousand sq. km	people per sq. km	% of total population	$ billions	Per capita $	$ billions	Per capita $	% growth	Per capita % growth
	2012	2012	2012	2012	2012	2012	2012	2012	2011–12	2011–12
Afghanistan	29.8	652.2	46	24	20.4	680	46.6[a]	1,560[a]	14.4	11.6
Albania	3.2	28.8	115	54	12.7	4,030[b]	29.3	9,280	1.6	1.3
Algeria	38.5	2,381.7	16	74	193.2	5,020	321.6[a]	8,360[a]	3.3	1.4
American Samoa	0.1	0.2	276	93	..	..[c]	..	..	..	..
Andorra	0.1	0.5	167	87	..	..[d]	..	..	..	..
Angola	20.8	1,246.7	17	60	95.4	4,580	112.4	5,400	6.8	3.5
Antigua and Barbuda	0.1	0.4	202	30	1.1	12,480[e]	1.7[a]	18,920[a]	2.8	1.8
Argentina	41.1	2,780.4	15	93	..[f]	..[c,f]	..[f]	..[f]	1.9[g]	..[f]
Armenia	3.0	29.7	104	64	11.0	3,720	20.4	6,860	7.2	7.0
Aruba	0.1	0.2	569	47	..	..[d]	..	..	..	..
Australia	22.7	7,741.2	3	89	1,346.6	59,260	966.6	42,540	3.4	1.7
Austria	8.4	83.9	102	68	403.4	47,850	369.7	43,850	0.9	0.6
Azerbaijan	9.3	86.6	112	54	57.9	6,220	86.5	9,310	2.2	0.9
Bahamas, The	0.4	13.9	37	84	7.7	20,600	10.8[a]	29,020[a]	1.8	0.3
Bahrain	1.3	0.8	1,734	89	25.8	19,560	27.8	22,250	3.4	1.4
Bangladesh	154.7	144.0	1,188	29	129.3	840	314.2	2,030	6.2	5.0
Barbados	0.3	0.4	659	45	4.3	15,080	7.3[a]	25,670[a]	0.0	−0.5
Belarus	9.5	207.6	47	75	61.8	6,530	141.6	14,960	1.5	1.6
Belgium	11.1	30.5	368	98	497.6	44,720	452.7	40,680	−0.1	−0.9
Belize	0.3	23.0	14	45	1.4	4,490	2.5[a]	7,630[a]	5.3	2.8
Benin	10.1	114.8	89	46	7.5	750	15.6	1,550	5.4	2.6
Bermuda	0.1	0.1	1,296	100	6.8	104,590	..	..	−4.9	−5.2
Bhutan	0.7	38.4	19	36	1.8	2,420	4.6	6,200	9.4	7.6
Bolivia	10.5	1,098.6	10	67	23.3	2,220	51.2	4,880	5.2	3.5
Bosnia and Herzegovina	3.8	51.2	75	49	18.2	4,750	37.0	9,650	−0.7	−0.6
Botswana	2.0	581.7	4	62	15.3	7,650	32.2	16,060	4.2	3.3
Brazil	198.7	8,514.9	23	85	2,311.1	11,630	2,291.0	11,530	0.9	0.0
Brunei Darussalam	0.4	5.8	78	76	..	..[d]	..	..	2.2	0.7
Bulgaria	7.3	111.0	67	74	50.0	6,840	112.9	15,450	0.8	1.4
Burkina Faso	16.5	274.2	60	27	11.0	670	24.4	1,480	9.5	6.4
Burundi	9.8	27.8	384	11	2.4	240	5.4	550	4.0	0.8
Cabo Verde	0.5	4.0	123	63	1.9	3,830	2.4	4,930	2.5	1.7
Cambodia	14.9	181.0	84	20	13.0	880	34.6	2,330	7.3	5.4
Cameroon	21.7	475.4	46	53	25.3	1,170	49.3	2,270	4.6	2.0
Canada	34.8	9,984.7	4	81	1,792.3	51,570	1,469.0	42,270	1.7	0.5
Cayman Islands	0.1	0.3	240	100	..	..[d]	..	..	..	..
Central African Republic	4.5	623.0	7	39	2.3	510	4.9	1,080	6.9	4.8
Chad	12.4	1,284.0	10	22	9.6	770	20.1	1,620	8.9	5.7
Channel Islands	0.2	0.2	849	31	..	..[d]	..	..	..	..
Chile	17.5	756.1	23	89	249.9	14,310	357.2	20,450	5.6	4.6
China	1,350.7	9,600.0	145	52	7,731.3	5,720	12,205.8	9,040	7.8	7.3
Hong Kong SAR, China	7.2	1.1	6,866	100	261.6	36,560	373.4	52,190	1.5	0.3
Macao SAR, China	0.6	0.0[h]	19,885	100	30.4	55,720	37.1	68,000	9.9	7.9
Colombia	47.7	1,141.8	43	76	334.8	7,020	476.4	9,990	4.2	2.8
Comoros	0.7	1.9	386	28	0.6	840	0.9	1,210	3.0	0.5
Congo, Dem. Rep.	65.7	2,344.9	29	35	15.4	230	25.5	390	7.2	4.3
Congo, Rep.	4.3	342.0	13	64	11.1	2,550	15.0	3,450	3.8	1.1

 Front | User guide | World view | People | Environment

	Population	Surface area	Population density	Urban population	Gross national income				Gross domestic product	
					Atlas method		Purchasing power parity			
	millions 2012	thousand sq. km 2012	people per sq. km 2012	% of total population 2012	$ billions 2012	Per capita $ 2012	$ billions 2012	Per capita $ 2012	% growth 2011–12	Per capita % growth 2011–12
Costa Rica	4.8	51.1	94	65	42.4	8,820	60.1[a]	12,500[a]	5.1	3.6
Côte d'Ivoire	19.8	322.5	62	52	24.2	1,220	38.2	1,920	9.5	7.0
Croatia	4.3	56.6	76	58	57.6	13,490	86.2	20,200	−2.0	−1.7
Cuba	11.3	109.9	106	75	66.4	5,890	..	..	2.7	2.8
Curaçao	0.2	0.4	342	..	..	..[d]	..	..	..	..
Cyprus	1.1	9.3	122	71	22.8[i]	26,110[i]	26.1[i]	29,840[i]	−2.4[i]	−4.9[i]
Czech Republic	10.5	78.9	136	73	190.5	18,130	267.9	25,480	−1.0	−1.2
Denmark	5.6	43.1	132	87	334.8	59,870	246.4	44,070	−0.4	−0.7
Djibouti	0.9	23.2	37	77	..	..[j]	..	..	..	..
Dominica	0.1	0.8	96	67	0.5	6,440	0.9[a]	11,980[a]	−1.7	−2.1
Dominican Republic	10.3	48.7	213	70	56.3	5,470	99.3[a]	9,660[a]	3.9	2.6
Ecuador	15.5	256.4	62	68	80.1	5,170	147.0	9,490	5.1	3.5
Egypt, Arab Rep.	80.7	1,001.5	81	44	240.3	2,980	520.7	6,450	2.2	0.5
El Salvador	6.3	21.0	304	65	22.6	3,590	42.3[a]	6,720[a]	1.9	1.3
Equatorial Guinea	0.7	28.1	26	40	10.0	13,560	13.7	18,570	2.5	−0.3
Eritrea	6.1	117.6	61	22	2.8	450	3.4[a]	550[a]	7.0	3.6
Estonia	1.3	45.2	31	70	21.6	16,270	31.0	23,280	3.9	4.4
Ethiopia	91.7	1,104.3	92	17	34.7	380	101.5	1,110	8.5	5.7
Faeroe Islands	0.0[k]	1.4	35	41	..	..[d]	..	..	..	..
Fiji	0.9	18.3	48	53	3.6	4,110	4.1	4,690	2.3	1.5
Finland	5.4	338.4	18	84	251.7	46,490	212.0	39,150	−0.8	−1.3
France	65.7	549.2	120	86	2,742.9	41,750	2,458.1	37,420	0.0	−0.5
French Polynesia	0.3	4.0	75	51	..	..[d]	..	..	..	..
Gabon	1.6	267.7	6	86	16.4	10,040	23.0	14,090	5.6	3.1
Gambia, The	1.8	11.3	177	58	0.9	510	3.3	1,830	5.3	2.0
Georgia	4.5[l]	69.7	79[l]	53	14.8[l]	3,290[l]	26.0[l]	5,790[l]	6.0[l]	5.8[l]
Germany	80.4	357.1	231	74	3,624.6	45,070	3,516.2	43,720	0.7	2.4
Ghana	25.4	238.5	111	53	39.4	1,550	48.4	1,910	7.9	5.6
Greece	11.1	132.0	86	62	262.4	23,660	290.3	26,170	−6.4	−6.1
Greenland	0.1	410.5[m]	0[n]	85	..	..[d]	..	..	..	..
Grenada	0.1	0.3	310	39	0.8	7,220	1.1[a]	10,350[a]	0.6	0.2
Guam	0.2	0.5	302	93	..	..[d]	..	..	..	..
Guatemala	15.1	108.9	141	50	47.1	3,120	73.6[a]	4,880[a]	3.0	0.4
Guinea	11.5	245.9	47	36	5.0	440	11.1	970	3.9	1.3
Guinea-Bissau	1.7	36.1	59	45	0.9	510	1.8	1,100	−6.7	−8.9
Guyana	0.8	215.0	4	28	2.7	3,410	2.7[a]	3,340[a]	4.8	4.2
Haiti	10.2	27.8	369	55	7.7	760	12.4[a]	1,220[a]	2.8	1.4
Honduras	7.9	112.5	71	53	16.8	2,120	30.8[a]	3,880[a]	3.9	1.8
Hungary	9.9	93.0	110	70	123.1	12,410	211.8	21,350	−1.7	−1.2
Iceland	0.3	103.0	3	94	12.3	38,270	11.2	34,770	1.4	0.9
India	1,236.7	3,287.3	416	32	1,913.2	1,550	4,730.3	3,820	4.7	3.4
Indonesia	246.9	1,904.6	136	51	844.0	3,420	1,168.7	4,730	6.2	4.9
Iran, Islamic Rep.	76.4	1,745.2	47	69	..	..[c]	..	..	−1.9	−3.2
Iraq	32.6	435.2	75	66	199.8	6,130	242.9	7,460	9.3	6.5
Ireland	4.6	70.3	67	63	179.0	39,020	164.2	35,790	0.2	−0.1
Isle of Man	0.1	0.6	150	51	..	..[d]	..	..	..	..
Israel	7.9	22.1	366	92	253.4	32,030	240.2	30,370	3.4	1.5

1 World view

	Population	Surface area	Population density	Urban population	Gross national income: *Atlas* method		Gross national income: Purchasing power parity		Gross domestic product	
	millions	thousand sq. km	people per sq. km	% of total population	$ billions	Per capita $	$ billions	Per capita $	% growth	Per capita % growth
	2012	2012	2012	2012	2012	2012	2012	2012	2011–12	2011–12
Italy	59.5	301.3	202	69	2,062.5	34,640	2,065.9	34,700	–2.5	–0.6
Jamaica	2.7	11.0	250	52	13.9	5,130	..	..	–0.5	–0.7
Japan	127.6	378.0	350	92	6,106.7	47,870	4,687.6	36,750	2.0	2.2
Jordan	6.3	89.3	71	83	29.5	4,670	37.8	5,980	2.7	0.4
Kazakhstan	16.8	2,724.9	6	54	164.3	9,780	197.9	11,790	5.0	3.5
Kenya	43.2	580.4	76	24	37.2	860	74.7	1,730	4.6	1.8
Kiribati	0.1	0.8	124	44	0.3	2,520	0.4[a]	3,870[a]	2.8	1.2
Korea, Dem. People's Rep.	24.8	120.5	206	60	..	..[o]	..	..	..	..
Korea, Rep.	50.0	99.9	515	83	1,133.8	22,670	1,509.0	30,180	2.0	1.6
Kosovo	1.8	10.9	166	..	6.5	3,600	..	..	2.7	1.8
Kuwait	3.3	17.8	182	98	*140.2*	*44,880*	*149.2*	*47,750*	6.2	2.1
Kyrgyz Republic	5.6	199.9	29	35	5.5	990	12.4	2,220	–0.9	–2.5
Lao PDR	6.6	236.8	29	35	8.4	1,270	17.9	2,690	8.2	6.2
Latvia	2.0	64.5	33	68	28.6	14,060	44.4	21,820	5.0	6.3
Lebanon	4.4	10.5	433	87	40.7	9,190	62.7	14,160	1.4	0.4
Lesotho	2.1	30.4	68	28	2.8	1,380	4.5	2,170	4.0	2.8
Liberia	4.2	111.4	44	49	1.5	370	2.4	580	10.2	7.3
Libya	6.2	1,759.5	3	78	..	..[c]	..	..	..	..
Liechtenstein	0.0[k]	0.2	229	14	..	..[d]	..	..	..	..
Lithuania	3.0	65.3	48	67	41.3	13,820	70.3	23,540	3.7	5.1
Luxembourg	0.5	2.6	205	86	38.0	71,640	32.4	60,950	–0.2	–2.5
Macedonia, FYR	2.1	25.7	83	59	9.7	4,620	24.3	11,540	–0.3	–0.3
Madagascar	22.3	587.0	38	33	9.7	430	20.8	930	3.1	0.3
Malawi	15.9	118.5	169	16	5.0	320	11.6	730	1.9	–1.0
Malaysia	29.2	330.8	89	73	287.0	9,820	475.8	16,270	5.6	3.9
Maldives	0.3	0.3	1,128	42	1.9	5,750	2.6	7,560	3.4	1.4
Mali	14.9	1,240.2	12	36	9.8	660	16.9	1,140	–0.4	–3.3
Malta	0.4	0.3	1,311	95	8.3	19,710	11.3	26,930	1.0	0.2
Marshall Islands	0.1	0.2	292	72	0.2	4,040[b]	..	..	1.9	1.8
Mauritania	3.8	1,030.7	4	42	4.2	1,110	9.4	2,480	7.6	4.9
Mauritius	1.3	2.0	636	42	11.1	8,570	19.5	15,060	3.2	2.8
Mexico	120.8	1,964.4	62	78	1,165.1	9,640	1,951.1	16,140	3.8	2.5
Micronesia, Fed. Sts.	0.1	0.7	148	23	0.3	3,230	0.4[a]	3,920[a]	0.4	0.5
Moldova	3.6[p]	33.9	124[p]	48	7.4[p]	2,070[p]	12.9[p]	3,630[p]	–0.8[p]	–0.8[p]
Monaco	0.0[k]	0.0[h]	18,790	100	..	..[d]	..	..	..	..
Mongolia	2.8	1,564.1	2	69	8.8	3,160	14.0	5,020	12.3	10.6
Montenegro	0.6	13.8	46	63	4.5	7,220	9.1	14,590	–0.5	–0.6
Morocco	32.5	446.6	73	57	97.9[q]	2,960[q]	167.4[q]	5,060[q]	4.2[q]	2.7[q]
Mozambique	25.2	799.4	32	31	12.8	510	25.3	1,000	7.4	4.7
Myanmar	52.8	676.6	81	33	..	..[o]	..	..	..	..
Namibia	2.3	824.3	3	39	12.7	5,610	16.4	7,240	5.0	3.1
Nepal	27.5	147.2	192	17	19.2	700	40.4	1,470	4.9	3.6
Netherlands	16.8	41.5	497	84	804.3	48,000	733.0	43,750	–1.2	–1.6
New Caledonia	0.3	18.6	14	62	..	..[d]	..	..	..	..
New Zealand	4.4	267.7	17	86	163.6	36,900	144.6	32,620	3.2	2.6
Nicaragua	6.0	130.4	50	58	9.9	1,650	23.3[a]	3,890[a]	5.2	3.7
Niger	17.2	1,267.0	14	18	6.7	390	13.0	760	10.8	6.7

	Population	Surface area	Population density	Urban population	Gross national income				Gross domestic product	
					Atlas method		Purchasing power parity		product	
	millions	thousand sq. km	people per sq. km	% of total population	$ billions	Per capita $	$ billions	Per capita $	% growth	Per capita % growth
	2012	2012	2012	2012	2012	2012	2012	2012	2011–12	2011–12
Nigeria	168.8	923.8	185	50	242.7	1,440	404.8	2,400	6.5	3.6
Northern Mariana Islands	0.1	0.5	116	92	..	..d	..	..	..	..
Norway	5.0	323.8	16	80	495.7	98,780	338.5	67,450	2.9	1.6
Oman	3.3	309.5	11	74	58.8	19,450	71.0	25,330	5.0	-7.1
Pakistan	179.2	796.1	232	37	225.1	1,260	516.5	2,880	4.0	2.3
Palau	0.0k	0.5	45	85	0.2	9,860	0.4a	16,870a	5.3	4.5
Panama	3.8	75.4	51	76	32.4	8,510	57.6a	15,150a	10.7	8.9
Papua New Guinea	7.2	462.8	16	13	12.8	1,790	19.6a	2,740a	8.0	5.7
Paraguay	6.7	406.8	17	62	22.8	3,400	38.2	5,720	-1.2	-2.9
Peru	30.0	1,285.2	23	78	181.8	6,060	302.7	10,090	6.3	5.0
Philippines	96.7	300.0	324	49	241.7	2,500	423.6	4,380	6.8	5.0
Poland	38.5	312.7	127	61	488.0	12,660	838.6	21,760	1.8	1.8
Portugal	10.5	92.1	115	62	217.0	20,640	266.3	25,330	-3.2	-2.8
Puerto Rico	3.7	8.9	413	99	66.0	18,000	..	..	0.5	1.3
Qatar	2.1	11.6	177	99	142.6	74,600	168.8	88,350	6.2	-1.0
Romania	20.1	238.4	87	53	171.9	8,560	354.3	17,650	0.4	0.7
Russian Federation	143.5	17,098.2	9	74	1,822.7	12,700	3,272.9	22,800	3.4	3.0
Rwanda	11.5	26.3	464	19	6.9	600	15.1	1,320	8.0	5.0
Samoa	0.2	2.8	67	20	0.6	3,260	0.8a	4,250a	2.9	2.1
San Marino	0.0k	0.1	521	94	..	..d	..	..	..	..
São Tomé and Príncipe	0.2	1.0	196	63	0.2	1,310	0.3	1,810	4.0	1.3
Saudi Arabia	28.3	2,149.7r	13	82	687.8	24,310	837.4	30,160	5.1	3.2
Senegal	13.7	196.7	71	43	14.2	1,030s	25.8	1,880	3.5	0.5
Serbia	7.2	88.4	83	57	38.1	5,280	82.6	11,430	-1.7	-1.2
Seychelles	0.1	0.5	192	54	1.1	12,180	2.3a	25,580a	2.8	1.8
Sierra Leone	6.0	71.7	83	40	3.5	580	8.0	1,340	15.2	13.0
Singapore	5.3	0.7	7,589	100	250.8	47,210	319.3	60,110	1.3	-1.1
Sint Maarten (Dutch part)	0.0k	0.0h	1,150	..	..	..d	..	..	..	..
Slovak Republic	5.4	49.0	112	55	93.0	17,190	137.5	25,430	1.8	1.6
Slovenia	2.1	20.3	102	50	46.9	22,810	58.1	28,240	-2.5	-2.7
Solomon Islands	0.5	28.9	20	21	0.6	1,130	1.2a	2,130a	3.9	1.7
Somalia	10.2	637.7	16	38	..	..o	..	..	..	..
South Africa	52.3	1,219.1	43	62	389.8	7,460	563.3	10,780	2.5	1.2
South Sudan	10.8	644.3	..	18	8.6	790	..	..	-47.6	-49.8
Spain	46.8	505.6	94	78	1,368.8	29,270	1,485.1	31,760	-1.6	-1.7
Sri Lanka	20.3	65.6	324	15	59.3	2,920	122.5	6,030	6.4	9.2
St. Kitts and Nevis	0.1	0.3	206	32	0.7	13,610	0.9a	17,630a	6.9	5.7
St. Lucia	0.2	0.6	297	17	1.2	6,890	2.0a	11,300a	0.5	-0.4
St. Martin (French part)	0.0k	0.1	569	..	..	..d	..	..	..	..
St. Vincent & the Grenadines	0.1	0.4	280	50	0.7	6,400	1.2a	10,870a	2.3	2.3
Sudan	37.2t	1,879.4t	20	33t	55.9t	1,500t	77.1t	2,070t	-10.1u	0.6u
Suriname	0.5	163.8	3	70	4.6	8,680	4.5a	8,380a	3.9	2.9
Swaziland	1.2	17.4	72	21	3.5	2,860	5.9	4,760	-1.5	-3.0
Sweden	9.5	450.3	23	85	534.3	56,120	418.5	43,960	0.9	0.2
Switzerland	8.0	41.3	200	74	647.5	80,970	439.8	55,000	1.0	0.0
Syrian Arab Republic	22.4	185.2	122	56	..	..j	..	..	..	0.8
Tajikistan	8.0	142.6	57	27	7.1	880	17.4	2,180	7.5	4.9

1 World view

	Population	Surface area	Population density	Urban population	Gross national income — Atlas method		Gross national income — Purchasing power parity		Gross domestic product	
	millions	thousand sq. km	people per sq. km	% of total population	$ billions	Per capita $	$ billions	Per capita $	% growth	Per capita % growth
	2012	2012	2012	2012	2012	2012	2012	2012	2011–12	2011–12
Tanzania	47.8	947.3	54	27	26.7ᵛ	570ᵛ	72.4ᵛ	1,560ᵛ	6.9ᵛ	3.7ᵛ
Thailand	66.8	513.1	131	34	347.8	5,210	619.5	9,280	6.5	6.2
Timor-Leste	1.2	14.9	81	29	4.4	3,620	7.5ᵃ	6,230ᵃ	0.6	−2.3
Togo	6.6	56.8	122	39	3.3	500	6.0	900	5.6	2.9
Tonga	0.1	0.8	146	24	0.4	4,220	0.5ᵃ	5,020ᵃ	0.8	0.5
Trinidad and Tobago	1.3	5.1	261	14	19.7	14,710	30.6ᵃ	22,860ᵃ	1.5	1.2
Tunisia	10.8	163.6	69	67	44.8	4,150	99.2	9,210	3.6	2.6
Turkey	74.0	783.6	96	72	801.1	10,830	1,360.6	18,390	2.2	0.9
Turkmenistan	5.2	488.1	11	49	28.0	5,410	46.9ᵃ	9,070ᵃ	11.1	9.7
Turks and Caicos Islands	0.0ᵏ	1.0	34	94	..	..ᵈ	..	..	..	..
Tuvalu	0.0ᵏ	0.0ʰ	329	51	0.1	5,650	..	..	0.2	0.0
Uganda	36.3	241.6	182	16	17.6	480	47.1	1,300	3.4	0.0
Ukraine	45.6	603.6	79	69	159.6	3,500	327.1	7,180	0.2	0.4
United Arab Emirates	9.2	83.6	110	85	355.5	38,620	381.4	41,430	4.4	1.2
United Kingdom	63.6	243.6	263	80	2,448.8	38,500	2,266.0	35,620	0.3	−0.3
United States	313.9	9,831.5	34	83	16,430.4	52,340	16,514.5	52,610	2.8	2.0
Uruguay	3.4	176.2	19	93	46.1	13,580	52.0	15,310	3.9	3.6
Uzbekistan	29.8	447.4	70	36	51.2	1,720	109.1ᵃ	3,670ᵃ	8.2	6.6
Vanuatu	0.2	12.2	20	25	0.7	3,000	1.1ᵃ	4,300ᵃ	2.3	0.0
Venezuela, RB	30.0	912.1	34	94	373.3	12,460	386.9	12,920	5.6	4.0
Vietnam	88.8	331.0	286	32	137.5	1,550	321.4	3,620	5.2	4.1
Virgin Islands (U.S.)	0.1	0.4	301	96	..	..ᵈ	..	..	..	..
West Bank and Gaza	4.0	6.0	672	75	..	..ʲ	..	..	..	..
Yemen, Rep.	23.9	528.0	45	33	30.4	1,270	55.1	2,310	0.1	−2.2
Zambia	14.1	752.6	19	40	19.0	1,350	22.4	1,590	7.2	3.9
Zimbabwe	13.7	390.8	35	39	8.9	650	..	..	4.4	1.6
World	7,043.9 s	134,289.9 s	54 w	53 w	71,692.4 t	10,178 w	85,986.8 t	12,207 w	2.4 w	1.2 w
Low income	846.5	16,197.8	56	28	499.4	590	1,171.1	1,383	6.3	4.0
Middle income	4,897.6	64,212.0	77	50	21,404.7	4,370	35,099.0	7,167	4.9	3.7
Lower middle income	2,507.0	20,739.9	122	39	4,745.3	1,893	9,718.6	3,877	4.7	3.2
Upper middle income	2,390.6	43,472.2	56	61	16,661.1	6,969	25,389.9	10,621	5.0	4.2
Low & middle income	5,744.1	80,409.9	73	46	21,916.1	3,815	36,250.5	6,311	4.9	3.6
East Asia & Pacific	1,991.6	16,301.6	126	50	9,727.7	4,884	15,451.5	7,758	7.5	6.7
Europe & Central Asia	270.8	6,478.6	43	60	1,804.4	6,664	3,234.8	11,946	1.8	1.1
Latin America & Carib.	581.4	19,460.9	30	79	5,273.2	9,070	6,852.9	11,787	2.9	1.7
Middle East & N. Africa	339.6	8,775.4	39	60	..	..	..	..	1.9	0.2
South Asia	1,649.2	5,131.1	346	31	2,370.1	1,437	5,777.6	3,503	4.9	3.5
Sub-Saharan Africa	911.5	24,262.3	39	37	1,230.2	1,350	2,030.0	2,227	4.3	1.5
High income	1,299.8	53,880.1	25	80	49,905.7	38,394	50,055.1	38,509	1.5	1.2
Euro area	331.2	2,693.1	128	76	12,673.5	38,263	12,354.0	37,299	−0.6	0.0

a. Based on regression; others are extrapolated from the 2005 International Comparison Program benchmark estimates. b. Included in the aggregates for upper middle-income economies based on earlier data. c. Estimated to be upper middle income ($4,086–$12,615). d. Estimated to be high income ($12,616 or more). e. Included in the aggregates for high-income economies based on earlier data. f. Data series will be calculated once ongoing revisions to official statistics reported by the National Statistics and Censuses Institute of Argentina have been finalized. g. Data for Argentina are officially reported by the National Statistics and Censuses Institute of Argentina. The International Monetary Fund has, however, issued a declaration of censure and called on Argentina to adopt remedial measures to address the quality of official GDP and consumer price index data. Alternative data sources have shown significantly lower real growth and higher inflation than the official data since 2008. In this context, the World Bank is also using alternative data sources and estimates for the surveillance of macroeconomic developments in Argentina. h. Greater than 0 but less than 50. i. Data are for the area controlled by the government of Cyprus. j. Estimated to be lower middle income ($1,036–$4,085). k. Greater than 0 but less than 50,000. l. Excludes Abkhazia and South Ossetia. m. Refers to area free from ice. n. Greater than 0 but less than 0.5. o. Estimated to be low income ($1,035 or less). p. Excludes Transnistria. q. Includes Former Spanish Sahara. r. Provisional estimate. s. Included in the aggregates for lower middle-income economies based on earlier data. t. Excludes South Sudan. u. Excludes South Sudan after July 9, 2011. v. Covers mainland Tanzania only.

 Front | User guide | World view | People | Environment

About the data

Population, land area, income (as measured by gross national income, GNI), and output (as measured by gross domestic product, GDP) are basic measures of the size of an economy. They also provide a broad indication of actual and potential resources and are therefore used throughout *World Development Indicators* to normalize other indicators.

Population

Population estimates are usually based on national population censuses. Estimates for the years before and after the census are interpolations or extrapolations based on demographic models. Errors and undercounting occur even in high-income countries; in developing countries errors may be substantial because of limits in the transport, communications, and other resources required to conduct and analyze a full census.

The quality and reliability of official demographic data are also affected by public trust in the government, government commitment to full and accurate enumeration, confidentiality and protection against misuse of census data, and census agencies' independence from political influence. Moreover, comparability of population indicators is limited by differences in the concepts, definitions, collection procedures, and estimation methods used by national statistical agencies and other organizations that collect the data.

Of the 214 economies in the table, 180 (about 86 percent) conducted a census during the 2000 census round (1995–2004). As of January 2014, 175 countries (about 82 percent) have completed a census for the 2010 census round (2005–14). The currentness of a census and the availability of complementary data from surveys or registration systems are important indicators of demographic data quality. See *Primary data documentation* for the most recent census or survey year and for the completeness of registration. Some European countries' registration systems offer complete information on population in the absence of a census.

Current population estimates for developing countries that lack recent census data and pre- and post-census estimates for countries with census data are provided by the United Nations Population Division and other agencies. The cohort component method—a standard method for estimating and projecting population—requires fertility, mortality, and net migration data, often collected from sample surveys, which can be small or limited in coverage. Population estimates are from demographic modeling and so are susceptible to biases and errors from shortcomings in the model and in the data. Because the five-year age group is the cohort unit and five-year period data are used, interpolations to obtain annual data or single age structure may not reflect actual events or age composition.

Surface area

The surface area of an economy includes inland bodies of water and some coastal waterways. Surface area thus differs from land area, which excludes bodies of water, and from gross area, which may include offshore territorial waters. Land area is particularly important for understanding an economy's agricultural capacity and

the environmental effects of human activity. Innovations in satellite mapping and computer databases have resulted in more precise measurements of land and water areas.

Urban population

There is no consistent and universally accepted standard for distinguishing urban from rural areas, in part because of the wide variety of situations across countries. Most countries use an urban classification related to the size or characteristics of settlements. Some define urban areas based on the presence of certain infrastructure and services. And other countries designate urban areas based on administrative arrangements. Because the estimates in the table are based on national definitions of what constitutes a city or metropolitan area, cross-country comparisons should be made with caution. To estimate urban populations, ratios of urban to total population obtained from the United Nations were applied to the World Bank's estimates of total population.

Size of the economy

GNI measures total domestic and foreign value added claimed by residents. GNI comprises GDP plus net receipts of primary income (compensation of employees and property income) from nonresident sources. GDP is the sum of gross value added by all resident producers in the economy plus any product taxes (less subsidies) not included in the valuation of output. GNI is calculated without deducting for depreciation of fabricated assets or for depletion and degradation of natural resources. Value added is the net output of an industry after adding up all outputs and subtracting intermediate inputs. The industrial origin of value added is determined by the International Standard Industrial Classification revision 3 and revision 4. The World Bank uses GNI per capita in U.S. dollars to classify countries for analytical purposes and to determine borrowing eligibility. For definitions of the income groups in *World Development Indicators,* see *User guide.*

When calculating GNI in U.S. dollars from GNI reported in national currencies, the World Bank follows the *World Bank Atlas* conversion method, using a three-year average of exchange rates to smooth the effects of transitory fluctuations in exchange rates. (For further discussion of the *World Bank Atlas* method, see *Statistical methods.*)

Because exchange rates do not always reflect differences in price levels between countries, the table also converts GNI and GNI per capita estimates into international dollars using purchasing power parity (PPP) rates. PPP rates provide a standard measure allowing comparison of real levels of expenditure between countries, just as conventional price indexes allow comparison of real values over time.

PPP rates are calculated by simultaneously comparing the prices of similar goods and services among a large number of countries. In the most recent round of price surveys conducted by the International Comparison Program (ICP) in 2005, 146 countries and territories participated, including China for the first time, India for the first time since 1985, and almost all African countries. The PPP conversion factors presented in the table come from three sources. For

47 high- and upper middle-income countries conversion factors are provided by Eurostat and the Organisation for Economic Co-operation and Development (OECD); PPP estimates for these countries incorporate new price data collected since 2005. For the remaining 2005 ICP countries the PPP estimates are extrapolated from the 2005 ICP benchmark results, which account for relative price changes between each economy and the United States. For countries that did not participate in the 2005 ICP round, the PPP estimates are imputed using a statistical model. More information on the results of the 2005 ICP is available at www.worldbank.org/data/icp.

Growth rates of GDP and GDP per capita are calculated using the least squares method and constant price data in local currency. Constant price U.S. dollar series are used to calculate regional and income group growth rates. The growth rates in the table are annual averages. Methods of computing growth rates are described in *Statistical methods*.

Definitions

• **Population** is based on the de facto definition of population, which counts all residents regardless of legal status or citizenship—except for refugees not permanently settled in the country of asylum, who are generally considered part of the population of their country of origin. The values shown are midyear estimates. • **Surface area** is a country's total area, including areas under inland bodies of water and some coastal waterways. • **Population density** is midyear population divided by land area. • **Urban population** is the midyear population of areas defined as urban in each country and obtained by the United Nations. • **Gross national income, *Atlas* method,** is the sum of value added by all resident producers plus any product taxes (less subsidies) not included in the valuation of output plus net receipts of primary income (compensation of employees and property income) from abroad. Data are in current U.S. dollars converted using the *World Bank Atlas* method (see *Statistical methods*). • **Gross national income, purchasing power parity,** is GNI converted to international dollars using PPP rates. An international dollar has the same purchasing power over GNI that a U.S. dollar has in the United States. • **Gross national income per capita** is GNI divided by midyear population. • **Gross domestic product** is the sum of value added by all resident producers plus any product taxes (less subsidies) not included in the valuation of output. Growth is calculated from constant price GDP data in local currency. • **Gross domestic product per capita** is GDP divided by midyear population.

Data sources

The World Bank's population estimates are compiled and produced by its Development Data Group in consultation with its Human Development Network, operational staff, and country offices. The United Nations Population Division (2013) is a source of the demographic data for more than half the countries, most of them developing countries. Other important sources are census reports and other statistical publications from national statistical offices, Eurostat's *Demographic Statistics,* the United Nations Statistics Division's *Population and Vital Statistics Report,* the U.S. Bureau of the Census's International Data Base, and the Secretariat of the Pacific Community's Statistics and Demography Programme.

Data on surface and land area are from the Food and Agriculture Organization, which gathers these data from national agencies through annual questionnaires and by analyzing the results of national agricultural censuses.

Data on urban population shares are from United Nations Population Division (2012).

GNI, GNI per capita, GDP growth, and GDP per capita growth are estimated by World Bank staff based on national accounts data collected by World Bank staff during economic missions or reported by national statistical offices to other international organizations such as the OECD. PPP conversion factors are estimates by Eurostat/OECD and by World Bank staff based on data collected by the ICP.

References

Eurostat (Statistical Office of the European Communities). n.d. *Demographic Statistics.* [http://epp.eurostat.ec.europa.eu/portal/page /portal/eurostat/home/]. Luxembourg.

OECD (Organisation for Economic Co-operation and Development). n.d. OECD.StatExtracts database. [http://stats.oecd.org/]. Paris.

UNAIDS (Joint United Nations Programme on HIV/AIDS). 2013a. *AIDS by Numbers.* Geneva.

————. 2013b. *Global Report: UNAIDS Report on the Global AIDS Epidemic 2013.* [www.unaids.org/en/resources/publications/2013/]. Geneva.

UNFPA (United Nations Population Fund). 2014. Reproductive Health website. [www.unfpa.org/rh/planning.htm].

UNICEF (United Nations Children's Fund). 2013. *Committing to Child Survival: A Promise Renewed—Progress Report 2013.* [www.unicef .org/publications/files/APR_Progress_Report_2013_9_Sept_2013. pdf]. New York.

UN Inter-agency Group for Child Mortality Estimation. 2013. *Levels and Trends in Child Mortality: Report 2013.* [www.childinfo.org/files /Child_Mortality_Report_2013.pdf]. New York.

United Nations. 2013. *The Millennium Development Goals Report 2013.* [www.un.org/millenniumgoals/reports.shtml]. New York.

United Nations Population Division. 2012. *World Urbanization Prospects: The 2011 Revision.* New York: United Nations, Department of Economic and Social Affairs.

————. 2013. *World Population Prospects: The 2012 Revision.* New York: United Nations, Department of Economic and Social Affairs.

United Nations Statistics Division. Various years. *Population and Vital Statistics Report.* New York.

WHO (World Health Organization). 2013. *World Malaria Report 2013.* Geneva.

World Bank. 2011. *The Changing Wealth of Nations: Measuring Sustainable Development for the New Millennium.* Washington, DC.

————. 2013. *Global Monitoring Report 2013: Rural-Urban Dynamics and the Millennium Development Goals.* Washington, DC.

To access the World Development Indicators online tables, use the URL http://wdi.worldbank.org/table/ and the table number (for example, http://wdi.worldbank.org/table/1.1). To view a specific indicator online, use the URL http://data.worldbank.org/indicator/ and the indicator code (for example, http://data.worldbank.org/indicator/SP.POP.TOTL).

1.1 Size of the economy

Population ♀♂	SP.POP.TOTL
Surface area	AG.SRF.TOTL.K2
Population density	EN.POP.DNST
Gross national income, *Atlas* method	NY.GNP.ATLS.CD
Gross national income per capita, *Atlas* method	NY.GNP.PCAP.CD
Purchasing power parity gross national income	NY.GNP.MKTP.PP.CD
Purchasing power parity gross national income, Per capita	NY.GNP.PCAP.PP.CD
Gross domestic product	NY.GDP.MKTP.KD.ZG
Gross domestic product, Per capita	NY.GDP.PCAP.KD.ZG

1.2 Millennium Development Goals: eradicating poverty and saving lives

Share of poorest quintile in national consumption or income	SI.DST.FRST.20
Vulnerable employment ♀♂	SL.EMP.VULN.ZS
Prevalence of malnutrition, Underweight ♀♂	SH.STA.MALN.ZS
Primary completion rate ♀♂	SE.PRM.CMPT.ZS
Ratio of girls to boys enrollments in primary and secondary education ♀♂	SE.ENR.PRSC.FM.ZS
Under-five mortality rate ♀♂	SH.DYN.MORT

1.3 Millennium Development Goals: protecting our common environment

Maternal mortality ratio, Modeled estimate	SH.STA.MMRT
Contraceptive prevalence rate	SP.DYN.CONU.ZS
HIV prevalence	SH.DYN.AIDS.ZS
Incidence of tuberculosis	SH.TBS.INCD

Carbon dioxide emissions per capita	EN.ATM.CO2E.PC
Nationally protected terrestrial and marine areas	ER.PTD.TOTL.ZS
Access to improved sanitation facilities	SH.STA.ACSN
Internet users	IT.NET.USER.PZ

1.4 Millennium Development Goals: overcoming obstacles

This table provides data on net official development assistance by donor, least developed countries' access to high-income markets, and the Debt Initiative for Heavily Indebted Poor Countries. ..[a]

1.5 Women in development

Female population ♀♂	SP.POP.TOTL.FE.ZS
Life expectancy at birth, Male ♀♂	SP.DYN.LE00.MA.IN
Life expectancy at birth, Female ♀♂	SP.DYN.LE00.FE.IN
Pregnant women receiving prenatal care	SH.STA.ANVC.ZS
Teenage mothers	SP.MTR.1519.ZS
Women in wage employment in nonagricultural sector	SL.EMP.INSV.FE.ZS
Unpaid family workers, Male ♀♂	SL.FAM.WORK.MA.ZS
Unpaid family workers, Female ♀♂	SL.FAM.WORK.FE.ZS
Female part-time employment ♀♂	SL.TLF.PART.TL.FE.ZS
Female legislators, senior officials, and managers	SG.GEN.LSOM.ZS
Women in parliaments	SG.GEN.PARL.ZS
Female-headed households	SP.HOU.FEMA.ZS

♀♂ Data disaggregated by sex are available in the World Development Indicators database.
a. Available online only as part of the table, not as an individual indicator.

Poverty rates

	International poverty line in local currency			Population below international poverty lines[a]								
	$1.25 a day	$2 a day	Survey year[b]	Population below $1.25 a day %	Poverty gap at $1.25 a day %	Population below $2 a day %	Poverty gap at $2 a day %	Survey year[b]	Population below $1.25 a day %	Poverty gap at $1.25 a day %	Population below $2 a day %	Poverty gap at $2 a day %
	2005	2005										
Albania	75.5	120.8	2005	<2	<0.5	7.9	1.5	2008	<2	<0.5	4.3	0.9
Algeria	48.4[c]	77.5[c]	1988	7.6	1.2	24.6	6.7	1995	6.8	1.4	23.6	6.5
Angola	88.1	141.0	2000	54.3	29.9	70.2	42.4	2009	43.4	16.5	67.4	31.5
Argentina	1.7	2.7	2009[d,e]	2.0	1.2	3.4	1.7	2010[d,e]	<2	0.7	<2	0.9
Armenia	245.2	392.4	2008	<2	<0.5	12.4	2.3	2010	2.5	<0.5	19.9	4.0
Azerbaijan	2,170.9	3,473.5	2001	6.3	1.1	27.1	6.8	2008	<2	<0.5	2.8	0.6
Bangladesh	31.9	51.0	2005	50.5	14.2	80.3	34.3	2010	43.3	11.2	76.5	30.4
Belarus	949.5	1,519.2	2010	<2	<0.5	<2	<0.5	2011	<2	<0.5	<2	<0.5
Belize	1.8[c]	2.9[c]	1998[f]	11.3	4.7	26.3	10.0	1999[f]	12.2	5.5	22.0	9.9
Benin	344.0	550.4		..	..	..	..	2003	47.3	15.7	75.3	33.5
Bhutan	23.1	36.9	2007	10.2	1.8	29.8	8.5	2012	1.7	<0.5	12.6	2.6
Bolivia	3.2	5.1	2007[e]	13.1	6.6	24.7	10.9	2008[e]	15.6	8.6	24.9	13.1
Bosnia and Herzegovina	1.1	1.7	2004	<2	<0.5	<2	<0.5	2007	<2	<0.5	<2	<0.5
Botswana	4.2	6.8	1986	35.6	13.8	54.7	25.8	1994	31.2	11.0	49.4	22.3
Brazil	2.0	3.1	2008[f]	6.0	3.4	11.3	5.3	2009[f]	6.1	3.6	10.8	5.4
Bulgaria	0.9	1.5	2003	<2	<0.5	<2	<0.5	2007	<2	<0.5	<2	<0.5
Burkina Faso	303.0	484.8	2003	56.5	20.3	81.2	39.3	2009	44.6	14.7	72.6	31.7
Burundi	558.8	894.1	1998	86.4	47.3	95.4	64.1	2006	81.3	36.4	93.5	56.1
Cabo Verde	97.7	156.3		..	..	..	..	2002	21.0	6.1	40.9	15.2
Cambodia	2,019.1	3,230.6	2008	22.8	4.9	53.3	17.4	2009	18.6	3.6	49.5	15.1
Cameroon	368.1	589.0	2001	10.8	2.3	32.5	9.5	2007	9.6	1.2	30.4	8.2
Central African Republic	384.3	614.9	2003	62.4	28.3	81.9	45.3	2008	62.8	31.3	80.1	46.8
Chad	409.5	655.1		..	..	..	..	2003	61.9	25.6	83.3	43.9
Chile	484.2	774.7	2006[f]	<2	0.5	3.2	1.1	2009[f]	<2	0.7	2.7	1.2
China	5.1[g]	8.2[g]	2008[h]	13.1	3.2	29.8	10.1	2009[h]	11.8	2.8	27.2	9.1
Colombia	1,489.7	2,383.5	2009[f]	9.7	4.7	18.5	8.2	2010[f]	8.2	3.8	15.8	6.8
Comoros	368.0	588.8		..	..	..	..	2004	46.1	20.8	65.0	34.2
Congo, Dem. Rep.	395.3	632.5		..	..	..	..	2006	87.7	52.8	95.2	67.6
Congo, Rep.	469.5	751.1		..	..	..	..	2005	54.1	22.8	74.4	38.8
Costa Rica	348.7[c]	557.9[c]	2008[f]	2.4	1.5	5.0	2.3	2009[f]	3.1	1.8	6.0	2.7
Côte d'Ivoire	5.6	8.9	2004	<2	<0.5	<2	<0.5	2008	<2	<0.5	<2	<0.5
Croatia	19.0	30.4	1993[e]	<2	<0.5	<2	<0.5	1996[e]	<2	<0.5	<2	<0.5
Czech Republic	407.3	651.6	2002	23.3	6.8	46.8	17.6	2008	23.8	7.5	46.3	17.8
Djibouti	134.8	215.6		..	..	..	..	2002	18.8	5.3	41.2	14.6
Dominican Republic	25.5[c]	40.8[c]	2009[f]	3.0	0.7	10.0	2.7	2010[f]	2.2	<0.5	9.9	2.4
Ecuador	0.6	1.0	2009[f]	6.4	2.9	13.5	5.5	2010[f]	4.6	2.1	10.6	4.1
Egypt, Arab Rep.	2.5	4.0	2005	2.0	<0.5	18.5	3.5	2008	<2	<0.5	15.4	2.8
El Salvador	6.0[c]	9.6[c]	2008[f]	5.4	1.9	14.0	4.8	2009[f]	9.0	4.4	16.9	7.6
Estonia	11.0	17.7	2003	<2	<0.5	2.6	<0.5	2004	<2	<0.5	<2	0.5
Ethiopia	3.4	5.5	2005	39.0	9.6	77.6	28.9	2011	30.7	8.2	66.0	23.6
Fiji	1.9	3.1	2003	29.2	11.3	48.7	21.8	2009	5.9	1.1	22.9	6.0
Gabon	554.7	887.5		..	..	..	..	2005	4.8	0.9	19.6	5.0
Gambia, The	12.9	20.7	1998	65.6	33.8	81.2	49.1	2003	29.8	9.8	55.9	24.4
Georgia	1.0	1.6	2009	15.2	4.2	32.7	11.6	2010	18.0	5.8	35.6	13.7
Ghana	5,594.8	8,951.6	1998	39.1	14.4	63.3	28.5	2006	28.6	9.9	51.8	21.3
Guatemala	5.7[c]	9.1[c]	2004[f]	24.4	13.2	39.2	20.2	2006[f]	13.5	4.7	26.3	10.5
Guinea	1,849.5	2,959.1	2003	56.3	21.3	80.8	39.7	2007	43.3	15.0	69.6	31.0

	International poverty line in local currency		Population below international poverty lines[a]									
	$1.25 a day 2005	$2 a day 2005	Survey year[b]	Population below $1.25 a day %	Poverty gap at $1.25 a day %	Population below $2 a day %	Poverty gap at $2 a day %	Survey year[b]	Population below $1.25 a day %	Poverty gap at $1.25 a day %	Population below $2 a day %	Poverty gap at $2 a day %
Guinea-Bissau	355.3	568.6	1993	52.1	20.6	75.7	37.4	2002	48.9	16.6	78.0	34.9
Guyana	131.5[c]	210.3[c]	1993[e]	6.9	1.5	17.1	5.4	1998[e]	8.7	2.8	18.0	6.7
Haiti	24.2[c]	38.7[c]		..	..	..	..	2001	61.7	32.3	77.5	46.7
Honduras	12.1[c]	19.3[c]	2008[f]	21.4	11.8	32.6	17.5	2009[f]	17.9	9.4	29.8	14.9
Hungary	171.9	275.0	2004	<2	<0.5	<2	<0.5	2007	<2	<0.5	<2	<0.5
India	19.5[i]	31.2[i]	2005[h]	41.6	10.5	75.6	29.5	2010[h]	32.7	7.5	68.7	24.5
Indonesia	5,241.0[i]	8,385.7[i]	2010[h]	18.1	3.3	46.1	14.3	2011[h]	16.2	2.7	43.3	13.0
Iran, Islamic Rep.	3,393.5	5,429.6	1998	<2	<0.5	8.3	1.8	2005	<2	<0.5	8.0	1.8
Iraq	799.8	1,279.7		..	..	..	..	2007	2.8	<0.5	21.4	4.4
Jamaica	54.2[c]	86.7[c]	2002	<2	<0.5	8.5	1.5	2004	<2	<0.5	5.4	0.8
Jordan	0.6	1.0	2008	<2	<0.5	2.1	<0.5	2010	<2	<0.5	<2	<0.5
Kazakhstan	81.2	129.9	2008	<2	<0.5	<2	<0.5	2009	<2	<0.5	<2	<0.5
Kenya	40.9	65.4	1997	19.6	4.6	42.7	14.7	2005	43.4	16.9	67.2	31.8
Kyrgyz Republic	16.2	26.0	2010	6.7	1.5	22.9	6.4	2011	5.0	1.1	21.6	5.4
Lao PDR	4,677.0	7,483.2	2002	44.0	12.1	76.9	31.1	2008	33.9	9.0	66.0	24.8
Latvia	0.4	0.7	2008	<2	<0.5	<2	<0.5	2009	<2	<0.5	<2	<0.5
Lesotho	4.3	6.9	1994	46.2	25.6	59.7	36.1	2003	43.4	20.8	62.3	33.1
Liberia	0.6	1.0		..	..	..	..	2007	83.8	40.9	94.9	59.6
Lithuania	2.1	3.3	2004	<2	<0.5	<2	0.5	2008	<2	<0.5	<2	<0.5
Macedonia, FYR	29.5	47.2	2009	<2	<0.5	5.9	0.9	2010	<2	<0.5	6.9	1.2
Madagascar	945.5	1,512.8	2005	67.8	26.5	89.6	46.9	2010	81.3	43.3	92.6	60.1
Malawi	71.2	113.8	2004	73.9	32.3	90.5	51.8	2010	61.6	26.2	82.3	44.0
Malaysia	2.6	4.2	2007[e]	<2	<0.5	2.9	<0.5	2009[e]	<2	<0.5	2.3	<0.5
Maldives	358.3	573.5	1998	25.6	13.1	37.0	20.0	2004	<2	<0.5	12.2	2.5
Mali	362.1	579.4	2006	51.4	18.8	77.1	36.5	2010	50.4	16.4	78.7	35.2
Mauritania	157.1	251.3	2004	25.4	7.0	52.6	19.2	2008	23.4	6.8	47.7	17.7
Mexico	9.6	15.3	2008	<2	<0.5	5.2	1.3	2010	<2	<0.5	4.5	1.0
Micronesia, Fed. Sts.	0.8[c]	1.3[c]		..	..	..	..	2000[d]	31.2	16.3	44.7	24.5
Moldova	6.0	9.7	2009	<2	<0.5	7.1	1.2	2010	<2	<0.5	4.4	0.7
Montenegro	0.6	1.0	2009	<2	<0.5	<2	<0.5	2010	<2	<0.5	<2	<0.5
Morocco	6.9	11.0	2001	6.3	0.9	24.3	6.3	2007	2.5	0.5	14.0	3.2
Mozambique	14,532.1	23,251.4	2003	74.7	35.4	90.0	53.6	2008	59.6	25.1	81.8	42.9
Namibia	6.3	10.1	1993[e]	49.1	24.6	62.2	36.5	2004[e]	31.9	9.5	51.1	21.8
Nepal	33.1	52.9	2003	53.1	18.4	77.3	36.6	2010	24.8	5.6	57.3	19.0
Nicaragua	9.1[c]	14.6[c]	2001[e]	14.4	3.7	34.4	11.5	2005[e]	11.9	2.4	31.7	9.6
Niger	334.2	534.7	2005	50.2	18.3	75.3	35.6	2008	43.6	12.4	75.2	30.8
Nigeria	98.2	157.2	2004	63.1	28.7	83.1	45.9	2010	68.0	33.7	84.5	50.2
Pakistan	25.9	41.4	2006	22.6	4.1	61.0	18.8	2008	21.0	3.5	60.2	17.9
Panama	0.8[c]	1.2[c]	2009[f]	5.9	1.8	14.6	4.9	2010[f]	6.6	2.1	13.8	5.1
Papua New Guinea	2.1[c]	3.4[c]		..	..	..	..	1996	35.8	12.3	57.4	25.5
Paraguay	2,659.7	4,255.6	2009[f]	7.6	3.2	14.2	6.0	2010[f]	7.2	3.0	13.2	5.7
Peru	2.1	3.3	2009[f]	5.5	1.6	14.0	4.6	2010[f]	4.9	1.3	12.7	4.1
Philippines	30.2	48.4	2006	22.6	5.5	45.0	16.4	2009	18.4	3.7	41.5	13.8
Poland	2.7	4.3	2010	<2	<0.5	<2	<0.5	2011	<2	<0.5	<2	<0.5
Romania	2.1	3.4	2010	<2	<0.5	<2	0.5	2011	<2	<0.5	<2	<0.5
Russian Federation	16.7	26.8	2008	<2	<0.5	<2	<0.5	2009	<2	<0.5	<2	<0.5
Rwanda	295.9	473.5	2006	72.1	34.8	87.4	52.2	2011	63.2	26.6	82.4	44.6

Poverty rates

	International poverty line in local currency		Population below international poverty lines[a]									
	$1.25 a day 2005	$2 a day 2005	Survey year[b]	Population below $1.25 a day %	Poverty gap at $1.25 a day %	Population below $2 a day %	Poverty gap at $2 a day %	Survey year[b]	Population below $1.25 a day %	Poverty gap at $1.25 a day %	Population below $2 a day %	Poverty gap at $2 a day %
São Tomé and Príncipe	7,953.9	12,726.3		..	..	..	..	2001	28.2	7.9	54.2	20.6
Senegal	372.8	596.5	2005	33.5	10.8	60.4	24.7	2011	29.6	9.1	55.2	21.9
Serbia	42.9	68.6	2009	<2	<0.5	<2	<0.5	2010	<2	<0.5	<2	<0.5
Seychelles	5.6[c]	9.0[c]	2000	<2	<0.5	<2	<0.5	2007	<2	<0.5	<2	<0.5
Sierra Leone	1,745.3	2,792.4	2003	53.4	20.3	76.1	37.5	2011	51.7	16.6	79.6	35.8
Slovak Republic	23.5	37.7	2008[e]	<2	<0.5	<2	<0.5	2009[e]	<2	<0.5	<2	<0.5
Slovenia	198.2	317.2	2003	<2	<0.5	<2	<0.5	2004	<2	<0.5	<2	<0.5
South Africa	5.7	9.1	2006	17.4	3.3	35.7	12.3	2009	13.8	2.3	31.3	10.2
Sri Lanka	50.0	80.1	2007	7.0	1.0	29.1	7.4	2010	4.1	0.7	23.9	5.4
St. Lucia	2.4[c]	3.8[c]		..	..	..	..	1995	20.9	7.2	40.6	15.5
Sudan	154.4	247.0		..	..	..	..	2009	19.8	5.5	44.1	15.4
Suriname	2.3[c]	3.7[c]		..	..	..	..	1999	15.5	5.9	27.2	11.7
Swaziland	4.7	7.5	2001	62.9	29.4	81.0	45.8	2010	40.6	16.0	60.4	29.3
Syrian Arab Republic	30.8	49.3		..	..	..	..	2004	<2	<0.5	16.9	3.3
Tajikistan	1.2	1.9	2007	14.7	4.4	37.0	12.2	2009	6.6	1.2	27.7	7.0
Tanzania	603.1	964.9	2000	84.6	41.6	95.3	60.3	2007	67.9	28.1	87.9	47.5
Thailand	21.8	34.9	2009[j]	<2	<0.5	4.6	0.8	2010[j]	<2	<0.5	4.1	0.7
Togo	352.8	564.5	2006	38.7	11.4	69.3	27.9	2011	28.2	8.8	52.7	20.9
Trinidad and Tobago	5.8[c]	9.2[c]	1988[e]	<2	<0.5	8.6	1.9	1992[e]	4.2	1.1	13.5	3.9
Tunisia	0.9	1.4	2005	<2	<0.5	8.1	1.8	2010	<2	<0.5	4.3	1.1
Turkey	1.3	2.0	2009	<2	<0.5	2.7	0.7	2010	<2	<0.5	4.7	1.4
Turkmenistan	5,961.1[c]	9,537.7[c]	1993[e]	63.5	25.8	85.7	44.9	1998[e]	24.8	7.0	49.7	18.4
Uganda	930.8	1,489.2	2006	51.5	19.1	75.6	36.4	2009	38.0	12.2	64.7	27.4
Ukraine	2.1	3.4	2009	<2	<0.5	<2	<0.5	2010	<2	<0.5	<2	<0.5
Uruguay	19.1	30.6	2009[f]	<2	<0.5	<2	<0.5	2010[f]	<2	<0.5	<2	<0.5
Venezuela, RB	1,563.9	2,502.2	2005[f]	13.4	8.2	21.9	11.6	2006[f]	6.6	3.7	12.9	5.9
Vietnam	7,399.9	11,839.8	2006	21.4	5.3	48.1	16.3	2008	16.9	3.8	43.4	13.5
West Bank and Gaza	2.7[c]	4.3[c]	2007	<2	<0.5	2.5	0.5	2009	<2	<0.5	<2	<0.5
Yemen, Rep.	113.8	182.1	1998	12.9	3.0	36.4	11.1	2005	17.5	4.2	46.6	14.8
Zambia	3,537.9	5,660.7	2006	68.5	37.0	82.6	51.8	2010	74.5	41.9	86.6	56.8

a. Based on nominal per capita consumption averages and distributions estimated parametrically from grouped household survey data, unless otherwise noted. b. Refers to the year in which the underlying household survey data were collected or, when the data collection period bridged two calendar years, the year in which most of the data were collected. c. Based on purchasing power parity (PPP) dollars imputed using regression. d. Covers urban areas only. e. Based on per capita income averages and distribution data estimated parametrically from grouped household survey data. f. Estimated nonparametrically from nominal income per capita distributions based on unit-record household survey data. g. PPP conversion factor based on urban prices. h. Population-weighted average of urban and rural estimates. i. Based on benchmark national PPP estimate rescaled to account for cost-of-living differences in urban and rural areas. j. Estimated nonparametrically from nominal consumption per capita distributions based on unit-record household survey data.

Trends in poverty indicators by region, 1990–2015

Region	1990	1993	1996	1999	2002	2005	2008	2010 estimate	2015 forecast	Trend, 1990–2010
Share of population living on less than 2005 PPP $1.25 a day (%)										
East Asia & Pacific	56.2	50.7	35.9	35.6	27.6	17.1	14.3	12.5	5.5	
Europe & Central Asia	1.9	2.9	3.9	3.8	2.3	1.3	0.5	0.7	0.4	
Latin America & Caribbean	12.2	11.4	11.1	11.9	11.9	8.7	6.5	5.5	4.9	
Middle East & North Africa	5.8	4.8	4.8	5.0	4.2	3.5	2.7	2.4	2.6	
South Asia	53.8	51.7	48.6	45.1	44.3	39.4	36.0	31.0	23.2	
Sub-Saharan Africa	56.5	59.4	58.1	57.9	55.7	52.3	49.2	48.5	42.3	
Total	43.1	41.0	34.8	34.1	30.8	25.1	22.7	20.6	15.5	
People living on less than 2005 PPP $1.25 a day (millions)										
East Asia & Pacific	926	871	640	656	523	332	284	251	115	
Europe & Central Asia	9	14	18	18	11	6	2	3	2	
Latin America & Caribbean	53	53	54	60	63	48	37	32	30	
Middle East & North Africa	13	12	12	14	12	10	9	8	9	
South Asia	617	632	631	619	640	598	571	507	406	
Sub-Saharan Africa	290	330	349	376	390	395	399	414	408	
Total	1,908	1,910	1,704	1,743	1,639	1,389	1,302	1,215	970	
Regional distribution of people living on less than $1.25 a day (% of total population living on less than $1.25 a day)										
East Asia & Pacific	48.5	45.6	37.6	37.6	31.9	23.9	21.8	20.7	11.8	
Europe & Central Asia	0.5	0.7	1.1	1.0	0.6	0.5	0.2	0.3	0.2	
Latin America & Caribbean	2.8	2.7	3.1	3.4	3.8	3.4	2.9	2.7	3.1	
Middle East & North Africa	0.7	0.6	0.7	0.8	0.7	0.8	0.7	0.7	1.0	
South Asia	32.3	33.1	37.0	35.5	39.1	43.1	43.8	41.7	41.9	
Sub-Saharan Africa	15.2	17.3	20.5	21.6	23.8	28.4	30.7	34.1	42.1	
Average daily consumption or income of people living on less than 2005 PPP $1.25 a day (2005 PPP $)										
East Asia & Pacific	0.83	0.85	0.89	0.87	0.89	0.95	0.95	0.97	..	
Europe & Central Asia	0.90	0.90	0.91	0.92	0.93	0.88	0.88	0.85	..	
Latin America & Caribbean	0.71	0.69	0.68	0.67	0.65	0.63	0.62	0.60	..	
Middle East & North Africa	1.02	1.02	1.01	1.01	1.01	0.99	0.97	0.96	..	
South Asia	0.88	0.89	0.91	0.91	0.92	0.94	0.95	0.96	..	
Sub-Saharan Africa	0.69	0.68	0.69	0.69	0.70	0.71	0.71	0.71	..	
Total	0.82	0.83	0.85	0.84	0.85	0.87	0.87	0.87	..	
Survey coverage (% of total population represented by underlying survey data)										
East Asia & Pacific	92.4	93.3	93.7	93.4	93.5	93.2	93.6	93.5	..	
Europe & Central Asia	81.5	87.3	97.1	93.9	96.3	94.7	89.9	85.3	..	
Latin America & Caribbean	94.9	91.8	95.9	97.7	97.5	95.9	94.5	86.9	..	
Middle East & North Africa	76.8	65.3	81.7	70.0	21.5	85.7	46.7	30.8	..	
South Asia	96.5	98.2	98.1	20.1	98.0	98.0	97.9	94.5	..	
Sub-Saharan Africa	46.0	68.8	68.0	53.1	65.7	82.7	81.7	64.1	..	
Total	86.4	89.4	91.6	68.2	87.8	93.0	90.2	84.7	..	

Source: World Bank PovcalNet.

Poverty rates

The World Bank produced its first global poverty estimates for developing countries for *World Development Report 1990: Poverty* (World Bank 1990) using household survey data for 22 countries (Ravallion, Datt, and van de Walle 1991). Since then there has been considerable expansion in the number of countries that field household income and expenditure surveys. The World Bank's Development Research Group maintains a database that is updated regularly as new survey data become available (and thus may contain more recent data or revisions that are not incorporated into the table) and conducts a major reassessment of progress against poverty about every three years. The next comprehensive reassessment is due later this year, and revised and updated poverty data will be published in the *World Development Indicators* online tables and database.

Last year the World Bank published the 2010 extreme poverty estimates for developing country regions and the developing world as a whole (that is, countries classified as low and middle income in 1990). They are provisional due to low household survey data availability for recent years (2008–12). Because about 40 new surveys have become available this year, the provisional 2010 estimates will be revised into 2011 estimates during the aforementioned comprehensive reassessment. The projections to 2015, which will also be revised later this year, use the 2010 provisional estimates as a baseline and assume that average household income or consumption will grow in line with the aggregate economic projections reported in *Global Economic Prospects 2014* (World Bank 2014) but that inequality within countries will remain unchanged. Estimates of the number of people living in extreme poverty are based on population projections in the World Bank's HealthStats database (http://datatopics.worldbank.org/hnp).

PovcalNet (http://iresearch.worldbank.org/PovcalNet) is an interactive computational tool that allows users to replicate these internationally comparable $1.25 and $2 a day poverty estimates for countries, developing country regions, and the developing world as a whole and to compute poverty measures for custom country groupings and for different poverty lines. The Poverty and Equity Data portal (http://povertydata.worldbank.org/poverty/home) provides access to the database and user-friendly dashboards with graphs and interactive maps that visualize trends in key poverty and inequality indicators for different regions and countries. The country dashboards display trends in poverty measures based on the national poverty lines (see online table 2.7) alongside the internationally comparable estimates in the table, produced from and consistent with PovcalNet.

Data availability

The World Bank's internationally comparable poverty monitoring database now draws on income or detailed consumption data collected from interviews with 1.23 million randomly sampled households through more than 850 household surveys collected by national statistical offices in nearly 130 countries. Despite progress in the last decade, the challenges of measuring poverty remain. The timeliness, frequency, quality, and comparability of household surveys need to increase substantially, particularly in the poorest countries. The availability and quality of poverty monitoring data remain low in small states, fragile situations, and low-income countries and even some middle-income countries.

The low frequency and lack of comparability of the data available in some countries create uncertainty over the magnitude of poverty reduction. The table on trends in poverty indicators reports the percentage of the regional and global population represented by household survey samples collected during the reference year or during the two preceding or two subsequent years (in other words, within a five-year window centered on the reference year). Data coverage in Sub-Saharan Africa and the Middle East and North Africa remains low and variable. The need to improve household survey programs for monitoring poverty is clearly urgent. But institutional, political, and financial obstacles continue to limit data collection, analysis, and public access.

Data quality

Besides the frequency and timeliness of survey data, other data quality issues arise in measuring household living standards. The surveys ask detailed questions on sources of income and how it was spent, which must be carefully recorded by trained personnel. Income is generally more difficult to measure accurately, and consumption comes closer to the notion of living standards. And income can vary over time even if living standards do not. But consumption data are not always available: the latest estimates reported here use consumption for about two-thirds of countries.

However, even similar surveys may not be strictly comparable because of differences in timing, sampling frames, or the quality and training of enumerators. Comparisons of countries at different levels of development also pose a potential problem because of differences in the relative importance of the consumption of nonmarket goods. The local market value of all consumption in kind (including own production, particularly important in underdeveloped rural economies) should be included in total consumption expenditure, but may not be. Most survey data now include valuations for consumption or income from own production, but valuation methods vary.

The statistics reported here are based on consumption data or, when unavailable, on income data. Analysis of some 20 countries for which both consumption and income data were available from the same surveys found income to yield a higher mean than consumption but also higher inequality. When poverty measures based on consumption and income were compared, the two effects roughly cancelled each other out: there was no significant statistical difference.

Invariably some sampled households do not participate in surveys because they refuse to do so or because nobody is at home during the interview visit. This is referred to as "unit nonresponse" and is distinct from "item nonresponse," which occurs when some of the sampled respondents participate but refuse to answer certain questions, such as those pertaining to income or consumption. To the extent that survey nonresponse is random, there is no concern regarding biases in survey-based inferences; the sample will still be representative of the population. However, households with different income might not be equally likely to respond. Richer households may be less likely to participate because of the high opportunity cost of their time or concerns about intrusion in their affairs. It is conceivable that the poorest can likewise be underrepresented; some are homeless or nomadic and hard to reach in standard household survey designs, and some may be physically or socially isolated and thus less likely to be interviewed. This can bias both poverty and inequality measurement if not corrected for (Korinek, Mistiaen, and Ravallion 2007).

International poverty lines

International comparisons of poverty estimates entail both conceptual and practical problems. Countries have different definitions of poverty, and consistent comparisons across countries can be difficult. Local poverty lines tend to have higher purchasing power in rich countries, where more generous standards are used, than in poor countries. Poverty measures based on an international poverty line attempt to hold the real value of the poverty line constant across countries, as is done when making comparisons over time. Since *World Development Report 1990* the World Bank has aimed to apply a common standard in measuring extreme poverty, anchored to what *poverty* means in the world's poorest countries. The welfare of people living in different countries can be measured on a common scale by adjusting for differences in the purchasing power of currencies. The commonly used $1 a day standard, measured in 1985 international prices and adjusted to local currency using purchasing power parities (PPPs), was chosen for *World Development Report 1990* because it was typical of the poverty lines in low-income countries at the time. Early editions of *World Development Indicators* used PPPs from the Penn World Tables to convert values in local currency to equivalent purchasing power measured in U.S dollars. Later editions used 1993 consumption PPP estimates produced by the World Bank.

International poverty lines were recently revised using the new data on PPPs compiled in the 2005 round of the International Comparison Program, along with data from an expanded set of household income and expenditure surveys. The new extreme poverty line is set at $1.25 a day in 2005 PPP terms, which represents the mean of the poverty lines found in the poorest 15 countries ranked by per capita consumption. The new poverty line maintains the same standard for extreme poverty—the poverty line typical of the poorest countries in the world—but updates it using the latest information on the cost of living in developing countries. PPP exchange rates are used to estimate global poverty because they take into account the local prices of goods and services not traded internationally. But PPP rates were designed for comparing aggregates from national accounts, not for making international poverty comparisons. As a result, there is no certainty that an international poverty line measures the same degree of need or deprivation across countries. So-called poverty PPPs, designed to compare the consumption of the poorest people in the world, might provide a better basis for comparison of poverty across countries. Work on these measures is ongoing.

Definitions

• **International poverty line in local currency** is the international poverty lines of $1.25 and $2.00 a day in 2005 prices, converted to local currency using the PPP conversion factors estimated by the International Comparison Program. • **Survey year** is the year in which the underlying data were collected or, when the data collection period bridged two calendar years, the year in which most of the data were collected. • **Population below $1.25 a day** and **population below $2 a day** are the percentages of the population living on less than $1.25 a day and $2 a day at 2005 international prices. As a result of revisions in PPP exchange rates, consumer price indexes, or welfare aggregates, poverty rates for individual countries cannot be compared with poverty rates reported in earlier editions. The PovcalNet online database and tool (http://iresearch.worldbank .org/PovcalNet) always contain the most recent full time series of comparable country data. • **Poverty gap** is the mean shortfall from the poverty line (counting the nonpoor as having zero shortfall), expressed as a percentage of the poverty line. This measure reflects the depth of poverty as well as its incidence.

Data sources

The poverty measures are prepared by the World Bank's Development Research Group. The international poverty lines are based on nationally representative primary household surveys conducted by national statistical offices or by private agencies under the supervision of government or international agencies and obtained from government statistical offices and World Bank Group country departments. For details on data sources and methods used in deriving the World Bank's latest estimates, see http://iresearch.worldbank .org/povcalnet.

References

Chen, Shaohua, and Martin Ravallion. 2011. "The Developing World Is Poorer Than We Thought, But No Less Successful in the Fight Against Poverty." *Quarterly Journal of Economics* 125(4): 1577–625.

Korinek, Anton, Johan A. Mistiaen, and Martin Ravallion. 2007. "An Econometric Method of Correcting for Unit Nonresponse Bias in Surveys." *Journal of Econometrics* 136: 213–35.

Ravallion, Martin, Guarav Datt, and Dominique van de Walle. 1991. "Quantifying Absolute Poverty in the Developing World." *Review of Income and Wealth* 37(4): 345–61.

Ravallion, Martin, Shaohua Chen, and Prem Sangraula. 2009. "Dollar a Day Revisited." *World Bank Economic Review* 23(2): 163–84.

World Bank. 1990. *World Development Report 1990: Poverty.* Washington, DC.

———. 2008. *Poverty Data: A Supplement to World Development Indicators 2008.* Washington, DC.

———. 2014. *Global Economic Prospects: Coping with Policy Normalization in High-income Countries.* Volume 8, January 14. Washington, DC.

PEOPLE

The *People* section presents demographic trends and forecasts alongside indicators of education, health, jobs, social protection, poverty, and the distribution of income. Together they provide a multidimensional portrait of human development.

This edition includes estimates of extreme poverty rates for 2010—measured as the proportion of the population living on less than $1.25 a day. The availability, frequency, and quality of poverty monitoring data remain low, especially in small states and in countries and territories with fragile situations. While estimates may change marginally as additional country data become available, it is now clear that the first Millennium Development Goal target—cutting the global extreme poverty rate to half its 1990 level—was achieved before the 2015 target date. In 1990, the benchmark year for the Millennium Development Goals, the extreme poverty rate was 43.1 percent. Estimates for 2010 show that the extreme poverty rate had fallen to 20.6 percent. The World Bank is working to create a complementary dataset to measure the goal of promoting shared prosperity, using the per capita incomes of the bottom 40 percent of the population in each country. To be released at the 2014 Annual Meetings of the World Bank, the dataset will be included in future *World Development Indicators*.

In addition to extreme poverty rates, the *People* section includes many other indicators to monitor the Millennium Development Goals. Following the Millennium Declaration by the United Nations General Assembly in 2000, various international agencies, including the World Bank, resolved to monitor the Millennium Development Goals using a harmonized set of indicators and to invest in improving data availability and quality. These efforts range from providing technical and financial assistance for strengthening country statistical systems to fostering international collaboration through participation in the United Nations Inter-agency and Expert Group on the Millennium Development Goal Indicators and several thematic interagency groups.

For example, estimates of child mortality in 2000 varied by source, method, and availability, making comparisons across countries and over time difficult. To address this, a UN interagency group has improved methods and harmonization, shared sources, reported on progress, and helped boost countries' measurement capacity. This effort has produced consistent estimates of neonatal, infant, and under-five mortality rates that span 50 years. Similar interagency efforts are improving maternal mortality estimates and gender statistics. For gender an interagency and expert group has endorsed a set of indicators to guide national efforts to produce, compile, and disseminate comparable gender statistics. As part of this work, the World Bank is providing technical assistance and training to national statistical offices, and new partnerships and initiatives, such as Evidence and Data for Gender Statistics and Data2X, are facilitating international action and collaboration.

People includes indicators disaggregated by location and by socioeconomic and demographic variables, such as sex, age, subnational and regional location, and wealth. These data provide important perspectives on the disparities within countries. New for the 2014 edition is an indicator of severe wasting, disaggregated by sex. Other new indicators include national estimates for labor force participation rates and ratios of employment to population.

 Economy | States and markets | Global links | Back

Highlights

Lower secondary completion rates fell only in the Middle East and North Africa

Completion rate, lower secondary education
(% of relevant age group)

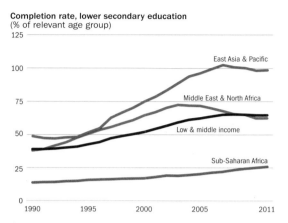

Source: United Nations Educational, Scientific and Cultural Organization Institute for Statistics.

Over the past 20 years lower secondary completion rates have increased 66 percent in low- and middle-income countries. East Asia and Pacific has seen the most progress, with the rate doubling to 99 percent over 1990–2011. Until the mid-1990s the Middle East and North Africa was on par with East Asia and Pacific, but upward trajectories in many of the region's countries have not been enough to offset Iran's decline since 2003. In Sub-Saharan Africa only 26 percent of students in the final grade of lower secondary education completed school in 2011, compared with 70 percent of students in the final grade of primary education. Given that these rates are an upper estimate of actual completion rates, the real situation is likely to be worse.

Europe and Central Asia has the lowest gap between net and gross enrollment rates

Gross enrollment ratio, primary education, 2011 (%)
■ Share of underage or overage students ■ Net enrollment rate

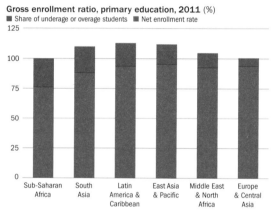

Source: United Nations Educational, Scientific and Cultural Organization Institute for Statistics.

The gap between net and gross enrollment rates captures the incidence of underage or overage students and is a measure of the efficiency of an education system. In Sub-Saharan Africa 42 percent of children enrolled in primary education dropped out in 2011, giving the region the highest dropout rate, repetition rate, and gap between gross and net enrollment. Latin America and Caribbean's net enrollment rate is almost the same as Europe and Central Asia's, but the gap is wider in the former. This suggests that the education system is more efficient Europe and Central Asia, which has the lowest repeater rate and drop-out rate.

In 2012 child wasting was most serious in South Asia

Prevalence of wasting among children ages 0–59 months, 2012 (%)
— 95% lower confidence limit ● Prevalence estimate — 95% upper confidence limit

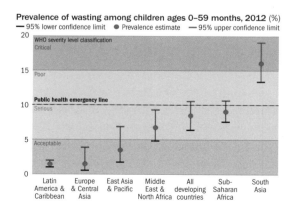

Source: UNICEF, WHO, and World Bank 2013.

Wasting, defined as weight for height more than two standard deviations below the median for the international reference population ages 0–59 months, is a measure for acute malnutrition. World Health Organization (WHO) member countries have endorsed a global nutrition target to reduce the prevalence of child wasting to less than 5 percent by 2025. In 2012 the prevalence was estimated at 8.5 percent for all developing countries and was below 5 percent in three out of the six World Bank developing regions. In the Middle East and North Africa and Sub-Saharan Africa the prevalence was above 5 percent but below the WHO Public Health Emergency Line of 10 percent. South Asia had the highest prevalence, 16 percent, which is considered critical in the WHO severity level classification.

Most maternal deaths are in Sub-Saharan Africa and South Asia

In 2010, 85 percent of the world's maternal deaths occurred in Sub-Saharan Africa and South Asia. Although the number of maternal deaths has been falling in every region—globally from 540,000 to 290,000 over 1990–2010—the share of maternal deaths is increasingly concentrated in these two regions. In 2010 more than half of maternal deaths occurred in Sub-Saharan Africa, and 29 percent occurred in South Asia. In Sub-Saharan Africa the share of global maternal deaths increased from 35 percent in 1990 to 57 percent in 2010, suggesting a rate of decline that is slower than in other regions. In South Asia the share decreased from 45 percent in 1990 to 29 percent in 2010, but it still has the second largest share of global maternal deaths.

Share of global maternal deaths (%)

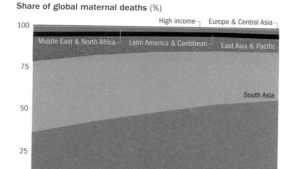

Source: WHO and others 2012.

Globally, a large proportion of under-five deaths occur in the first 28 days of life

The first 28 days of life (the neonatal period) are the most vulnerable time for a child's survival. The proportion of deaths among children under age 5 that occur in the neonatal period is large and has increased in all regions since 1990, although neonatal mortality rates have been falling in every region. Declines in the neonatal mortality rate are slower than those in the under-five mortality rate: between 1990 and 2012 global neonatal mortality rates fell from 33 deaths per 1,000 births to 21, but the proportion of neonatal deaths in under-five deaths increased from 37 percent to 44 percent. In 2012 the proportion was more than 50 percent in four regions: Middle East and North Africa, East Asia and Pacific, South Asia, and Latin America and the Caribbean.

Proportion of deaths among children under age 5 that occur during the neonatal period (%)

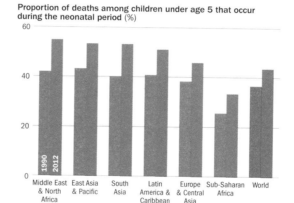

Source: UN Inter-agency Group for Child Mortality Estimation 2013.

Over 20 percent of ministers in Latin America and Sub-Saharan Africa are women

With over 20 percent of ministers being women, Latin America and Caribbean and Sub-Saharan Africa lead developing regions in women's participation in ministerial positions. Women occupy over 40 percent of ministerial positions in Cabo Verde, Ecuador, Bolivia, Nicaragua, and South Africa. However, even with these achievements, men still dominate leadership and decisionmaking positions in politics, business, and households. There are still 14 countries, including 5 high-income countries, that have no female representation in ministerial positions. Gender equality in decisionmaking not only benefits women and girls, but also matters for society more broadly. Empowering women as economic, political, and social actors can change policy choices and make institutions more representative of a range of voices.

Women in ministerial positions (% of total)

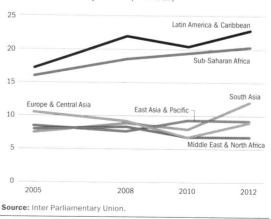

Source: Inter Parliamentary Union.

2 People

	Prevalence of child malnutrition, underweight % of children under age 5 2005–12ª	Under-five mortality rate per 1,000 live births 2012	Maternal mortality ratio Modeled estimate per 100,000 live births 2010	Adolescent fertility rate births per 1,000 women ages 15–19 2012	Prevalence of HIV % of population ages 15–49 2012	Primary completion rate % of relevant age group 2008–12ª	Youth literacy rate % ages 15–24 2005–12ª	Labor force participation rate Modeled ILO estimate % ages 15 and older 2012	Vulnerable employment Unpaid family workers and own-account workers % of total employment 2008–12ª	Unemployment % of total labor force 2008–12ª	Female legislators, senior officials, and managers % of total 2008–12ª
Afghanistan	..	99	460	87	<0.1	..	..	48	..	..	..
Albania	6.3	17	27	15	..	..	99	55	..	14	..
Algeria	3.7	20	97	10	..	100	92	44	30	10	..
American Samoa	..	..	..	..	..	..	..	..	..	..	..
Andorra	..	3	..	..	..	..	..	..	..	..	..
Angola	15.6	164	450	170	2.3	54	73	70	..	..	..
Antigua and Barbuda	..	10	..	49	..	100	..	..	..	..	..
Argentina	2.3	14	77	54	0.4	109	99	61	19	7	..
Armenia	5.3	16	30	27	0.2	100	100	63	30	18	22
Aruba	..	..	..	27	..	95	99	..	..	..	..
Australia	0.2	5	7	12	..	..	..	65	9	5	37
Austria	..	4	4	4	..	97	..	61	9	4	27
Azerbaijan	8.4	35	43	40	0.2	92	100	66	55	5	7
Bahamas, The	..	17	47	28	3.3	93	..	74	..	14	52
Bahrain	..	10	20	14	..	..	98	71	2	1	..
Bangladesh	36.8	41	240	81	<0.1	75	79	71	..	5	..
Barbados	..	18	51	48	0.9	104	..	71	..	12	47
Belarus	1.3	5	4	21	0.4	103	100	56	2	6	..
Belgium	..	4	8	7	..	91	..	53	10	8	30
Belize	6.2	18	53	71	1.4	116	..	66	..	8	..
Benin	20.2	90	350	90	1.1	71	42	73	..	..	..
Bermuda	..	..	..	..	..	91	..	..	..	..	..
Bhutan	12.8	45	180	41	0.2	101	74	72	53	2	27
Bolivia	4.5	41	190	72	0.3	92	99	72	55	3	..
Bosnia and Herzegovina	1.5	7	8	15	..	..	100	45	27	28	..
Botswana	11.2	53	160	44	23.0	95	95	77	..	..	..
Brazil	2.2	14	56	71	..	..	98	70	25	7	..
Brunei Darussalam	..	8	24	23	..	102	100	64	..	..	..
Bulgaria	..	12	11	36	..	104	98	53	8	12	37
Burkina Faso	26.2	102	300	115	1.0	58	39	84	..	..	..
Burundi	29.1	104	800	30	1.3	62	89	83	..	..	..
Cabo Verde	..	22	79	71	0.2	99	98	67	..	..	..
Cambodia	29.0	40	250	44	0.8	98	87	83	64	0	21
Cameroon	15.1	95	690	116	4.5	73	81	70	76	4	..
Canada	..	5	12	14	..	..	..	66	..	7	36
Cayman Islands	..	..	..	..	..	..	99	..	..	4	44
Central African Republic	28.0	129	890	98	..	45	66	79	..	..	..
Chad	..	150	1,100	152	2.7	35	48	72	..	..	..
Channel Islands	..	..	..	8	..	..	..	..	..	..	..
Chile	0.5	9	25	55	0.4	97	99	62	24	6	..
China	3.4	14	37	9	..	..	100	71	..	4	..
Hong Kong SAR, China	..	..	..	3	..	98	..	59	7	3	32
Macao SAR, China	..	..	..	4	..	98	100	71	4	3	31
Colombia	3.4	18	92	69	0.5	105	98	67	49	11	..
Comoros	..	78	280	51	2.1	80	86	58	..	..	..
Congo, Dem. Rep.	24.2	146	540	135	1.1	73	66	72	..	..	..
Congo, Rep.	11.8	96	560	127	2.8	73	..	71	..	..	..

 Front | User guide | World view | People | Environment

	Prevalence of child malnutrition, underweight — % of children under age 5 — 2005–12a	Under-five mortality rate — per 1,000 live births — 2012	Maternal mortality ratio — Modeled estimate per 100,000 live births — 2010	Adolescent fertility rate — births per 1,000 women ages 15–19 — 2012	Prevalence of HIV — % of population ages 15–49 — 2012	Primary completion rate — % of relevant age group — 2008–12a	Youth literacy rate — % ages 15–24 — 2005–12a	Labor force participation rate — Modeled ILO estimate % ages 15 and older — 2012	Vulnerable employment — Unpaid family workers and own-account workers % of total employment — 2008–12a	Unemployment — % of total labor force — 2008–12a	Female legislators, senior officials, and managers — % of total — 2008–12a
Costa Rica	1.1	10	40	61	0.3	95	98	63	20	8	35
Côte d'Ivoire	29.4	108	400	130	3.2	61	68	67	..	..	..
Croatia	..	5	17	13	..	94	100	51	17	16	25
Cuba	..	6	73	43	<0.1	96	100	57	..	3	..
Curaçao	..	..	..	28	..	..	..	..	..	..	..
Cyprus	..	3	10	5	..	102	100	64	13	12	14
Czech Republic	..	4	5	5	..	102	..	59	15	7	26
Denmark	..	4	12	5	..	99	..	63	6	8	28
Djibouti	29.8	81	200	19	1.2	52b	..	52	..	..	..
Dominica	..	13	..	..	..	104	..	..	..	..	..
Dominican Republic	3.4	27	150	100	0.7	90	97	65	37	15	..
Ecuador	..	23	110	77	0.6	111	99	68	51	4	..
Egypt, Arab Rep.	6.8	21	66	43	<0.1	107	89	49	23	13	..
El Salvador	6.6	16	81	76	0.6	101	96	62	38	6	29
Equatorial Guinea	..	100	240	113	6.2	55	98	87	..	..	..
Eritrea	..	52	240	65	0.7	31	90	85	..	..	..
Estonia	..	4	2	17	..	96	100	62	5	10	36
Ethiopia	29.2	68	350	78	1.3	..	55	84	..	..	..
Faeroe Islands	..	..	..	..	..	..	..	..	..	..	..
Fiji	..	22	26	43	0.2	103	..	55	39	9	..
Finland	..	3	5	9	..	97	..	60	10	8	32
France	..	4	8	6	..	..	..	56	7	10	39
French Polynesia	..	..	..	38	..	..	..	56	..	..	..
Gabon	6.5	62	230	103	4.0	..	98	61	..	..	..
Gambia, The	15.8	73	360	116	1.3	70	68	78	..	..	..
Georgia	1.1	20	67	47	0.3	108	100	65	61	15	..
Germany	1.1	4	7	4	..	100	..	60	7	5	30
Ghana	14.3	72	350	58	1.4	98b	86	69	77	4	..
Greece	..	5	3	12	..	100	99	53	30	24	23
Greenland	..	..	..	..	..	..	..	..	..	..	..
Grenada	..	14	24	35	..	112	..	..	..	..	..
Guam	..	..	..	50	..	..	..	63	..	12	..
Guatemala	13.0	32	120	97	0.7	88	87	68	..	3	..
Guinea	16.3	101	610	131	1.7	61	31	72	..	..	..
Guinea-Bissau	16.6	129	790	99	3.9	64	73	73	..	..	..
Guyana	11.1	35	280	88	1.3	85	93	61	..	..	..
Haiti	18.9	76	350	42	2.1	..	72	66	..	..	..
Honduras	8.6	23	100	84	0.5	100	96	63	53	4	..
Hungary	..	6	21	12	..	99	99	52	6	11	40
Iceland	..	2	5	11	..	99	..	74	8	6	40
India	43.5	56	200	33	0.3	96	81	56	81	4	14
Indonesia	18.6	31	220	48	0.4	100	99	68	57	7	22
Iran, Islamic Rep.	..	18	21	32	0.2	102	99	45	42	11	13
Iraq	7.1	34	63	69	..	..	82	42	..	15	..
Ireland	..	4	6	8	..	..	..	60	12	15	33
Isle of Man	..	..	..	..	..	..	..	..	..	..	..
Israel	..	4	7	8	..	102	..	64	7	7	32

	Prevalence of child malnutrition, underweight	Under-five mortality rate	Maternal mortality ratio	Adolescent fertility rate	Prevalence of HIV	Primary completion rate	Youth literacy rate	Labor force participation rate	Vulnerable employment	Unemployment	Female legislators, senior officials, and managers
	% of children under age 5	per 1,000 live births	Modeled estimate per 100,000 live births	births per 1,000 women ages 15–19	% of population ages 15–49	% of relevant age group	% ages 15–24	Modeled ILO estimate % ages 15 and older	Unpaid family workers and own-account workers % of total employment	% of total labor force	% of total
	2005–12a	2012	2010	2012	2012	2008–12a	2005–12a	2012	2008–12a	2008–12a	2008–12a
Italy	..	4	4	4	..	103	100	49	18	11	25
Jamaica	3.2	17	110	70	1.7	..	96	63	38	14	..
Japan	..	3	5	5	..	102	..	59	11	4	..
Jordan	1.9	19	63	26	..	93	99	41	10	12	..
Kazakhstan	3.7	19	51	30	..	102b	100	72	29	5	38
Kenya	16.4	73	360	94	6.1	..	82	67	..	..	..
Kiribati	..	60	..	17	..	115	..	..	..	..	..
Korea, Dem. People's Rep.	18.8	29	81	1	..	..	100	78	..	..	..
Korea, Rep.	..	4	16	2	..	103	..	61	25	3	10
Kosovo	..	..	..	..	..	..	..	..	17	31	..
Kuwait	2.2	11	14	14	..	..	99	68	2	4	..
Kyrgyz Republic	2.7	27	71	29	0.3	98	100	67	..	8	..
Lao PDR	31.6	72	470	65	0.3	95	84	78	..	..	..
Latvia	..	9	34	14	..	99	100	60	8	15	45
Lebanon	..	9	25	12	..	86	99	47	..	25	..
Lesotho	13.5	100	620	89	23.1	72	83	66	..	25	..
Liberia	20.4	75	770	117	0.9	65	49	61	79	4	..
Libya	5.6	15	58	3	..	..	100	53	..	..	..
Liechtenstein	..	..	..	..	..	101	..	..	..	..	..
Lithuania	..	5	8	11	..	101	100	61	9	13	38
Luxembourg	..	2	20	8	..	84	..	58	6	5	24
Macedonia, FYR	2.1	7	10	18	..	94	99	55	22	31	28
Madagascar	..	58	240	123	0.5	70	65	89	..	..	..
Malawi	13.8	71	460	145	10.8	74	72	83	..	..	..
Malaysia	12.9	9	29	6	0.4	..	98	59	21	3	25
Maldives	17.8	11	60	4	<0.1	110	99	67	..	..	..
Mali	27.9	128	540	176	0.9	59	47	66	..	..	..
Malta	..	7	8	18	..	92	98	52	9	6	23
Marshall Islands	..	38	..	..	..	100	..	..	..	..	..
Mauritania	19.5	84	510	73	0.4	69	69	54	..	31	..
Mauritius	..	15	60	31	1.2	99	97	59	17	9	23
Mexico	2.8	16	50	63	0.2	93	98	62	29	5	31
Micronesia, Fed. Sts.	..	39	100	19	..	..	..	..	..	..	..
Moldova	3.2	18	41	29	0.7	90	100	40	29	6	44
Monaco	..	4	..	..	..	..	..	..	..	..	..
Mongolia	5.3	28	63	19	<0.1	130	96	62	55	5	47
Montenegro	2.2	6	8	15	..	101	99	50	..	20	30
Morocco	3.1	31	100	36	0.1	99b	82	50	51	9	13
Mozambique	15.6	90	490	138	11.1	52	67	84	..	..	..
Myanmar	22.6	52	200	12	0.6	95	96	79	..	..	..
Namibia	17.5	39	200	55	13.3	85	87	59	33	17	37
Nepal	29.1	42	170	74	0.3	100b	82	83	..	3	..
Netherlands	..	4	6	6	..	..	..	65	12	5	30
New Caledonia	..	..	..	21	..	..	100	57	..	..	..
New Zealand	..	6	15	25	..	..	..	68	12	7	40
Nicaragua	5.7	24	95	101	0.3	80	87	63	47	8	..
Niger	39.9	114	590	205	0.5	49	37	65	..	..	..

People 2

	Prevalence of child malnutrition, underweight % of children under age 5 2005–12ᵃ	Under-five mortality rate per 1,000 live births 2012	Maternal mortality ratio Modeled estimate per 100,000 live births 2010	Adolescent fertility rate births per 1,000 women ages 15–19 2012	Prevalence of HIV % of population ages 15–49 2012	Primary completion rate % of relevant age group 2008–12ᵃ	Youth literacy rate % ages 15–24 2005–12ᵃ	Labor force participation rate Modeled ILO estimate % ages 15 and older 2012	Vulnerable employment Unpaid family workers and own-account workers % of total employment 2008–12ᵃ	Unemployment % of total labor force 2008–12ᵃ	Female legislators, senior officials, and managers % of total 2008–12ᵃ
Nigeria	24.4	124	630	120	3.1	76	66	56	..	..	..
Northern Mariana Islands	..	..	..	..	..	..	..	..	..	..	..
Norway	..	3	7	8	..	98	..	66	5	3	31
Oman	8.6	12	32	11	..	104	98	64	..	..	..
Pakistan	30.9	86	260	27	<0.1	72	71	54	63	5	3
Palau	..	21	..	..	..	..	..	..	..	..	..
Panama	3.9	19	92	79	0.7	98	98	66	29	4	46
Papua New Guinea	18.1	63	230	62	0.5	..	71	72	..	..	..
Paraguay	3.4	22	99	67	0.3	86	99	70	43	5	34
Peru	4.5	18	67	51	0.4	91	97	76	46	4	19
Philippines	20.2	30	99	47	<0.1	91	98	65	40	7	55
Poland	..	5	5	12	..	95	100	57	18	10	38
Portugal	..	4	8	13	..	..	100	61	17	16	33
Puerto Rico	..	..	20	47	..	..	87	42	..	15	43
Qatar	..	7	7	10	..	..	97	87	..	1	4
Romania	..	12	27	31	..	97	97	56	32	7	31
Russian Federation	..	10	34	26	..	98	100	64	6	6	37
Rwanda	11.7	55	340	34	2.9	58	77	86	..	..	..
Samoa	..	18	100	28	..	102	100	41	38	6	36
San Marino	..	3	..	..	..	93	..	..	..	..	18
São Tomé and Príncipe	14.4	53	70	65	1.0	104ᵇ	80	61	..	..	..
Saudi Arabia	5.3	9	24	10	..	106	98	52	..	6	5
Senegal	14.4	60	370	94	0.5	60	65	77	..	..	..
Serbia	1.6	7	12	17	..	93	99	52	26	24	33
Seychelles	..	13	..	56	..	105	99	..	..	..	..
Sierra Leone	21.1	182	890	101	1.5	72	61	67	..	..	..
Singapore	..	3	3	6	..	..	100	68	9	3	34
Sint Maarten	..	..	..	..	..	..	..	..	..	..	..
Slovak Republic	..	8	6	16	..	95	..	60	12	14	31
Slovenia	..	3	12	1	..	101	100	58	13	9	38
Solomon Islands	11.5	31	93	65	..	85	..	66	..	..	..
Somalia	32.8	147	1,000	110	0.5	..	..	56	..	..	..
South Africa	8.7	45	300	51	17.9	..	99	52	10	25	31
South Sudan	32.5	104	..	75	2.7	..	..	..	..	..	..
Spain	..	5	6	11	..	102	100	59	12	25	30
Sri Lanka	21.6	10	35	17	<0.1	97	98	55	41	4	24
St. Kitts and Nevis	..	9	..	..	..	93	..	..	..	..	..
St. Lucia	..	18	35	56	..	92	..	69	..	21	..
St. Martin	..	..	..	..	..	..	..	..	..	..	..
St. Vincent & the Grenadines	..	23	48	55	..	99	..	67	8	19	..
Sudan	27.0ᶜ	73ᶜ	730	84ᶜ	..	..	87	54	..	15	..
Suriname	5.8	21	130	35	1.1	88	98	55	..	..	..
Swaziland	5.8	80	320	72	26.5	77	94	57	..	..	..
Sweden	..	3	4	7	..	102	..	64	7	8	35
Switzerland	..	4	8	2	..	96	..	68	9	4	33
Syrian Arab Republic	10.1	15	70	42	..	107	95	44	33	8	9
Tajikistan	15.0	58	65	43	0.3	98	100	68	47	12	..

 Economy | States and markets | Global links | ○ Back

2 People

	Prevalence of child malnutrition, underweight	Under-five mortality rate	Maternal mortality ratio	Adolescent fertility rate	Prevalence of HIV	Primary completion rate	Youth literacy rate	Labor force participation rate	Vulnerable employment	Unemployment	Female legislators, senior officials, and managers
			Modeled estimate	births per 1,000 women ages	% of			Modeled ILO estimate	Unpaid family workers and own-account workers		
	% of children under age 5	per 1,000 live births	per 100,000 live births	15–19	population ages 15–49	% of relevant age group	% ages 15–24	% ages 15 and older	% of total employment	% of total labor force	% of total
	2005–12ᵃ	2012	2010	2012	2012	2008–12ᵃ	2005–12ᵃ	2012	2008–12ᵃ	2008–12ᵃ	2008–12ᵃ
Tanzania	16.2	54	460	123	5.1	81	75	89	..	4	..
Thailand	7.0	13	48	41	1.1	..	98	72	54	1	25
Timor-Leste	45.3	57	300	52	..	71	80	38	70	4	10
Togo	16.5	96	300	92	2.9	74	80	81	..	..	..
Tonga	..	13	110	18	..	100	99	64	..	..	..
Trinidad and Tobago	..	21	46	35	1.6	95	100	64	..	5	..
Tunisia	3.3	16	56	5	<0.1	102	97	48	29	18	..
Turkey	..	14	20	31	..	103	99	49	32	9	10
Turkmenistan	..	53	67	18	..	..	100	61	..	..	..
Turks and Caicos Islands	..	..	..	..	..	..	..	..	..	..	..
Tuvalu	1.6	30	..	..	..	..	..	..	..	..	..
Uganda	14.1	69	310	127	7.2	53	87	78	..	4	..
Ukraine	..	11	32	26	0.9	103	100	59	18	8	39
United Arab Emirates	..	8	12	28	..	111	95	79	1	4	10
United Kingdom	..	5	12	26	..	..	..	62	12	8	34
United States	..	7	21	31	..	98	..	63	..	8	43
Uruguay	4.5	7	29	58	0.7	104	99	66	22	7	..
Uzbekistan	4.4	40	28	39	0.1	92	100	61	..	..	..
Vanuatu	11.7	18	110	45	..	84	95	71	70	5	29
Venezuela, RB	2.9	15	92	83	0.6	96	99	65	32	8	..
Vietnam	12.0	23	59	29	0.4	101	97	77	63	2	..
Virgin Islands (U.S.)	..	..	..	51	..	..	..	63	..	..	..
West Bank and Gaza	2.2	23	..	46	..	90	99	41	27	23	10
Yemen, Rep.	..	60	200	47	0.1	70	86	49	30	18	5
Zambia	14.9	89	440	125	12.7	91	64	79	..	..	..
Zimbabwe	10.1	90	570	60	14.7	..	91	86	..	..	..
World	**15.1 w**	**48 w**	**210 w**	**45 w**	**0.8 w**	**91 w**	**89 w**	**64 w**	**.. w**	**6 w**	
Low income	21.8	82	410	93	2.3	67	73	76	..	..	
Middle income	15.7	45	190	40	..	94	91	63	..	5	
Lower middle income	24.1	61	260	47	0.6	91	84	58	65	5	
Upper middle income	2.8	20	64	31	..	..	98	67	..	5	
Low & middle income	17.0	53	240	49	1.2	89	88	64	..	5	
East Asia & Pacific	5.3	21	83	20	..	..	99	71	..	4	
Europe & Central Asia	1.8	22	32	31	..	99	99	57	27	9	
Latin America & Carib.	2.9	19	82	69	..	102	97	67	32	7	
Middle East & N. Africa	6.2	26	81	37	..	91	92	46	34	11	
South Asia	32.2	60	220	39	0.3	88	80	57	78	4	
Sub-Saharan Africa	20.8	98	500	108	4.7	69	70	70	..	..	
High income	1.4	6	16	18	..	100	..	61	11	8	
Euro area	..	4	6	6	..	99	100	57	11	11	

a. Data are for the most recent year available. b. Data are for 2013. c. Excludes South Sudan.

 Front | User guide | World view | People | Environment

About the data

Though not included in the table due to space limitations, many indicators in this section are available disaggregated by sex, place of residence, wealth, and age in the World Development Indicators database.

Child malnutrition

Good nutrition is the cornerstone for survival, health, and development. Well-nourished children perform better in school, grow into healthy adults, and in turn give their children a better start in life. Well-nourished women face fewer risks during pregnancy and childbirth, and their children set off on firmer developmental paths, both physically and mentally. Undernourished children have lower resistance to infection and are more likely to die from common childhood ailments such as diarrheal diseases and respiratory infections. Frequent illness saps the nutritional status of those who survive, locking them into a vicious cycle of recurring sickness and faltering growth.

The proportion of underweight children is the most common child malnutrition indicator. Being even mildly underweight increases the risk of death and inhibits cognitive development in children. And it perpetuates the problem across generations, as malnourished women are more likely to have low-birthweight babies. Estimates of prevalence of underweight children are from the World Health Organization's (WHO) Global Database on Child Growth and Malnutrition, a standardized compilation of child growth and malnutrition data from national nutritional surveys. To better monitor global child malnutrition, the United Nations Children's Fund (UNICEF), WHO, and the World Bank have jointly produced estimates for 2012 and trends since 1990 for regions, income groups, and the world, using a harmonized database and aggregation method.

Under-five mortality

Mortality rates for children and others are important indicators of health status. When data on the incidence and prevalence of diseases are unavailable, mortality rates may be used to identify vulnerable populations. And they are among the indicators most frequently used to compare socioeconomic development across countries.

The main sources of mortality data are vital registration systems and direct or indirect estimates based on sample surveys or censuses. A complete vital registration system—covering at least 90 percent of vital events in the population—is the best source of age-specific mortality data. But complete vital registration systems are fairly uncommon in developing countries. Thus estimates must be obtained from sample surveys or derived by applying indirect estimation techniques to registration, census, or survey data (see *Primary data documentation*). Survey data are subject to recall error.

To make estimates comparable and to ensure consistency across estimates by different agencies, the UN Inter-agency Group for Child Mortality Estimation, which comprises UNICEF, WHO, the United Nations Population Division, the World Bank, and other universities

and research institutes, has developed and adopted a statistical method that uses all available information to reconcile differences. Trend lines are obtained by fitting a country-specific regression model of mortality rates against their reference dates. (For further discussion of childhood mortality estimates, see UN Inter-agency Group for Child Mortality Estimation [2013]; for detailed background data and for a graphic presentation, see www.childmortality.org).

Maternal mortality

Measurements of maternal mortality are subject to many types of errors. In countries with incomplete vital registration systems, deaths of women of reproductive age or their pregnancy status may not be reported, or the cause of death may not be known. Even in high-income countries with reliable vital registration systems, misclassification of maternal deaths has been found to lead to serious underestimation. Surveys and censuses can be used to measure maternal mortality by asking respondents about survivorship of sisters. But these estimates are retrospective, referring to a period approximately five years before the survey, and may be affected by recall error. Further, they reflect pregnancy-related deaths (deaths while pregnant or within 42 days of pregnancy termination, irrespective of the cause of death) and need to be adjusted to conform to the strict definition of maternal death.

Maternal mortality ratios in the table are modeled estimates based on work by WHO, UNICEF, United Nations Population Fund (UNFPA), and the World Bank and include country-level time series data. For countries without complete registration data but with other types of data and for countries with no data, maternal mortality is estimated with a multilevel regression model using available national maternal mortality data and socioeconomic information, including fertility, birth attendants, and gross domestic product. The methodology differs from that used for previous estimates, so data presented here should not be compared across editions (WHO and others 2012).

Adolescent fertility

Reproductive health is a state of physical and mental well-being in relation to the reproductive system and its functions and processes. Means of achieving reproductive health include education and services during pregnancy and childbirth, safe and effective contraception, and prevention and treatment of sexually transmitted diseases. Complications of pregnancy and childbirth are the leading cause of death and disability among women of reproductive age in developing countries.

Adolescent pregnancies are high risk for both mother and child. They are more likely to result in premature delivery, low birthweight, delivery complications, and death. Many adolescent pregnancies are unintended, but young girls may continue their pregnancies, giving up opportunities for education and employment, or seek unsafe abortions. Estimates of adolescent fertility rates are based on vital registration systems or, in their absence, censuses or sample

2 People

surveys and are generally considered reliable measures of fertility in the recent past. Where no empirical information on age-specific fertility rates is available, a model is used to estimate the share of births to adolescents. For countries without vital registration systems fertility rates are generally based on extrapolations from trends observed in censuses or surveys from earlier years.

Prevalence of HIV

HIV prevalence rates reflect the rate of HIV infection in each country's population. Low national prevalence rates can be misleading, however. They often disguise epidemics that are initially concentrated in certain localities or population groups and threaten to spill over into the wider population. In many developing countries most new infections occur in young adults, with young women especially vulnerable.

Data on HIV prevalence are from the Joint United Nations Programme on HIV/AIDS. Changes in procedures and assumptions for estimating the data and better coordination with countries have resulted in improved estimates. The models, which are routinely updated, track the course of HIV epidemics and their impacts, making full use of information on HIV prevalence trends from surveillance data as well as survey data. The models take into account reduced infectivity among people receiving antiretroviral therapy (which is having a larger impact on HIV prevalence and allowing HIV-positive people to live longer) and allow for changes in urbanization over time in generalized epidemics (important because prevalence is higher in urban areas and because many countries have seen rapid urbanization over the past two decades). The estimates include plausibility bounds, available at http://data.worldbank.org, which reflect the certainty associated with each of the estimates.

Primary completion

Many governments publish statistics that indicate how their education systems are working and developing—statistics on enrollment and efficiency indicators such as repetition rates, pupil–teacher ratios, and cohort progression. The primary completion rate, also called the gross intake ratio to last grade of primary education, is a core indicator of an education system's performance. It reflects an education system's coverage and the educational attainment of students. It is a key measure of progress toward the Millennium Development Goals and the Education for All initiative. However, a high primary completion rate does not necessarily mean high levels of student learning.

The indicator reflects the primary cycle as defined by the International Standard Classification of Education (ISCED97), ranging from three or four years of primary education (in a very small number of countries) to five or six years (in most countries) and seven (in a small number of countries). It is a proxy that should be taken as an upper estimate of the actual primary completion rate, since data limitations preclude adjusting for students who drop out during the final year of primary education. There are many reasons why the primary completion rate may exceed 100 percent. The numerator may include late entrants and overage children who have repeated one or more grades of primary education as well as children who entered school early, while the denominator is the number of children at the entrance age for the last grade of primary education.

Youth literacy

The youth literacy rate for ages 15–24 is a standard measure of recent progress in student achievement. It reflects the accumulated outcomes of primary education by indicating the proportion of the population that has acquired basic literacy and numeracy skills over the previous 10 years or so. In practice, however, literacy is difficult to measure. Estimating literacy rates requires census or survey measurements under controlled conditions. Many countries estimate the number of literate people from self-reported data. Some use educational attainment data as a proxy but apply different lengths of school attendance or levels of completion. Because definitions and methods of data collection differ across countries, data should be used cautiously. Generally, literacy encompasses numeracy, the ability to make simple arithmetic calculations.

Data on youth literacy are compiled by the United Nations Educational, Scientific and Cultural Organization (UNESCO) Institute for Statistics based on national censuses and household surveys during 1985–2012 and, for countries without recent literacy data, using the Global Age-Specific Literacy Projection Model.

Labor force participation

The labor force is the supply of labor available for producing goods and services in an economy. It includes people who are currently employed, people who are unemployed but seeking work, and first-time job-seekers. Not everyone who works is included, however. Unpaid workers, family workers, and students are often omitted, and some countries do not count members of the armed forces. Labor force size tends to vary during the year as seasonal workers enter and leave.

Data on the labor force are compiled by the International Labour Organization (ILO) from labor force surveys, censuses, and establishment censuses and surveys and from administrative records such as employment exchange registers and unemployment insurance schemes. Labor force surveys are the most comprehensive source for internationally comparable labor force data. Labor force data from population censuses are often based on a limited number of questions on the economic characteristics of individuals, with little scope to probe. Establishment censuses and surveys provide data on the employed population only, not unemployed workers, workers in small establishments, or workers in the informal sector (ILO, *Key Indicators of the Labour Market 2001–2002*).

Besides the data sources, there are other important factors that affect data comparability, such as census or survey reference period, definition of working age, and geographic coverage. For country-level information on source, reference period, or definition, consult the footnotes in the World Development Indicators database or the ILO's Key Indicators of the Labour Market, 8th edition, database.

The labor force participation rates in the table are modeled estimates from the ILO's Key Indicators of the Labour Market, 8th edition, database. These harmonized estimates use strict data selection criteria and enhanced methods to ensure comparability across countries and over time to avoid the inconsistencies mentioned above. Estimates are based mainly on labor force surveys, with other sources (population censuses and nationally reported estimates) used only when no survey data are available. National estimates of labor force participation rates are available in the World Development Indicators online database. Because other employment data are mostly national estimates, caution should be used when comparing the modeled labor force participation rate and other employment data.

Vulnerable employment

The proportion of unpaid family workers and own-account workers in total employment is derived from information on status in employment. Each group faces different economic risks, and unpaid family workers and own-account workers are the most vulnerable—and therefore the most likely to fall into poverty. They are the least likely to have formal work arrangements, are the least likely to have social protection and safety nets to guard against economic shocks, and are often incapable of generating enough savings to offset these shocks. A high proportion of unpaid family workers in a country indicates weak development, little job growth, and often a large rural economy.

Data on vulnerable employment are drawn from labor force and general household sample surveys, censuses, and official estimates. Besides the limitation mentioned for calculating labor force participation rates, there are other reasons to limit comparability. For example, information provided by the Organisation for Economic Co-operation and Development relates only to civilian employment, which can result in an underestimation of "employees" and "workers not classified by status," especially in countries with large armed forces. While the categories of unpaid family workers and own-account workers would not be affected, their relative shares would be.

Unemployment

The ILO defines the unemployed as members of the economically active population who are without work but available for and seeking work, including people who have lost their jobs or who have voluntarily left work. Some unemployment is unavoidable. At any time some workers are temporarily unemployed—between jobs as employers look for the right workers and workers search for better jobs. Such unemployment, often called frictional unemployment, results from the normal operation of labor markets.

Changes in unemployment over time may reflect changes in the demand for and supply of labor, but they may also reflect changes in reporting practices. In countries without unemployment or welfare benefits people eke out a living in vulnerable employment. In countries with well-developed safety nets workers can afford to wait for suitable or desirable jobs. But high and sustained unemployment indicates serious inefficiencies in resource allocation.

The criteria for people considered to be seeking work, and the treatment of people temporarily laid off or seeking work for the first time, vary across countries. In many developing countries it is especially difficult to measure employment and unemployment in agriculture. The timing of a survey can maximize the effects of seasonal unemployment in agriculture. And informal sector employment is difficult to quantify where informal activities are not tracked.

Data on unemployment are drawn from labor force sample surveys and general household sample surveys, censuses, and official estimates. Administrative records, such as social insurance statistics and employment office statistics, are not included because of their limitations in coverage.

Women tend to be excluded from the unemployment count for various reasons. Women suffer more from discrimination and from structural, social, and cultural barriers that impede them from seeking work. Also, women are often responsible for the care of children and the elderly and for household affairs. They may not be available for work during the short reference period, as they need to make arrangements before starting work. Further, women are considered to be employed when they are working part-time or in temporary jobs, despite the instability of these jobs or their active search for more secure employment.

Female legislators, senior officials, and managers

Despite much progress in recent decades, gender inequalities remain pervasive in many dimensions of life. But while gender inequalities exist throughout the world, they are most prevalent in developing countries. Inequalities in the allocation of education, health care, nutrition, and political voice matter because of their strong association with well-being, productivity, and economic growth. These patterns of inequality begin at an early age, with boys usually receiving a larger share of education and health spending than girls, for example. The share of women in high-skilled occupations such as legislators, senior officials, and managers indicates women's status and role in the labor force and society at large. Women are vastly underrepresented in decisionmaking positions in government, although there is some evidence of recent improvement.

Data on female legislators, senior officials, and managers are based on the employment by occupation estimates, classified according to the International Standard Classification of Occupations 1988. Data are drawn mostly from labor force surveys, supplemented in limited cases with other household surveys, population censuses, and official estimates. Countries could apply different practice whether or where the armed forces are included. Armed forces constitute a separate major group, but in some countries they are included in the most closely matching civilian occupation or in nonclassifiable workers. For country-level information on classification, source, reference period, or definition, consult the footnotes in the World Development Indicators database or the ILO's Key Indicators of the Labour Market, 8th edition, database.

Definitions

• **Prevalence of child malnutrition, underweight,** is the percentage of children under age 5 whose weight for age is more than two standard deviations below the median for the international reference population ages 0–59 months. Data are based on the WHO child growth standards released in 2006. • **Under-five mortality rate** is the probability of a child born in a specific year dying before reaching age 5, if subject to the age-specific mortality rates of that year. The probability is expressed as a rate per 1,000 live births. • **Maternal mortality ratio, modeled estimate,** is the number of women who die from pregnancy-related causes while pregnant or within 42 days of pregnancy termination, per 100,000 live births. • **Adolescent fertility rate** is the number of births per 1,000 women ages 15–19. • **Prevalence of HIV** is the percentage of people who are infected with HIV in the relevant age group. • **Primary completion rate** is the number of new entrants (enrollments minus repeaters) in the last grade of primary education, regardless of age, divided by the population at the entrance age for the last grade of primary education. Data limitations preclude adjusting for students who drop out during the final year of primary education. • **Youth literacy rate** is the percentage of the population ages 15–24 that can, with understanding, both read and write a short simple statement about their everyday life. • **Labor force participation rate** is the proportion of the population ages 15 and older that engages actively in the labor market, by either working or looking for work during a reference period. Data are modeled ILO estimates. • **Vulnerable employment** is unpaid family workers and own-account workers as a percentage of total employment. • **Unemployment** is the share of the labor force without work but available for and seeking employment. Definitions of labor force and unemployment may differ by country. • **Female legislators, senior officials, and managers** are the percentage of legislators, senior officials, and managers (International Standard Classification of Occupations–88 category 1) who are female.

Data sources

Data on child malnutrition prevalence are from WHO's Global Database on Child Growth and Malnutrition (www.who.int/nutgrowthdb). Data on under-five mortality rates are from the UN Inter-agency Group for Child Mortality Estimation (www.childmortality.org) and are based mainly on household surveys, censuses, and vital registration data. Modeled estimates of maternal mortality ratios are from the UN Maternal Mortality Estimation Inter-agency Group (www.maternalmortalitydata.org). Data on adolescent fertility rates are from United Nations Population Division (2013), with annual data linearly interpolated by the World Bank's Development Data Group. Data on HIV prevalence are from UNAIDS (2013). Data on primary completion rates and literacy rates are from the UNESCO Institute for Statistics (www.uis.unesco.org). Data on labor force participation rates, vulnerable employment, unemployment, and female legislators, senior officials, and managers are from the ILO's Key Indicators of the Labour Market, 8th edition, database.

References

ILO (International Labour Organization).Various years. *Key Indicators of the Labour Market*. Geneva: International Labour Office.

UNAIDS (Joint United Nations Programme on HIV/AIDS). 2013. *Global Report: UNAIDS Report on the Global AIDS Epidemic 2013*. Geneva.

UNICEF (United Nations Children's Fund), WHO (World Health Organization), and the World Bank. 2013. *2012 Joint Child Malnutrition Estimates - Levels and Trends*. New York: UNICEF. [www.who.int/nutgrowthdb/estimates2012/en/].

UN Inter-agency Group for Child Mortality Estimation. 2013. *Levels and Trends in Child Mortality: Report 2013*. New York.

United Nations Population Division. 2013. *World Population Prospects: The 2012 Revision*. New York: United Nations, Department of Economic and Social Affairs.

WHO (World Health Organization), UNICEF (United Nations Children's Fund), UNFPA (United Nations Population Fund), and World Bank. 2012. *Trends in Maternal Mortality: 1990 to 2010*. Geneva: WHO.

World Bank. 2011. *World Development Report 2012: Gender Equality and Development*. Washington, DC.

———. n.d. PovcalNet online database. [http://iresearch.worldbank.org/PovcalNet]. Washington, DC.

To access the World Development Indicators online tables, use the URL http://wdi.worldbank.org/table/ and the table number (for example, http://wdi.worldbank.org/table/2.1). To view a specific indicator online, use the URL http://data.worldbank.org/indicator/ and the indicator code (for example, http://data.worldbank.org/indicator/SP.POP.TOTL).

2.1 Population dynamics

Population ♀♂	SP.POP.TOTL
Population growth	SP.POP.GROW
Population ages 0–14 ♀♂	SP.POP.0014.TO.ZS
Population ages 15–64 ♀♂	SP.POP.1564.TO.ZS
Population ages 65+ ♀♂	SP.POP.65UP.TO.ZS
Dependency ratio, Young	SP.POP.DPND.YG
Dependency ratio, Old	SP.POP.DPND.OL
Crude death rate	SP.DYN.CDRT.IN
Crude birth rate	SP.DYN.CBRT.IN

2.2 Labor force structure

Labor force participation rate, Male ♀♂	SL.TLF.CACT.MA.ZS
Labor force participation rate, Female ♀♂	SL.TLF.CACT.FE.ZS
Labor force, Total ♀♂	SL.TLF.TOTL.IN
Labor force, Average annual growth	..[a,b]
Labor force, Female ♀♂	SL.TLF.TOTL.FE.ZS

2.3 Employment by sector

Agriculture, Male ♀♂	SL.AGR.EMPL.MA.ZS
Agriculture, Female ♀♂	SL.AGR.EMPL.FE.ZS
Industry, Male ♀♂	SL.IND.EMPL.MA.ZS
Industry, Female ♀♂	SL.IND.EMPL.FE.ZS
Services, Male ♀♂	SL.SRV.EMPL.MA.ZS
Services, Female ♀♂	SL.SRV.EMPL.FE.ZS

2.4 Decent work and productive employment

Employment to population ratio, Total ♀♂	SL.EMP.TOTL.SP.ZS
Employment to population ratio, Youth ♀♂	SL.EMP.1524.SP.ZS
Vulnerable employment, Male ♀♂	SL.EMP.VULN.MA.ZS
Vulnerable employment, Female ♀♂	SL.EMP.VULN.FE.ZS
GDP per person employed	SL.GDP.PCAP.EM.KD

2.5 Unemployment

Unemployment, Male ♀♂	SL.UEM.TOTL.MA.ZS
Unemployment, Female ♀♂	SL.UEM.TOTL.FE.ZS
Youth unemployment, Male ♀♂	SL.UEM.1524.MA.ZS
Youth unemployment, Female ♀♂	SL.UEM.1524.FE.ZS
Long-term unemployment, Total ♀♂	SL.UEM.LTRM.ZS
Long-term unemployment, Male ♀♂	SL.UEM.LTRM.MA.ZS
Long-term unemployment, Female ♀♂	SL.UEM.LTRM.FE.ZS
Unemployment by educational attainment, Primary ♀♂	SL.UEM.PRIM.ZS
Unemployment by educational attainment, Secondary ♀♂	SL.UEM.SECO.ZS
Unemployment by educational attainment, Tertiary ♀♂	SL.UEM.TERT.ZS

2.6 Children at work

Children in employment, Total ♀♂	SL.TLF.0714.ZS
Children in employment, Male ♀♂	SL.TLF.0714.MA.ZS
Children in employment, Female ♀♂	SL.TLF.0714.FE.ZS
Work only ♀♂	SL.TLF.0714.WK.ZS
Study and work ♀♂	SL.TLF.0714.SW.ZS
Employment in agriculture ♀♂	SL.AGR.0714.ZS
Employment in manufacturing ♀♂	SL.MNF.0714.ZS
Employment in services ♀♂	SL.SRV.0714.ZS
Self-employed ♀♂	SL.SLF.0714.ZS
Wage workers ♀♂	SL.WAG.0714.ZS
Unpaid family workers ♀♂	SL.FAM.0714.ZS

2.7 Poverty rates at national poverty lines

Poverty headcount ratio, Rural	SI.POV.RUHC
Poverty headcount ratio, Urban	SI.POV.URHC
Poverty headcount ratio, National	SI.POV.NAHC
Poverty gap, Rural	SI.POV.RUGP
Poverty gap, Urban	SI.POV.URGP
Poverty gap, National	SI.POV.NAGP

2.8 Poverty rates at international poverty lines

Population living below 2005 PPP $1.25 a day	SI.POV.DDAY
Poverty gap at 2005 PPP $1.25 a day	SI.POV.2DAY
Population living below 2005 PPP $2 a day	SI.POV.GAPS
Poverty gap at 2005 PPP $2 a day	SI.POV.GAP2

2.9 Distribution of income or consumption

Gini index	SI.POV.GINI
Share of consumption or income, Lowest 10% of population	SI.DST.FRST.10
Share of consumption or income, Lowest 20% of population	SI.DST.FRST.20
Share of consumption or income, Second 20% of population	SI.DST.02ND.20
Share of consumption or income, Third 20% of population	SI.DST.03RD.20
Share of consumption or income, Fourth 20% of population	SI.DST.04TH.20

 Economy | States and markets | Global links | Back

2 People

Share of consumption or income, Highest 20% of population	SI.DST.05TH.20
Share of consumption or income, Highest 10% of population	SI.DST.10TH.10

2.10 Education inputs

Public expenditure per student, Primary	SE.XPD.PRIM.PC.ZS
Public expenditure per student, Secondary	SE.XPD.SECO.PC.ZS
Public expenditure per student, Tertiary	SE.XPD.TERT.PC.ZS
Public expenditure on education, % of GDP	SE.XPD.TOTL.GD.ZS
Public expenditure on education, % of total government expenditure	SE.XPD.TOTL.GB.ZS
Trained teachers in primary education ♀♂	SE.PRM.TCAQ.ZS
Primary school pupil-teacher ratio	SE.PRM.ENRL.TC.ZS

2.11 Participation in education

Gross enrollment ratio, Preprimary ♀♂	SE.PRE.ENRR
Gross enrollment ratio, Primary ♀♂	SE.PRM.ENRR
Gross enrollment ratio, Secondary ♀♂	SE.SEC.ENRR
Gross enrollment ratio, Tertiary ♀♂	SE.TER.ENRR
Net enrollment rate, Primary ♀♂	SE.PRM.NENR
Net enrollment rate, Secondary ♀♂	SE.SEC.NENR
Adjusted net enrollment rate, Primary, Male ♀♂	SE.PRM.TENR.MA
Adjusted net enrollment rate, Primary, Female ♀♂	SE.PRM.TENR.FE
Primary school-age children out of school, Male ♀♂	SE.PRM.UNER.MA
Primary school-age children out of school, Female ♀♂	SE.PRM.UNER.FE

2.12 Education efficiency

Gross intake ratio in first grade of primary education, Male ♀♂	SE.PRM.GINT.MA.ZS
Gross intake ratio in first grade of primary education, Female ♀♂	SE.PRM.GINT.FE.ZS
Cohort survival rate, Reaching grade 5, Male ♀♂	SE.PRM.PRS5.MA.ZS
Cohort survival rate, Reaching grade 5, Female ♀♂	SE.PRM.PRS5.FE.ZS
Cohort survival rate, Reaching last grade of primary education, Male ♀♂	SE.PRM.PRSL.MA.ZS
Cohort survival rate, Reaching last grade of primary education, Female ♀♂	SE.PRM.PRSL.FE.ZS
Repeaters in primary education, Male ♀♂	SE.PRM.REPT.MA.ZS
Repeaters in primary education, Female ♀♂	SE.PRM.REPT.FE.ZS
Transition rate to secondary education, Male ♀♂	SE.SEC.PROG.MA.ZS
Transition rate to secondary education, Female ♀♂	SE.SEC.PROG.FE.ZS

2.13 Education completion and outcomes

Primary completion rate, Total ♀♂	SE.PRM.CMPT.ZS
Primary completion rate, Male ♀♂	SE.PRM.CMPT.MA.ZS
Primary completion rate, Female ♀♂	SE.PRM.CMPT.FE.ZS
Youth literacy rate, Male ♀♂	SE.ADT.1524.LT.MA.ZS
Youth literacy rate, Female ♀♂	SE.ADT.1524.LT.FE.ZS
Adult literacy rate, Male ♀♂	SE.ADT.LITR.MA.ZS
Adult literacy rate, Female ♀♂	SE.ADT.LITR.FE.ZS

2.14 Education gaps by income and gender

This table provides education survey data for the poorest and richest quintiles.	..[b]

2.15 Health systems

Total health expenditure	SH.XPD.TOTL.ZS
Public health expenditure	SH.XPD.PUBL
Out-of-pocket health expenditure	SH.XPD.OOPC.TO.ZS
External resources for health	SH.XPD.EXTR.ZS
Health expenditure per capita, $	SH.XPD.PCAP
Health expenditure per capita, PPP $	SH.XPD.PCAP.PP.KD
Physicians	SH.MED.PHYS.ZS
Nurses and midwives	SH.MED.NUMW.P3
Community health workers	SH.MED.CMHW.P3
Hospital beds	SH.MED.BEDS.ZS
Completeness of birth registration	SP.REG.BRTH.ZS

2.16 Disease prevention coverage and quality

Access to an improved water source	SH.H2O.SAFE.ZS
Access to improved sanitation facilities	SH.STA.ACSN
Child immunization rate, Measles	SH.IMM.MEAS
Child immunization rate, DTP3	SH.IMM.IDPT
Children with acute respiratory infection taken to health provider	SH.STA.ARIC.ZS
Children with diarrhea who received oral rehydration and continuous feeding	SH.STA.ORCF.ZS
Children sleeping under treated bed nets	SH.MLR.NETS.ZS
Children with fever receiving antimalarial drugs	SH.MLR.TRET.ZS
Tuberculosis treatment success rate	SH.TBS.CURE.ZS
Tuberculosis case detection rate	SH.TBS.DTEC.ZS

2.17 Reproductive health

Total fertility rate	SP.DYN.TFRT.IN
Adolescent fertility rate	SP.ADO.TFRT
Unmet need for contraception	SP.UWT.TFRT
Contraceptive prevalence rate	SP.DYN.CONU.ZS
Pregnant women receiving prenatal care	SH.STA.ANVC.ZS
Births attended by skilled health staff	SH.STA.BRTC.ZS
Maternal mortality ratio, National estimate	SH.STA.MMRT.NE
Maternal mortality ratio, Modeled estimate	SH.STA.MMRT
Lifetime risk of maternal mortality	SH.MMR.RISK

2.18 Nutrition and growth

Prevalence of undernourishment	SN.ITK.DEFC.ZS
Prevalence of underweight, Male ♀♂	SH.STA.MALN.MA.ZS
Prevalence of underweight, Female ♀♂	SH.STA.MALN.FE.ZS
Prevalence of stunting, Male ♀♂	SH.STA.STNT.MA.ZS
Prevalence of stunting, Female ♀♂	SH.STA.STNT.FE.ZS
Prevalence of wasting, Male ♀♂	SH.STA.WAST.MA.ZS
Prevalence of wasting, Female ♀♂	SH.STA.WAST.FE.ZS
Prevalence of severe wasting, Male ♀♂	SH.SVR.WAST.MA.ZS
Prevalence of severe wasting, Female ♀♂	SH.SVR.WAST.FE.ZS
Prevalence of overweight children, Male ♀♂	SH.STA.OWGH.MA.ZS
Prevalence of overweight children, Female ♀♂	SH.STA.OWGH.FE.ZS

2.19 Nutrition intake and supplements

Low-birthweight babies	SH.STA.BRTW.ZS
Exclusive breastfeeding	SH.STA.BFED.ZS
Consumption of iodized salt	SN.ITK.SALT.ZS
Vitamin A supplementation	SN.ITK.VITA.ZS
Prevalence of anemia among children under age 5	SH.ANM.CHLD.ZS
Prevalence of anemia among pregnant women	SH.PRG.ANEM

2.20 Health risk factors and future challenges

Prevalence of smoking, Male ♀♂	SH.PRV.SMOK.MA
Prevalence of smoking, Female ♀♂	SH.PRV.SMOK.FE
Incidence of tuberculosis	SH.TBS.INCD
Prevalence of diabetes	SH.STA.DIAB.ZS

Prevalence of HIV, Total	SH.DYN.AIDS.ZS
Women's share of population ages 15+ living with HIV ♀♂	SH.DYN.AIDS.FE.ZS
Prevalence of HIV, Youth male ♀♂	SH.HIV.1524.MA.ZS
Prevalence of HIV, Youth female ♀♂	SH.HIV.1524.FE.ZS
Antiretroviral therapy coverage	SH.HIV.ARTC.ZS
Death from communicable diseases and maternal, prenatal, and nutrition conditions	SH.DTH.COMM.ZS
Death from non-communicable diseases	SH.DTH.NCOM.ZS
Death from injuries	SH.DTH.INJR.ZS

2.21 Mortality

Life expectancy at birth ♀♂	SP.DYN.LE00.IN
Neonatal mortality rate	SH.DYN.NMRT
Infant mortality rate ♀♂	SP.DYN.IMRT.IN
Under-five mortality rate, Total ♀♂	SH.DYN.MORT
Under-five mortality rate, Male ♀♂	SH.DYN.MORT.MA
Under-five mortality rate, Female ♀♂	SH.DYN.MORT.FE
Adult mortality rate, Male ♀♂	SP.DYN.AMRT.MA
Adult mortality rate, Female ♀♂	SP.DYN.AMRT.FE

2.22 Health gaps by income

This table provides health survey data for the poorest and richest quintiles. .. [b]

♀♂ Data disaggregated by sex are available in the World Development Indicators database.
a. Derived from data elsewhere in the World Development Indicators database.
b. Available online only as part of the table, not as an individual indicator.

ENVIRONMENT

A healthy environment is integral to meeting the Millennium Development Goals, which call for reversing environmental losses and inserting principles of environmental sustainability into country policies and programs. Whether the world sustains itself depends largely on properly managing natural resources. The indicators in the *Environment* section measure resource use and the way human activities affect the natural and built environment. They include measures of environmental goods (forest, water, cultivable land) and of degradation (pollution, deforestation, loss of habitat, and loss of biodiversity). They show that growing populations and expanding economies have placed greater demands on land, water, forest, minerals, and energy sources. But better policies, rising productivity, and new technologies can ensure that future development is environmentally and socially sustainable.

Economic growth and greater energy use are positively correlated—access to electricity and the use of energy are essential in raising people's standard of living. Economic development has improved the quality of life for many people, yielding gains unparalleled in human history. But the gains have been uneven, and economic growth has often had negative environmental consequences, with a drastic impact on poor people. Generating energy from fossil fuels produces emissions of carbon dioxide, the main greenhouse gas contributing to climate change.

The World Bank Group has joined the UN Sustainable Energy for All, which calls on governments, businesses, and civil societies to achieve three goals by 2030. First is universal access to electricity and clean cooking fuels. Second is doubling the share of the world's energy supply from renewable sources. And third is doubling the rate of improvement in energy efficiency. Several indicators in the *Environment* section cover energy use and efficiency, electricity use and production, greenhouse gas emissions, carbon dioxide emissions by economic sector, and access to electricity.

Other indicators describe land use, agriculture and food production, forests and biodiversity, threatened species, water resources, climate variability, exposure to impact, resilience, urbanization, traffic and congestion, air pollution, and natural resources rents. Where possible, the indicators come from international sources and have been standardized to facilitate comparisons across countries. But ecosystems span national boundaries, and access to natural resources may vary within countries. For example, water may be abundant in some parts of a country but scarce in others, and countries often share water resources. Land productivity and optimal land use may be location-specific, but widely separated regions can have common characteristics. Greenhouse gas emissions and climate change are measured globally, but their effects are experienced locally, shaping people's lives and livelihoods. Measuring environmental phenomena and their effects at the subnational, national, and supranational levels thus remains a major challenge.

Highlights

Agricultural land use increases while industry's share of GDP declines

Land under cereal production (million hectares)

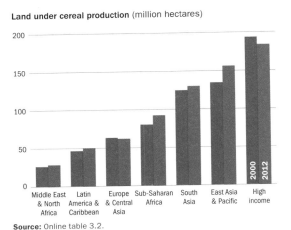

Source: Online table 3.2.

The share of agriculture in GDP is declining in all regions and income groups. Between 2000 and 2012 it fell 20 percentage points globally. Even in low-income countries the share fell 6 percentage points, from 34 percent to 28 percent, as most economies gradually shifted to industry and services. Over the last decade, apart from developing countries in Europe and Central Asia, low- and middle-income countries in general are increasing land under cereal production. Both East Asia and Pacific and Sub-Saharan Africa saw land under cereal production increase more than 15 percent. Since most of the land available for current and future food requirements is already in production, further expansion will likely involve fragile and marginal land—a strategy that cannot be sustained for long.

Forest shrinking but protected areas increasing

Terrestrial and marine protected areas (% of total territorial area)

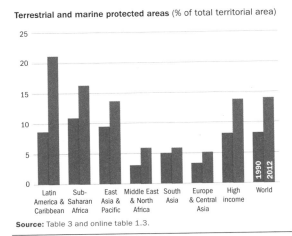

Source: Table 3 and online table 1.3.

At the beginning of the 20th century the Earth's forest area was about 5 billion hectares. That has since shrunk to about 4 billion hectares, with the decline concentrated in developing countries. Low- and middle-income countries lost 14.6 million hectares of forest a year between 1990 and 2011. Latin America and the Caribbean—with the largest share of forest areas at about a quarter of the earth's forest resources—lost some 99 million hectares, about 11 percent of its total forest area. But high-income economies have gained about 17.7 million hectares of forest area since 1990. Many countries designate protected areas to preserve valuable habitat and the plant and animal species that live there. And by 2012 more than 14 percent of the world's land area and its oceans had been protected.

High-income countries use more energy, but growth is faster in developing countries

Global energy use, 2011 (%)

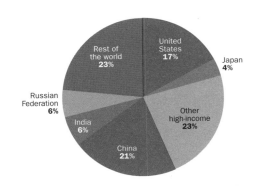

Source: Online table 3.6.

Economic growth and energy use move together, and energy producers tend to be energy users. With only 18 percent of the world's population, high-income economies use about half the world's energy production each year—more than 4 times more energy per person than middle-income economies and almost 14 times more than low-income economies. But low- and middle-income economies more than doubled their energy consumption and production over 1990–2011, as high-income countries increased consumption 16 percent and production 21 percent. The average growth in energy use over 1990–2011 was 2 percent globally—3.6 percent for developing countries and 0.9 percent for high-income economies.

Front | ? User guide | World view | People | Environment

Per capita carbon dioxide emissions are not highest in countries with the highest total emissions

Global per capita carbon dioxide emissions rose 16 percent between 1990 and 2010 to a record 4.9 metric tons. The countries with the highest per capita emissions are not among the countries with the highest total emissions. In 2010 the top five per capita emitters were Qatar, Trinidad and Tobago, Kuwait, Brunei Darussalam, and Aruba, all high-income countries, whereas the top five total emitters were China, the United States, India, the Russian Federation, and Japan. Europe and Central Asia had the highest per capita emissions among developing country regions (5.3 metric tons), followed by East Asia and Pacific (4.9 metric tons). While high-income countries saw per capita carbon dioxide emissions fall 2.5 percent between 1990 and 2010, to 11.6 metric tons, they remain the world's highest per capita emitters.

Per capita carbon dioxide emissions (metric tons per capita)

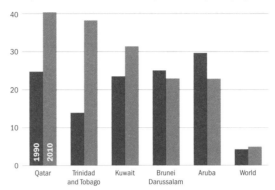

Source: Online table 3.8.

Sub-Saharan Africa's fast-growing urban population

Home to more than half the world's people, urban areas will accommodate almost all population growth over the next four decades. The pace will be fastest in developing countries, where the urban population is forecast to rise from 2.7 billion in 2012 to 5.2 billion in 2050. At 4 percent a year between 1990 and 2012, Sub-Saharan Africa had the fastest pace of urban growth rate of all developing regions. Urbanization can yield important social benefits, such as improving people's access to public services. In Sub-Saharan Africa 83 percent of the urban population has access to an improved water source, compared with 51 percent of the rural population. And access to improved sanitation facilities in urban areas is almost twice that in rural areas. But urbanization can also have adverse environmental effects, concentrating pollution, harming health, and reducing productivity.

Urban and rural population, 2012 (% of total population)

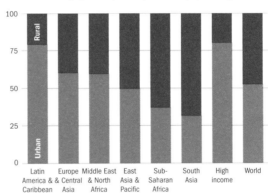

Source: Online table 3.12.

Developing countries join the WAVES partnership

The Wealth Accounting and the Valuation of Ecosystem Services (WAVES) is a global partnership that promotes sustainable development by mainstreaming natural resources in development planning and national economic accounts. Water accounts, a subset of natural capital accounts, collect data on water stocks and flows and water rights and use. They provide a conceptual framework for organizing water resources data for use in resource allocation policies at the national and regional levels. Botswana, Colombia, Costa Rica, Madagascar, and the Philippines joined WAVES in 2012. Using the System of Environmental-Economic Accounting methodology approved by the UN Statistics Commission, Botswana updated its water accounts from the 1990s using natural capital accounting. In addition to water accounts, Botswana's natural capital accounts will include land and ecosystem accounts, with a focus on tourism, minerals, and energy.

Botswana's sector shares of water use, formal employment, and GDP, 2011–12 (%)   ■ Water consumption ■ Formal employment ■ GDP

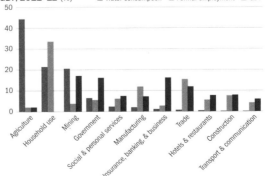

Source: Wealth Accounting and the Valuation of Ecosystem Services and Botswana Department of Water Affairs.

3 Environment

	Deforestation[a] average annual % 2000–10	Nationally protected areas Terrestrial and marine areas % of total territorial area 2012	Internal renewable freshwater resources[b] Per capita cubic meters 2011	Access to improved water source % of total population 2012	Access to improved sanitation facilities % of total population 2012	Urban population % growth 2011–12	Particulate matter concentration urban-population-weighted PM10 micrograms per cubic meter 2011	Carbon dioxide emissions million metric tons 2010	Energy use Per capita kilograms of oil equivalent 2011	Electricity production billion kilowatt hours 2011
Afghanistan	0.00	0.4	1,620	64	29	3.7	63	8.2	..	..
Albania	−0.10	9.5	8,529	96	91	2.2	43	4.3	689	4.2
Algeria	0.57	7.4	298	84	95	3.0	34	123.5	1,108	51.2
American Samoa	0.19	16.8	..	100	62	0.0	..	..	..	..
Andorra	0.00	9.8	4,053	100	100	0.0	31	0.5	..	..
Angola	0.21	12.1	7,334	54	60	4.4	21	30.4	673	5.7
Antigua and Barbuda	0.20	1.2	590	98	91	1.0	9	0.5	..	..
Argentina	0.81	6.6	6,777	99	97	1.0	35	180.5	1,967	129.6
Armenia	1.48	8.1	2,314	100	91	0.2	13	4.2	916	7.4
Aruba	0.00	0.0	..	98	98	0.6	..	2.3	..	..
Australia	0.37	15.0	22,023	100	100	1.9	14	373.1	5,501	252.6
Austria	−0.13	23.6	6,543	100	100	0.6	28	66.9	3,928	62.2
Azerbaijan	0.00	7.4	885	80	82	1.8	20	45.7	1,369	20.3
Bahamas, The	0.00	1.0	55	98	92	1.8	..	2.5	..	..
Bahrain	−3.55	6.8	3	100	99	2.0	24	24.2	7,353	13.8
Bangladesh	0.18	4.2	687	85	57	2.9	121	56.2	205	44.1
Barbados	0.00	0.1	284	100	..	1.6	11	1.5	..	..
Belarus	−0.43	8.3	3,927	100	94	0.4	20	62.2	3,114	32.2
Belgium	−0.16	24.5	1,086	100	100	0.8	29	108.9	5,349	89.0
Belize	0.67	26.4	50,588	99	91	2.0	18	0.4	..	..
Benin	1.04	25.5	1,053	76	14	4.2	69	5.2	385	0.2
Bermuda	0.00	5.1	..	..	..	0.4	..	0.5	..	..
Bhutan	−0.34	28.4	106,933	98	47	3.8	16	0.5	..	..
Bolivia	0.50	20.8	29,396	88	46	2.3	78	15.5	746	7.2
Bosnia and Herzegovina	0.00	1.5	9,246	100	95	1.0	84	31.1	1,848	15.3
Botswana	0.99	37.2	1,208	97	64	1.9	199	5.2	1,115	0.4
Brazil	0.50	26.0	27,512	98	81	1.2	36	419.8	1,371	531.8
Brunei Darussalam	0.44	29.6	20,910	..	..	1.9	9	9.2	9,427	3.7
Bulgaria	−1.53	35.4	2,858	99	100	0.2	41	44.7	2,615	50.0
Burkina Faso	1.01	15.2	781	82	19	6.0	51	1.7	..	..
Burundi	1.40	4.9	1,054	75	47	5.8	30	0.3	..	..
Cabo Verde	−0.36	0.2	612	89	65	2.0	..	0.4	..	..
Cambodia	1.34	23.8	8,257	71	37	2.7	89	4.2	365	1.1
Cameroon	1.05	10.9	12,904	74	45	3.6	26	7.2	318	6.0
Canada	0.00	7.0	82,987	100	100	1.3	14	499.1	7,333	636.9
Cayman Islands	0.00	1.5	..	96	96	1.7	..	0.6	..	..
Central African Republic	0.13	18.0	31,784	68	22	2.6	32	0.3	..	..
Chad	0.66	16.6	1,242	51	12	3.4	50	0.5	..	..
Channel Islands	..	0.5	..	..	..	1.0	..	..	..	..
Chile	−0.25	15.0	51,073	99	99	1.1	60	72.3	1,940	65.7
China	−1.57	16.1	2,093	92	65	3.0	82	8,286.9	2,029	4,715.7
Hong Kong SAR, China	..	41.9	..	..	..	1.2	30	36.3	2,106	39.0
Macao SAR, China	..	..	..	..	..	1.9	33	1.0	..	..
Colombia	0.17	20.8	44,861	91	80	1.7	53	75.7	671	61.8
Comoros	9.34	4.0	1,714	95	35	2.8	21	0.1	..	..
Congo, Dem. Rep.	0.20	12.0	14,078	46	31	4.3	46	3.0	383	7.9
Congo, Rep.	0.07	30.4	52,540	75	15	3.3	29	2.0	393	1.3

	Deforestation[a] average annual % 2000–10	Nationally protected areas Terrestrial and marine areas % of total territorial area 2012	Internal renewable freshwater resources[b] Per capita cubic meters 2011	Access to improved water source % of total population 2012	Access to improved sanitation facilities % of total population 2012	Urban population % growth 2011–12	Particulate matter concentration urban-population- weighted PM10 micrograms per cubic meter 2011	Carbon dioxide emissions million metric tons 2010	Energy use Per capita kilograms of oil equivalent 2011	Electricity production billion kilowatt hours 2011
Costa Rica	−0.93	22.6	23,725	97	94	2.1	48	7.8	983	9.8
Côte d'Ivoire	−0.15	22.2	3,963	80	22	3.7	21	5.8	579	6.1
Croatia	−0.19	10.3	8,807	99	98	0.2	30	20.9	1,971	10.7
Cuba	−1.66	9.9	3,381	94	93	−0.1	37	38.4	992	17.8
Curaçao	..	..	..	..	..	..	..	..	..	..
Cyprus	−0.09	17.1	699	100	100	1.4	42	7.7	2,121	4.9
Czech Republic	−0.08	22.4	1,253	100	100	0.1	29	111.8	4,138	86.8
Denmark	−1.14	23.6	1,077	100	100	0.5	25	46.3	3,231	35.2
Djibouti	0.00	0.2	354	92	61	1.6	40	0.5	..	..
Dominica	0.58	3.7	..	..	..	0.6	15	0.1	..	..
Dominican Republic	0.00	20.8	2,069	81	82	2.1	31	21.0	727	13.0
Ecuador	1.81	37.0	28,334	86	83	2.4	32	32.6	849	20.3
Egypt, Arab Rep.	−1.73	11.3	23	99	96	2.0	120	204.8	978	156.6
El Salvador	1.45	8.7	2,837	90	70	1.4	46	6.2	690	5.8
Equatorial Guinea	0.69	15.1	36,313	..	..	3.2	21	4.7	..	..
Eritrea	0.28	3.8	472	..	..	5.4	77	0.5	129	0.3
Estonia	0.12	23.2	9,521	99	95	−0.3	17	18.3	4,197	12.9
Ethiopia	1.08	18.4	1,365	52	24	4.1	86	6.5	381	5.2
Faeroe Islands	0.00	1.0	..	..	..	0.4	21	0.7	..	..
Fiji	−0.34	6.0	32,895	96	87	1.5	27	1.3	..	..
Finland	0.14	15.2	19,858	100	100	0.6	16	61.8	6,449	73.5
France	−0.39	28.7	3,059	100	100	1.1	24	361.3	3,868	556.9
French Polynesia	−3.97	0.1	..	100	97	1.1	..	0.9	..	..
Gabon	0.00	19.1	102,884	92	41	2.7	12	2.6	1,253	1.8
Gambia, The	−0.41	4.4	1,729	90	60	4.2	39	0.5	..	..
Georgia	0.09	3.7	12,966	99	93	0.4	35	6.2	790	10.2
Germany	0.00	49.0	1,308	100	100	−1.5	24	745.4	3,811	602.4
Ghana	2.08	14.4	1,221	87	14	3.4	82	9.0	425	11.2
Greece	−0.81	21.5	5,214	100	99	0.1	35	86.7	2,402	59.2
Greenland	0.00	40.6	..	100	100	0.2	..	0.6	..	..
Grenada	0.00	0.3	..	97	98	1.3	9	0.3	..	..
Guam	0.00	5.3	..	100	90	1.2	..	..	..	..
Guatemala	1.40	29.8	7,425	94	80	3.4	75	11.1	691	8.1
Guinea	0.54	26.8	20,248	75	19	3.9	37	1.2	..	..
Guinea-Bissau	0.48	27.1	9,851	74	20	3.9	34	0.2	..	..
Guyana	0.00	5.0	304,723	98	84	0.9	17	1.7	..	..
Haiti	0.76	0.1	1,297	62	24	3.8	56	2.1	320	0.7
Honduras	2.06	16.2	12,336	90	80	3.1	84	8.1	609	7.1
Hungary	−0.62	23.1	602	100	100	0.2	32	50.6	2,503	36.0
Iceland	−4.99	13.3	532,892	100	100	0.6	18	2.0	17,964	17.2
India	−0.46	5.0	1,184	93	36	2.4	100	2,008.8	614	1,052.3
Indonesia	0.51	9.1	8,281	85	59	2.7	47	434.0	857	182.4
Iran, Islamic Rep.	0.00	7.0	1,704	96	89	1.5	115	571.6	2,813	239.7
Iraq	−0.09	0.4	1,108	85	85	2.5	36	114.7	1,266	54.2
Ireland	−1.53	12.8	10,706	100	99	0.7	18	40.0	2,888	27.7
Isle of Man	0.00	..	..	..	..	0.7	..	..	..	..
Israel	−0.07	14.7	97	100	100	1.9	47	70.7	2,994	59.6

3 Environment

	Deforestation[a] average annual % 2000–10	Nationally protected areas Terrestrial and marine areas % of total territorial area 2012	Internal renewable freshwater resources[b] Per capita cubic meters 2011	Access to improved water source % of total population 2012	Access to improved sanitation facilities % of total population 2012	Urban population % growth 2011–12	Particulate matter concentration urban-population-weighted PM10 micrograms per cubic meter 2011	Carbon dioxide emissions million metric tons 2010	Energy use Per capita kilograms of oil equivalent 2011	Electricity production billion kilowatt hours 2011
Italy	–0.90	21.0	3,005	100	..	–1.7	34	406.3	2,757	300.6
Jamaica	0.11	7.1	3,483	93	80	0.5	41	7.2	1,135	5.1
Japan	–0.05	11.0	3,364	100	100	0.4	19	1,170.7	3,610	1,042.7
Jordan	0.00	0.0	110	96	98	2.5	38	20.8	1,143	14.6
Kazakhstan	0.17	3.3	3,887	93	97	1.2	47	248.7	4,717	86.6
Kenya	0.33	11.6	493	62	30	4.4	66	12.4	480	7.8
Kiribati	0.00	20.2	..	67	40	1.8	..	0.1	..	..
Korea, Dem. People's Rep.	2.00	1.7	2,720	98	82	0.8	124	71.6	773	21.6
Korea, Rep.	0.11	5.3	1,303	98	100	0.8	46	567.6	5,232	520.1
Kosovo	..	..	..	..	..	..	48	..	1,411	5.8
Kuwait	–2.57	12.9	–	99	100	4.0	89	93.7	10,408	57.5
Kyrgyz Republic	–1.07	6.3	8,873	88	92	1.9	50	6.4	562	15.2
Lao PDR	0.49	16.7	29,197	72	65	5.1	46	1.9	..	..
Latvia	–0.34	17.6	8,127	98	..	–1.2	39	7.6	2,122	6.1
Lebanon	–0.45	0.5	1,095	100	..	1.1	43	20.4	1,449	16.4
Lesotho	–0.47	0.5	2,577	81	30	3.7	42	0.0	..	..
Liberia	0.67	2.4	49,023	75	17	3.5	25	0.8	..	..
Libya	0.00	0.1	115	..	97	1.1	74	59.0	2,186	27.6
Liechtenstein	0.00	43.1	..	..	..	0.5	30	..	..	..
Lithuania	–0.68	17.2	5,139	96	94	–1.2	32	13.6	2,406	4.2
Luxembourg	0.00	39.7	1,929	100	100	2.7	17	10.8	8,046	2.6
Macedonia, FYR	–0.41	7.3	2,567	99	91	0.3	82	10.9	1,484	6.9
Madagascar	0.45	4.7	15,545	50	14	4.7	48	2.0	..	..
Malawi	0.97	18.3	1,044	85	10	3.8	49	1.2	..	..
Malaysia	0.54	13.9	20,168	100	96	2.6	47	216.8	2,639	130.1
Maldives	0.00	..	90	99	99	4.6	21	1.1	..	..
Mali	0.61	6.0	4,162	67	22	4.8	55	0.6	..	..
Malta	0.00	2.2	121	100	100	0.9	41	2.6	2,060	2.2
Marshall Islands	0.00	0.7	..	95	76	0.5	..	0.1	..	..
Mauritania	2.66	1.2	108	50	27	3.2	46	2.2	..	..
Mauritius	1.00	0.7	2,139	100	91	0.5	11	4.1	..	..
Mexico	0.30	13.7	3,427	95	85	1.6	46	443.7	1,560	295.8
Micronesia, Fed. Sets.	–0.04	0.1	..	89	57	0.4	..	0.1	..	..
Moldova	–1.77	3.8	281	97	87	1.5	44	4.9	936	5.8
Monaco	0.00	98.4	..	100	100	0.8	18	..	..	..
Mongolia	0.73	13.8	12,635	85	56	2.8	284	11.5	1,310	4.8
Montenegro	0.00	12.8	..	98	90	0.4	30	2.6	1,900	2.7
Morocco	–0.23	19.9	905	84	75	2.1	66	50.6	539	24.9
Mozambique	0.54	16.4	4,080	49	21	3.3	34	2.9	415	16.8
Myanmar	0.93	6.0	19,159	86	77	2.6	67	9.0	268	7.3
Namibia	0.97	42.6	2,778	92	32	3.3	55	3.2	717	1.4
Nepal	0.70	16.4	7,298	88	37	3.1	110	3.8	383	3.3
Netherlands	–0.14	31.5	659	100	100	0.8	25	182.1	4,638	113.0
New Caledonia	0.00	30.5	..	98	100	1.4	29	3.9	..	..
New Zealand	–0.01	21.3	74,230	100	..	0.7	16	31.6	4,124	44.5
Nicaragua	2.01	32.5	32,125	85	52	2.0	49	4.5	515	3.8
Niger	0.98	16.7	212	52	9	5.2	50	1.4	..	..

 Front | ? User guide | World view | People | Environment

	Deforestation[a] average annual % 2000–10	Nationally protected areas Terrestrial and marine areas % of total territorial area 2012	Internal renewable freshwater resources[b] Per capita cubic meters 2011	Access to improved water source % of total population 2012	Access to improved sanitation facilities % of total population 2012	Urban population % growth 2011–12	Particulate matter concentration urban-population-weighted PM10 micrograms per cubic meter 2011	Carbon dioxide emissions million metric tons 2010	Energy use Per capita kilograms of oil equivalent 2011	Electricity production billion kilowatt hours 2011
Nigeria	3.67	13.8	1,346	64	28	4.0	149	78.9	721	27.0
Northern Mariana Islands	0.53	19.9	..	98	80	0.3	..	..	..	..
Norway	−0.80	12.2	77,124	100	100	1.7	24	57.2	5,681	126.9
Oman	0.00	9.3	463	93	97	9.5	32	57.2	8,356	21.9
Pakistan	2.24	10.6	312	91	48	2.6	171	161.4	482	95.3
Palau	−0.18	28.2	..	95	100	1.6	..	0.2	..	..
Panama	0.36	14.1	39,409	94	73	2.4	49	9.6	1,085	7.9
Papua New Guinea	0.48	1.4	114,217	40	19	2.7	32	3.1	..	..
Paraguay	0.97	6.4	14,301	94	80	2.6	32	5.1	739	57.6
Peru	0.18	18.3	54,567	87	73	1.7	63	57.6	695	39.2
Philippines	−0.75	5.1	5,039	92	74	2.2	45	81.6	426	69.2
Poland	−0.31	34.8	1,391	..	..	−0.1	34	317.3	2,629	163.1
Portugal	−0.11	14.7	3,599	100	100	0.5	28	52.4	2,187	51.9
Puerto Rico	−1.76	4.6	1,922	..	99	−0.6	15	..	..	..
Qatar	0.00	2.4	29	100	100	7.2	28	70.5	17,419	30.7
Romania	−0.32	19.2	2,100	..	..	−0.3	35	78.7	1,778	62.0
Russian Federation	0.00	11.3	30,169	97	70	0.6	27	1,740.8	5,113	1,053.0
Rwanda	−2.38	10.5	852	71	64	4.4	30	0.6	..	..
Samoa	0.00	2.3	..	99	92	−0.2	..	0.2	..	..
San Marino	0.00	..	..	..	..	0.7	20	..	..	..
São Tomé and Príncipe	0.00	0.0	11,901	97	34	3.7	14	0.1	..	..
Saudi Arabia	0.00	29.9	86	97	100	2.1	108	464.5	6,738	250.1
Senegal	0.49	24.2	1,935	74	52	3.6	147	7.1	264	3.0
Serbia	−0.99	6.3	1,158	99	97	0.1	43	46.0	2,230	38.0
Seychelles	0.00	1.3	..	96	97	1.7	..	0.7	..	..
Sierra Leone	0.69	10.3	27,278	60	13	2.9	29	0.7	..	..
Singapore	0.00	3.4	116	100	100	2.5	25	13.5	6,452	46.0
Sint Maarten	..	..	..	..	..	..	..	..	..	..
Slovak Republic	−0.06	36.1	2,334	100	100	0.1	30	36.1	3,214	28.3
Slovenia	−0.16	54.9	9,095	100	100	0.2	31	15.3	3,531	15.9
Solomon Islands	0.25	1.1	83,086	81	29	4.3	25	0.2	..	..
Somalia	1.07	0.5	606	31	23	4.1	32	0.6	..	..
South Africa	0.00	6.6	869	95	74	2.0	40	460.1	2,741	259.6
South Sudan	..	..	..	57	9	5.4	..	..	..	..
Spain	−0.68	25.3	2,379	100	100	0.2	27	269.7	2,686	289.0
Sri Lanka	1.12	15.4	2,530	94	92	−2.1	62	12.7	499	11.6
St. Kitts and Nevis	0.00	0.8	453	98	..	1.4	9	0.2	..	..
St. Lucia	−0.07	2.5	..	94	65	−3.0	11	0.4	..	..
St. Martin	0.00	..	..	..	..	..	..	..	..	..
St. Vincent & the Grenadines	−0.27	1.2	..	95	..	0.8	14	0.2	..	..
Sudan	0.08	7.1	641	55[c]	24[c]	2.5[c]	62	14.2	355	8.6
Suriname	0.01	15.2	166,113	95	80	1.5	18	2.4	..	..
Swaziland	−0.84	3.0	2,178	74	57	1.4	52	1.0	..	..
Sweden	−0.30	13.9	18,097	100	100	0.9	20	52.5	5,190	150.3
Switzerland	−0.38	26.3	5,106	100	100	1.2	21	38.8	3,207	62.9
Syrian Arab Republic	−1.29	0.7	325	90	96	2.7	27	61.9	910	41.1
Tajikistan	0.00	4.8	8,120	72	94	2.7	15	2.9	306	16.2

3 Environment

	Deforestation[a]	Nationally protected areas	Internal renewable freshwater resources[b]	Access to improved water source	Access to improved sanitation facilities	Urban population	Particulate matter concentration	Carbon dioxide emissions	Energy use	Electricity production
	average annual % 2000–10	Terrestrial and marine areas % of total territorial area 2012	Per capita cubic meters 2011	% of total population 2012	% of total population 2012	% growth 2011–12	urban-population-weighted PM10 micrograms per cubic meter 2011	million metric tons 2010	Per capita kilograms of oil equivalent 2011	billion kilowatt hours 2011
Tanzania	1.13	31.7	1,812	53	12	4.8	62	6.8	448	5.3
Thailand	0.02	16.4	3,372	96	93	1.4	45	295.3	1,790	156.0
Timor-Leste	1.40	6.2	6,986	70	39	4.2	..	0.2	..	..
Togo	5.13	24.2	1,777	61	11	3.9	34	1.5	427	0.1
Tonga	0.00	9.5	..	99	91	0.8	..	0.2	..	..
Trinidad and Tobago	0.32	10.1	2,881	94	92	2.3	16	50.7	15,691	8.9
Tunisia	–1.86	4.8	393	97	90	1.3	79	25.9	890	16.1
Turkey	–1.11	2.1	3,107	100	91	2.6	65	298.0	1,539	229.4
Turkmenistan	0.00	3.2	275	71	99	2.0	21	53.1	4,839	17.2
Turks and Caicos Islands	0.00	3.6	..	..	..	2.6	..	0.2	..	..
Tuvalu	0.00	0.3	..	98	83	1.0	..	..	..	..
Uganda	2.56	11.5	1,110	75	34	6.0	29	3.8	..	..
Ukraine	–0.21	4.5	1,162	98	94	0.0	47	304.8	2,766	194.9
United Arab Emirates	–0.24	15.5	17	100	98	3.4	132	167.6	7,407	99.1
United Kingdom	–0.31	23.4	2,292	100	100	0.7	20	493.5	2,973	364.9
United States	–0.13	15.1	9,044	99	100	1.0	18	5,433.1	7,032	4,326.6
Uruguay	–2.14	2.6	17,438	99	96	0.4	33	6.6	1,309	10.3
Uzbekistan	–0.20	3.4	557	87	100	1.6	35	104.4	1,628	52.4
Vanuatu	0.00	0.5	..	91	58	3.5	23	0.1	..	..
Venezuela, RB	0.60	49.5	24,488	..	..	1.7	38	201.7	2,380	122.1
Vietnam	–1.65	4.7	4,092	95	75	3.1	69	150.2	697	99.2
Virgin Islands (U.S.)	0.80	2.8	..	100	96	–0.3	..	..	..	..
West Bank and Gaza	–0.10	0.6	207	82	94	3.3	..	2.4	..	..
Yemen, Rep.	0.00	1.1	90	55	53	4.1	78	21.9	312	6.2
Zambia	0.33	37.8	5,882	63	43	4.3	46	2.4	621	11.5
Zimbabwe	1.88	27.2	918	80	40	4.0	104	9.4	697	8.9
World	**0.11 w**	**14.0 w**	**6,122 s**	**89 w**	**64 w**	**2.0 w**	**61 w**	**33,615.4[d] w**	**1,890 w**	**22,158.5 w**
Low income	0.61	13.5	5,121	69	37	3.7	74	229.3	360	209.7
Middle income	0.13	14.4	4,931	90	60	2.4	75	16,548.5	1,281	9,778.8
Lower middle income	0.31	11.1	3,144	88	48	2.6	90	3,827.0	687	2,211.0
Upper middle income	0.04	15.8	6,791	93	74	2.3	65	12,721.1	1,893	7,566.7
Low & middle income	0.22	14.2	4,958	87	57	2.5	75	16,777.5	1,179	10,005.1
East Asia & Pacific	–0.44	13.7	4,438	91	67	2.9	75	9,570.5	1,671	5,410.8
Europe & Central Asia	–0.48	5.2	2,744	95	94	1.3	48	1,416.7	2,078	908.6
Latin America & Carib.	0.46	21.2	21,735	94	81	1.5	43	1,553.7	1,292	1,348.0
Middle East & N. Africa	–0.15	5.9	679	90	88	2.2	79	1,277.9	1,376	654.4
South Asia	–0.29	5.9	1,217	91	40	2.5	110	2,252.6	555	1,215.8
Sub-Saharan Africa	0.48	16.3	4,391	64	30	3.9	77	703.8	681	445.2
High income	–0.03	13.8	11,335	99	96	0.7	27	14,901.7	4,872	12,198.4
Euro area	–0.31	27.0	2,962	100	100	–0.2	27	2,472.4	3,480	2,292.2

a. Negative values indicate an increase in forest area. b. River flows from other countries are not included because of data unreliability. c. Excludes South Sudan. d. Includes emissions not allocated to specific countries.

About the data

Environmental resources are needed to promote growth and poverty reduction, but growth can create new stresses on the environment. Deforestation, loss of biologically diverse habitat, depletion of water resources, pollution, urbanization, and ever increasing demand for energy production are some of the factors that must be considered in shaping development strategies.

Loss of forests

Forests provide habitat for many species and act as carbon sinks. If properly managed they also provide a livelihood for people who manage and use forest resources. FAO (2010) provides information on forest cover in 2010 and adjusted estimates of forest cover in 1990 and 2000. Data presented here do not distinguish natural forests from plantations, a breakdown the FAO provides only for developing countries. Thus, data may underestimate the rate at which natural forest is disappearing in some countries.

Habitat protection and biodiversity

Deforestation is a major cause of loss of biodiversity, and habitat conservation is vital for stemming this loss. Conservation efforts have focused on protecting areas of high biodiversity. The World Conservation Monitoring Centre (WCMC) and the United Nations Environment Programme (UNEP) compile data on protected areas. Differences in definitions, reporting practices, and reporting periods limit cross-country comparability. Nationally protected areas are defined using the six International Union for Conservation of Nature (IUCN) categories for areas of at least 1,000 hectares—scientific reserves and strict nature reserves with limited public access, national parks of national or international significance and not materially affected by human activity, natural monuments and natural landscapes with unique aspects, managed nature reserves and wildlife sanctuaries, protected landscapes (which may include cultural landscapes), and areas managed mainly for the sustainable use of natural systems to ensure long-term protection and maintenance of biological diversity—as well as terrestrial protected areas not assigned to an IUCN category. Designating an area as protected does not mean that protection is in force. For small countries with protected areas smaller than 1,000 hectares, the size limit in the definition leads to underestimation of protected areas. Due to variations in consistency and methods of collection, data quality is highly variable across countries. Some countries update their information more frequently than others, some have more accurate data on extent of coverage, and many underreport the number or extent of protected areas.

Freshwater resources

The data on freshwater resources are derived from estimates of runoff into rivers and recharge of groundwater. These estimates are derived from different sources and refer to different years, so cross-country comparisons should be made with caution. Data are collected intermittently and may hide substantial year-to-year variations in total renewable water resources. Data do not distinguish between seasonal and geographic variations in water availability within countries. Data for small countries and countries in arid and semiarid zones are less reliable than data for larger countries and countries with greater rainfall.

Water and sanitation

A reliable supply of safe drinking water and sanitary disposal of excreta are two of the most important means of improving human health and protecting the environment. Improved sanitation facilities prevent human, animal, and insect contact with excreta.

Data on access to an improved water source measure the percentage of the population with ready access to water for domestic purposes, based on surveys and estimates of service users provided by governments to the Joint Monitoring Programme of the World Health Organization (WHO) and the United Nations Children's Fund (UNICEF). The coverage rates are based on information from service users on household use rather than on information from service providers, which may include nonfunctioning systems. Access to drinking water from an improved source does not ensure that the water is safe or adequate, as these characteristics are not tested at the time of survey. While information on access to an improved water source is widely used, it is extremely subjective; terms such as "safe," "improved," "adequate," and "reasonable" may have different meanings in different countries despite official WHO definitions (see *Definitions*). Even in high-income countries treated water may not always be safe to drink. Access to an improved water source is equated with connection to a supply system; it does not account for variations in the quality and cost of the service.

Urbanization

There is no consistent and universally accepted standard for distinguishing urban from rural areas and, by extension, calculating their populations. Most countries use a classification related to the size or characteristics of settlements. Some define areas based on the presence of certain infrastructure and services. Others designate areas based on administrative arrangements. Because data are based on national definitions, cross-country comparisons should be made with caution.

Air pollution

Indoor and outdoor air pollution place a major burden on world health. More than half the world's people rely on dung, wood, crop waste, or coal to meet basic energy needs. Cooking and heating with these fuels on open fires or stoves without chimneys lead to indoor air pollution, which is responsible for 1.6 million deaths a year—one every 20 seconds. In many urban areas air pollution exposure is the main environmental threat to health. Long-term exposure to high levels of soot and small particles contributes to such health effects as respiratory diseases, lung cancer, and heart disease. Particulate pollution, alone or with sulfur dioxide, creates an enormous burden of ill health.

3 Environment

Data on particulate matter are estimated average annual concentrations in residential areas away from air pollution "hotspots," such as industrial districts and transport corridors. Data are estimates of annual ambient concentrations of particulate matter in cities of more than 100,000 people by the World Bank's Agriculture and Environmental Services Department.

Pollutant concentrations are sensitive to local conditions, and even monitoring sites in the same city may register different levels. Thus these data should be considered only a general indication of air quality, and comparisons should be made with caution. They allow for cross-country comparisons of the relative risk of particulate matter pollution facing urban residents. Major sources of urban outdoor particulate matter pollution are traffic and industrial emissions, but nonanthropogenic sources such as dust storms may also be a substantial contributor for some cities. Country technology and pollution controls are important determinants of particulate matter. Current WHO air quality guidelines are annual mean concentrations of 20 micrograms per cubic meter for particulate matter less than 10 microns in diameter.

Carbon dioxide emissions

Carbon dioxide emissions are the primary source of greenhouse gases, which contribute to global warming, threatening human and natural habitats. Fossil fuel combustion and cement manufacturing are the primary sources of anthropogenic carbon dioxide emissions, which the U.S. Department of Energy's Carbon Dioxide Information Analysis Center (CDIAC) calculates using data from the United Nations Statistics Division's World Energy Data Set and the U.S. Bureau of Mines's Cement Manufacturing Data Set. Carbon dioxide emissions, often calculated and reported as elemental carbon, were converted to actual carbon dioxide mass by multiplying them by 3.667 (the ratio of the mass of carbon to that of carbon dioxide). Although estimates of global carbon dioxide emissions are probably accurate within 10 percent (as calculated from global average fuel chemistry and use), country estimates may have larger error bounds. Trends estimated from a consistent time series tend to be more accurate than individual values. Each year the CDIAC recalculates the entire time series since 1949, incorporating recent findings and corrections. Estimates exclude fuels supplied to ships and aircraft in international transport because of the difficulty of apportioning the fuels among benefiting countries.

Energy use

In developing economies growth in energy use is closely related to growth in the modern sectors—industry, motorized transport, and urban areas—but also reflects climatic, geographic, and economic factors. Energy use has been growing rapidly in low- and middle-income economies, but high-income economies still use more than four times as much energy per capita.

Total energy use refers to the use of primary energy before transformation to other end-use fuels (such as electricity and refined petroleum products). It includes energy from combustible renewables and waste—solid biomass and animal products, gas and liquid from biomass, and industrial and municipal waste. Biomass is any plant matter used directly as fuel or converted into fuel, heat, or electricity. Data for combustible renewables and waste are often based on small surveys or other incomplete information and thus give only a broad impression of developments and are not strictly comparable across countries. The International Energy Agency (IEA) reports include country notes that explain some of these differences (see *Data sources*). All forms of energy—primary energy and primary electricity—are converted into oil equivalents. A notional thermal efficiency of 33 percent is assumed for converting nuclear electricity into oil equivalents and 100 percent efficiency for converting hydroelectric power.

Electricity production

Use of energy is important in improving people's standard of living. But electricity generation also can damage the environment. Whether such damage occurs depends largely on how electricity is generated. For example, burning coal releases twice as much carbon dioxide—a major contributor to global warming—as does burning an equivalent amount of natural gas. Nuclear energy does not generate carbon dioxide emissions, but it produces other dangerous waste products.

The IEA compiles data and data on energy inputs used to generate electricity. Data for countries that are not members of the Organisation for Economic Co-operation and Development (OECD) are based on national energy data adjusted to conform to annual questionnaires completed by OECD member governments. In addition, estimates are sometimes made to complete major aggregates from which key data are missing, and adjustments are made to compensate for differences in definitions. The IEA makes these estimates in consultation with national statistical offices, oil companies, electric utilities, and national energy experts. It occasionally revises its time series to reflect political changes. For example, the IEA has constructed historical energy statistics for countries of the former Soviet Union. In addition, energy statistics for other countries have undergone continuous changes in coverage or methodology in recent years as more detailed energy accounts have become available. Breaks in series are therefore unavoidable.

Definitions

• **Deforestation** is the permanent conversion of natural forest area to other uses, including agriculture, ranching, settlements, and infrastructure. Deforested areas do not include areas logged but intended for regeneration or areas degraded by fuelwood gathering, acid precipitation, or forest fires. • **Nationally protected areas** are terrestrial and marine protected areas as a percentage of total territorial area and include all nationally designated protected areas with known location and extent. All overlaps between different designations and categories, buffered points, and polygons are removed, and all undated protected areas are dated. • **Internal renewable freshwater resources** are the average annual flows of rivers and groundwater from rainfall in the country. Natural incoming flows originating outside a country's borders and overlapping water resources between surface runoff and groundwater recharge are excluded.
• **Access to an improved water source** is the percentage of the population with reasonable access to an adequate amount of water from an improved source, such as piped water into a dwelling, plot, or yard; public tap or standpipe; tubewell or borehole; protected dug well or spring; and rainwater collection. Unimproved sources include unprotected dug wells or springs, carts with small tank or drum, bottled water, and tanker trucks. • **Access to improved sanitation facilities** is the percentage of the population with at least adequate access to excreta disposal facilities (private or shared, but not public) that can effectively prevent human, animal, and insect contact with excreta (facilities do not have to include treatment to render sewage outflows innocuous). Improved facilities range from simple but protected pit latrines to flush toilets with a sewerage connection. To be effective, facilities must be correctly constructed and properly maintained. • **Urban population** is the midyear population of areas defined as urban in each country and reported to the United Nations divided by the World Bank estimate of total population. • **Particulate matter concentration** is fine suspended particulates of less than 10 microns in diameter (PM10) that are capable of penetrating deep into the respiratory tract and causing severe health damage. Data are urban-population-weighted PM10 levels in residential areas of cities with more than 100,000 residents. • **Carbon dioxide emissions** are emissions from the burning of fossil fuels and the manufacture of cement and include carbon dioxide produced during consumption of solid, liquid, and gas fuels and gas flaring. • **Energy use** refers to the use of primary energy before transformation to other end use fuels, which equals indigenous production plus imports and stock changes, minus exports and fuels supplied to ships and aircraft engaged in international transport. • **Electricity production** is measured at the terminals of all alternator sets in a station. In addition to hydropower, coal, oil, gas, and nuclear power generation, it covers generation by geothermal, solar, wind, and tide and wave energy as well as that from combustible renewables and waste. Production includes the output of electric plants designed to produce electricity only, as well as that of combined heat and power plants.

Data sources

Data on deforestation are from FAO (2010) and the FAO's data website. Data on protected areas, derived from the UNEP and WCMC online databases, are based on data from national authorities, national legislation, and international agreements. Data on freshwater resources are from the FAO's AQUASTAT database. Data on access to water and sanitation are from the WHO/UNICEF Joint Monitoring Programme for Water Supply and Sanitation (www .wssinfo.org). Data on urban population are from the United Nations Population Division (2011). Data on particulate matter concentrations are World Bank estimates. Data on carbon dioxide emissions are from CDIAC online databases. Data on energy use and electricity production are from IEA online databases and published in IEA's annual publications, *Energy Statistics of Non-OECD Countries, Energy Balances of Non-OECD Countries, Energy Statistics of OECD Countries,* and *Energy Balances of OECD Countries.*

References

Botswana Department of Water Affairs. n.d. Various reports. [www .water.gov.bw]. Gaborone.

CDIAC (Carbon Dioxide Information Analysis Center). n.d. Online database. [http://cdiac.ornl.gov/home.html]. Oak Ridge National Laboratory, Environmental Science Division, Oak Ridge, TN.

FAO (Food and Agriculture Organization of the United Nations). 2010. *Global Forest Resources Assessment 2010.* Rome.

———. n.d. AQUASTAT. Online database. [www.fao.org/nr/water /aquastat/data/query/index.html]. Rome.

IEA (International Energy Agency). Various years. *Energy Balances of Non-OECD Countries.* Paris.

———.Various years. *Energy Balances of OECD Countries.* Paris.

———. Various years. *Energy Statistics of Non-OECD Countries.* Paris.

———.Various years. *Energy Statistics of OECD Countries.* Paris.

UNEP (United Nations Environment Programme) and WCMC (World Conservation Monitoring Centre). 2013. Online databases [www .unep-wcmc.org/datasets-tools–reports_15.html?&types=Data,We bsite,Tool&ctops=]. Cambridge, UK.

United Nations Population Division. 2012. *World Urbanization Prospects: The 2011 Revision.* New York: United Nations, Department of Economic and Social Affairs. [http://esa.un.org/unpd/wup /CD-ROM/Urban-Agglomerations.htm].

WAVES (Wealth Accounting and the Valuation of Ecosystem Services). n.d. Online reports. [www.wavespartnership.org]. Washington, DC.

3 Environment

To access the World Development Indicators online tables, use the URL http://wdi.worldbank.org/table/ and the table number (for example, http://wdi.worldbank.org/table/3.1). To view a specific indicator online, use the URL http://data.worldbank.org/indicator/ and the indicator code (for example, http://data.worldbank.org/indicator/SP.RUR.TOTL.ZS).

3.1 Rural environment and land use

Rural population	SP.RUR.TOTL.ZS
Rural population growth	SP.RUR.TOTL.ZG
Land area	AG.LND.TOTL.K2
Forest area	AG.LND.FRST.ZS
Permanent cropland	AG.LND.CROP.ZS
Arable land, % of land area	AG.LND.ARBL.ZS
Arable land, hectares per person	AG.LND.ARBL.HA.PC

3.2 Agricultural inputs

Agricultural land, % of land area	AG.LND.AGRI.ZS
Agricultural land, % irrigated	AG.LND.IRIG.AG.ZS
Average annual precipitation	AG.LND.PRCP.MM
Land under cereal production	AG.LND.CREL.HA
Fertilizer consumption, % of fertilizer production	AG.CON.FERT.PT.ZS
Fertilizer consumption, kilograms per hectare of arable land	AG.CON.FERT.ZS
Agricultural employment	SL.AGR.EMPL.ZS
Tractors	AG.LND.TRAC.ZS

3.3 Agricultural output and productivity

Crop production index	AG.PRD.CROP.XD
Food production index	AG.PRD.FOOD.XD
Livestock production index	AG.PRD.LVSK.XD
Cereal yield	AG.YLD.CREL.KG
Agriculture value added per worker	EA.PRD.AGRI.KD

3.4 Deforestation and biodiversity

Forest area	AG.LND.FRST.K2
Average annual deforestation	..[a,b]
Threatened species, Mammals	EN.MAM.THRD.NO
Threatened species, Birds	EN.BIR.THRD.NO
Threatened species, Fishes	EN.FSH.THRD.NO
Threatened species, Higher plants	EN.HPT.THRD.NO
Terrestrial protected areas	ER.LND.PTLD.ZS
Marine protected areas	ER.MRN.PTMR.ZS

3.5 Freshwater

Internal renewable freshwater resources	ER.H2O.INTR.K3
Internal renewable freshwater resources, Per capita	ER.H2O.INTR.PC
Annual freshwater withdrawals, cu. m	ER.H2O.FWTL.K3
Annual freshwater withdrawals, % of internal resources	ER.H2O.FWTL.ZS

Annual freshwater withdrawals, % for agriculture	ER.H2O.FWAG.ZS
Annual freshwater withdrawals, % for industry	ER.H2O.FWIN.ZS
Annual freshwater withdrawals, % of domestic	ER.H2O.FWDM.ZS
Water productivity, GDP/water use	ER.GDP.FWTL.M3.KD
Access to an improved water source, % of rural population	SH.H2O.SAFE.RU.ZS
Access to an improved water source, % of urban population	SH.H2O.SAFE.UR.ZS

3.6 Energy production and use

Energy production	EG.EGY.PROD.KT.OE
Energy use	EG.USE.COMM.KT.OE
Energy use, Average annual growth	..[a,b]
Energy use, Per capita	EG.USE.PCAP.KG.OE
Fossil fuel	EG.USE.COMM.FO.ZS
Combustible renewable and waste	EG.USE.CRNW.ZS
Alternative and nuclear energy production	EG.USE.COMM.CL.ZS

3.7 Electricity production, sources, and access

Electricity production	EG.ELC.PROD.KH
Coal sources	EG.ELC.COAL.ZS
Natural gas sources	EG.ELC.NGAS.ZS
Oil sources	EG.ELC.PETR.ZS
Hydropower sources	EG.ELC.HYRO.ZS
Renewable sources	EG.ELC.RNWX.ZS
Nuclear power sources	EG.ELC.NUCL.ZS
Access to electricity	EG.ELC.ACCS.ZS

3.8 Energy dependency, efficiency and carbon dioxide emissions

Net energy imports	EG.IMP.CONS.ZS
GDP per unit of energy use	EG.GDP.PUSE.KO.PP.KD
Carbon dioxide emissions, Total	EN.ATM.CO2E.KT
Carbon dioxide emissions, Carbon intensity	EN.ATM.CO2E.EG.ZS
Carbon dioxide emissions, Per capita	EN.ATM.CO2E.PC
Carbon dioxide emissions, kilograms per 2005 PPP $ of GDP	EN.ATM.CO2E.PP.GD.KD

3.9 Trends in greenhouse gas emissions

Carbon dioxide emissions, Total	EN.ATM.CO2E.KT
Carbon dioxide emissions, % change	..[a,b]
Methane emissions, Total	EN.ATM.METH.KT.CE
Methane emissions, % change	..[a,b]

 Front | User guide | World view | People | Environment

Methane emissions, From energy processes	EN.ATM.METH.EG.ZS
Methane emissions, Agricultural	EN.ATM.METH.AG.ZS
Nitrous oxide emissions, Total	EN.ATM.NOXE.KT.CE
Nitrous oxide emissions, % change	..a,b
Nitrous oxide emissions, Energy and industry	EN.ATM.NOXE.EI.ZS
Nitrous oxide emissions, Agriculture	EN.ATM.NOXE.AG.ZS
Other greenhouse gas emissions, Total	EN.ATM.GHGO.KT.CE
Other greenhouse gas emissions, % change	..a,b

3.10 Carbon dioxide emissions by sector

Electricity and heat production	EN.CO2.ETOT.ZS
Manufacturing industries and construction	EN.CO2.MANF.ZS
Residential buildings and commercial and public services	EN.CO2.BLDG.ZS
Transport	EN.CO2.TRAN.ZS
Other sectors	EN.CO2.OTHX.ZS

3.11 Climate variability, exposure to impact, and resilience

Average daily minimum/maximum temperature	..b
Projected annual temperature	..b
Projected annual cool days/cold nights	..b
Projected annual hot days/warm nights	..b
Projected annual precipitation	..b
Land area with an elevation of 5 meters or less	AG.LND.EL5M.ZS
Population living in areas with elevation of 5 meters or less	EN.POP.EL5M.ZS
Population affected by droughts, floods, and extreme temperatures	EN.CLC.MDAT.ZS
Disaster risk reduction progress score	EN.CLC.DRSK.XQ

3.12 Urbanization

Urban population	SP.URB.TOTL
Urban population, % of total population	SP.URB.TOTL.IN.ZS
Urban population, Average annual growth	SP.URB.GROW
Population in urban agglomerations of more than 1 million	EN.URB.MCTY.TL.ZS

Population in the largest city	EN.URB.LCTY.UR.ZS
Access to improved sanitation facilities, % of urban population	SH.STA.ACSN.UR
Access to improved sanitation facilities, % of rural population	SH.STA.ACSN.RU

3.13 Traffic and congestion

Motor vehicles, Per 1,000 people	IS.VEH.NVEH.P3
Motor vehicles, Per kilometer of road	IS.VEH.ROAD.K1
Passenger cars	IS.VEH.PCAR.P3
Road density	IS.ROD.DNST.K2
Road sector energy consumption, % of total consumption	IS.ROD.ENGY.ZS
Road sector energy consumption, Per capita	IS.ROD.ENGY.PC
Diesel fuel consumption	IS.ROD.DESL.PC
Gasoline fuel consumption	IS.ROD.SGAS.PC
Pump price for super grade gasoline	EP.PMP.SGAS.CD
Pump price for diesel	EP.PMP.DESL.CD
Urban-population-weighted particulate matter concentrations (PM10)	EN.ATM.PM10.MC.M3

3.14 Air pollution

This table provides air pollution data for major cities. ..b

3.15 Contribution of natural resources to gross domestic product

Total natural resources rents	NY.GDP.TOTL.RT.ZS
Oil rents	NY.GDP.PETR.RT.ZS
Natural gas rents	NY.GDP.NGAS.RT.ZS
Coal rents	NY.GDP.COAL.RT.ZS
Mineral rents	NY.GDP.MINR.RT.ZS
Forest rents	NY.GDP.FRST.RT.ZS

a. Derived from data elsewhere in the World Development Indicators database.
b. Available online only as part of the table, not as an individual indicator.

ECONOMY

The *Economy* section provides a picture of the global economy and the economic activity of more than 200 countries and territories that produce, trade, and consume the world's output. It includes measures of macroeconomic performance and stability and broader measures of income and saving adjusted for pollution, depreciation, and resource depletion.

The world economy grew 2.4 percent in 2013 to reach $73 trillion in current prices, and growth is projected to accelerate to 3.2 percent in 2014. The share from low- and middle-income economies increased to 32.2 percent from 31.0 percent in 2012. Low- and middle-income economies, estimated to have grown 4.9 percent in 2013, are projected to expand 5.3 percent in 2014. Growth in high-income economies has been upgraded from earlier forecasts to 1.3 percent in 2013 and 2.2 percent in 2014.

During 2014 many countries are expected to switch to the *System of National Accounts 2008* (2008 SNA)—the latest version of the internationally agreed standard set of recommendations on how to compile measures of economic activity, adopted by the United Nations Statistical Commission. The 2008 SNA is an update of the *System of National Accounts 1993* and retains the basic theoretical framework of its predecessor.

In line with the commission's mandate, the 2008 SNA introduces treatments for new aspects of the economy that have come into prominence, elaborates on aspects that have increasingly become the focus of analytical attention, and clarifies guidance on a wide range of issues. The changes in the 2008 SNA include further specification of assets, capital formation, and consumption of fixed capital; concepts related to statistical units and institutional sectoring; the scope of transactions, including the production boundary; the scope of transactions by government and the public sector; and the treatment and definition of financial instruments and assets. The 2008 SNA and the sixth edition of the IMF's *Balance of Payments Manual* have harmonized concepts and classifications.

These changes bring the accounts into line with developments in the economic environment, advances in methodological research, and the needs of users. As of 2013, Australia; Canada; Hong Kong SAR, China; Mexico; Timor-Leste; and the United States have switched to the 2008 SNA.

A detailed explanation of the changes from the 1993 SNA are in annex 3 of the 2008 SNA manual (http://unstats.un.org /unsd/nationalaccount/docs/SNA2008.pdf). The complete 2008 SNA methodology can be accessed through the United Nations Statistics Division website (http://unstats.un.org/unsd /nationalaccount/sna2008.asp).

East Asia & Pacific: Deterioration of current account balances

Current account balance (% of GDP)

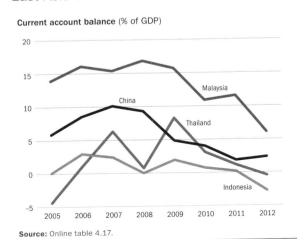

In 2012 Indonesia posted its first current account deficit since the Asian financial crisis. Private savings are under pressure from lower commodity prices, and public savings are suffering from slow revenue growth and high subsidy spending despite recent reductions. Thailand's current account balance turned negative in 2012, and savings rates have declined due to rising household leverage and fiscal support, driving private consumption higher. Malaysia's current account surplus, in double digits since 2003, dropped to 6 percent of GDP in 2012. Public savings are also lower following stimulus packages implemented since the global financial crisis. China's current account balance fell from a high of 10.1 percent of GDP in 2007 to 2.3 percent in 2012 (World Bank 2013a).

Source: Online table 4.17.

South Asia: Growth has slowed but is stabilizing

Annual GDP growth (%)

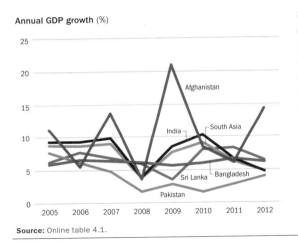

South Asian economies managed the financial and economic crisis reasonably well. But real GDP growth has moderated and remains far below pre-crisis levels. Regional growth slowed from 6.3 percent in 2011 to 4.9 percent in 2012, driven mainly by the slowdown in India, which accounts for about 80 percent of the region's GDP. India's real GDP growth for 2012 was 4.7 percent, down from 6.6 percent in 2011. In Bangladesh, with slower export and investment growth, GDP growth was 6.2 percent in 2012, down from 6.7 percent in 2011. Sri Lanka, facing prudent macroeconomic policies and dampened demand in its main export markets, recorded 6.4 percent growth in 2012, down from 8.2 percent in 2011. In Afghanistan, the regional outlier, real GDP growth for 2012 is estimated at 14.4 percent, up from 6.1 percent in 2011. Bhutan, Nepal, and Pakistan recorded higher growth rates in 2012 than in 2011, but GDP growth in the Maldives in 2011 was half that in 2011 (World Bank 2013b).

Source: Online table 4.1.

Middle East and North Africa: Diverging trends in adjusted net savings

Adjusted net savings (% of GNI)

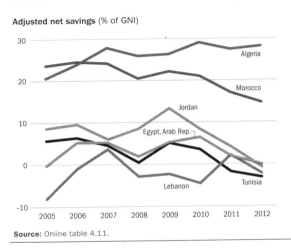

Adjusted net savings measure the real difference between national income and consumption—in other words, the change in a country's real wealth. It takes into account investment in human capital, depreciation of fixed capital, depletion of natural resources, and damage caused by pollution. Savings rates below zero suggest declining wealth and, as a result, unsustainable development. Higher savings lay the basis for building wealth and future growth. Recent trends in the Middle East and North Africa show diverging pathways. Adjusted net savings are positive and high for Algeria and Morocco but below zero for Jordan, Lebanon, and Tunisia. The central negative factor affecting saving rates is depletion of energy resources, which reached 25 percent of gross national income in Middle East and North African countries in 2008 before falling back to around 13 percent in 2012.

Source: Online table 4.11.

Sub-Saharan Africa: More than 10 years of steady growth

Sub-Saharan Africa averaged GDP growth of 5.5 percent a year between 1999 and 2010 (6.5 percent excluding South Africa), nearly 1 percentage point higher than the rest of the developing world (excluding China). In 2012, 5 of the world's 10 fastest growing economies were in Sub-Saharan Africa: Sierra Leone, Niger, Liberia, Burkina Faso, and Côte d'Ivoire. But growth varied widely—from a severe contraction in South Sudan and Sudan to over 10 percent growth in Liberia, Niger, and Sierra Leone, thanks largely to new mineral production. Many countries have seen high growth for several years, with about a third growing 6 percent or more annually (World Bank 2013c).

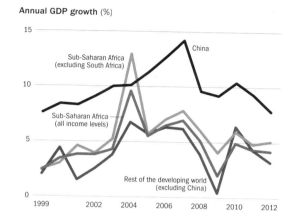

Annual GDP growth (%)

Source: Online table 4.1.

Latin America and the Caribbean: Growth present but slowing

Latin America and the Caribbean was the third slowest growing region in 2012, ahead of Europe and Central Asia and the Middle East and North Africa. Growth decelerated, part of a 3 percentage point decline from 2010 peaks across all developing countries. In much of the Caribbean growth was constrained by higher debt and lower tourism activity. Weak external conditions and contractions in domestic demand were largely responsible for causing the region's GDP growth to fall from 6 percent in 2010 to an estimated 3 percent in 2012. The drop was pronounced in the region's largest economies, Brazil and Argentina, but other countries continued to grow, in most cases with robust domestic demand helping offset some of the slowdown in exports (De la Torre, Yeyati, and Pienknagura 2013).

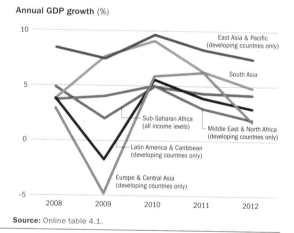

Annual GDP growth (%)

Source: Online table 4.1.

Europe and Central Asia: Multispeed recovery

Europe and Central Asia saw economic growth fall sharply, from 6.3 percent in 2011 to 1.8 percent in 2012 because of poor harvests, higher inflation, weak external demand, and European banks' shrinking balance sheets. The slowdown was severe in Eastern Europe, where GDP grew less than 1 percent (and declined in Serbia). The adjustment in the Commonwealth of Independent States was less severe, but they grew more slowly in 2012 than in 2011. Many developing countries have yet to recover from the 2008 crisis. The recovery of the 11 EU member states that joined after 2004 stalled in 2012, as domestic demand fell and the external environment weakened, leaving net exports as the sole driver of growth. That group's GDP growth of 0.6 percent in 2012 was a fifth that of the year before, and Bosnia and Herzegovina, the Czech Republic, Hungary, the Kyrgyz Republic, and Moldova joined Croatia and Slovenia in a recession (World Bank 2013d,e,f).

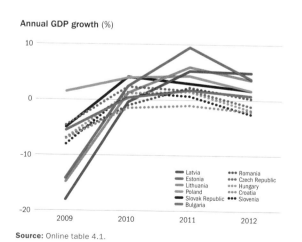

Annual GDP growth (%)

Source: Online table 4.1.

 Economy | States and markets |  Global links | Back

4 Economy

	Gross domestic product			Gross savings	Adjusted net savings	Current account balance	Central government cash surplus or deficit	Central government debt	Consumer price index	Broad money
	average annual % growth	Estimate	Forecast	% of GDP	% of GNI	% of GDP	% of GDP	% of GDP	% growth	% of GDP
	2000–12	2012–13	2013–14	2012	2012	2012	2012	2012	2012	2012
Afghanistan	9.4	3.1	3.5	–14.9	..	–35.5	–0.6	..	7.2	31.9
Albania	5.0	1.3	2.1	14.5	–1.3	–10.4	–3.4	56.6	2.0	82.1
Algeria	3.7	2.8	3.3	47.5	28.3	6.0	–0.3	..	8.9	61.0
American Samoa	..	..	..	..	..	..	..	..	..	..
Andorra	5.9	..	..	..	..	..	..	..	..	..
Angola	11.8	5.1	8.0	18.0	–25.2	12.1	..	..	10.3	34.9
Antigua and Barbuda	2.2	..	..	24.9	..	–6.9	–1.4	..	3.4	102.6
Argentina	5.8[a]	5.0	2.8	21.9	10.1	0.0	..	..	10.0[a]	33.0
Armenia	7.6	3.2	5.0	11.7	–3.7	–11.1	–1.4	..	2.6	33.7
Aruba	–0.1	..	..	..	..	–9.5	..	..	0.6	68.3
Australia	3.1	..	..	25.5	12.0	–3.7	–3.7	30.6	1.8	102.8
Austria[b]	1.7	..	..	24.6	13.1	1.6	–2.2	75.3	2.5	..
Azerbaijan	14.8	4.9	5.3	41.9	15.9	22.5	6.1	6.4	1.1	31.1
Bahamas, The	0.6	..	..	8.4	..	–18.4	–4.1	47.9	2.0	76.6
Bahrain	5.4	..	..	19.5	–0.8	9.7	–0.5	35.6	2.8	74.1
Bangladesh	6.0	6.0	5.7	39.8	21.3	2.3	–0.9	..	6.2	69.7
Barbados	1.2	..	..	8.4	3.6	–4.9	–8.0	96.8	4.5	..
Belarus	7.5	1.0	1.5	31.5	19.7	–2.7	1.7	40.8	59.2	30.5
Belgium[b]	1.4	..	..	20.3	7.9	–2.0	–3.6	91.1	2.8	..
Belize	3.8	1.8	2.7	15.8	9.3	–1.3	–0.2	74.2	1.3	77.4
Benin	3.8	4.2	4.1	7.1	–5.2	–7.1	–1.4	..	6.8	37.9
Bermuda	0.9	..	..	..	..	14.1	..	..	..	..
Bhutan	8.7	7.6	8.1	44.5	23.7	–19.7	..	..	10.9	61.2
Bolivia	4.2	5.3	4.7	25.7	5.5	7.9	..	..	4.6	73.8
Bosnia and Herzegovina	3.8	0.8	2.0	14.5	..	–9.3	–1.2	..	2.0	58.1
Botswana	4.2	4.6	4.9	40.7	33.2	–7.4	–1.9	..	7.5	44.2
Brazil	3.7	2.2	2.4	14.8	4.3	–2.4	–2.6	52.8	5.4	80.8
Brunei Darussalam	1.2	..	..	..	..	..	..	..	0.5	65.9
Bulgaria	4.0	0.6	1.7	21.7	10.9	–1.4	–2.0	15.4	3.0	79.6
Burkina Faso	5.9	7.0	7.0	22.9	8.5	–2.0	–3.2	..	3.8	30.3
Burundi	3.6	4.3	4.5	17.5	–13.7	–10.3	..	..	18.0	23.0
Cabo Verde	6.7	2.6	2.9	35.0	..	–11.5	–9.0	..	2.5	78.7
Cambodia	8.1	7.0	7.0	10.6	–7.5	–8.6	–4.4	..	2.9	50.1
Cameroon	3.3	4.8	5.0	15.8	–1.6	–3.8	..	..	2.9	21.2
Canada	1.9	..	..	23.6	13.0	–3.5	–1.3	53.8	1.5	..
Cayman Islands	..	..	..	..	..	..	..	..	..	..
Central African Republic	4.8	–18.0	–1.8	..	..	..	0.7	..	5.8	18.1
Chad	9.6	5.0	8.7	..	..	..	..	..	10.2	11.9
Channel Islands	0.5	..	..	..	..	..	..	..	..	..
Chile	4.1	..	..	21.4	–0.2	–3.5	1.3	..	3.0	77.3
China	10.6	7.7	7.7	51.2	35.0	2.3	..	..	2.7	187.6
Hong Kong SAR, China	4.4	..	..	28.3	..	2.3	3.8	39.2	4.1	335.3
Macao SAR, China	12.7	..	..	57.4	..	42.9	23.8	..	6.1	107.6
Colombia	4.5	4.0	4.3	18.9	–3.2	–3.3	–1.1	62.6	3.2	42.9
Comoros	1.9	3.3	3.5	..	..	..	..	..	1.8	38.3
Congo, Dem. Rep.	5.7	7.5	7.5	..	..	..	3.8	..	85.1	18.3
Congo, Rep.	4.6	5.6	5.4	..	..	..	..	..	3.9	31.5

 Front | User guide | World view | People | Environment

	Gross domestic product			Gross savings	Adjusted net savings	Current account balance	Central government cash surplus or deficit	Central government debt	Consumer price index	Broad money
	average annual % growth			% of GDP	% of GNI	% of GDP	% of GDP	% of GDP	% growth	% of GDP
	2000–12	Estimate 2012–13	Forecast 2013–14	2012	2012	2012	2012	2012	2012	2012
Costa Rica	4.7	3.4	4.3	15.9	15.1	−5.3	−3.5	..	4.5	49.4
Côte d'Ivoire	1.2	8.7	8.2	..	..	2.0	−3.1	..	1.3	39.0
Croatia	2.1	..	..	18.9	9.3	−0.3	−4.7	..	3.4	80.7
Cuba	5.8	..	..	..	..	..	..	..	..	..
Curaçao	..	..	..	..	..	..	..	..	..	..
Cyprus[b]	2.6[c]	..	..	8.8[c]	3.9[c]	−6.9	−6.3	113.3	2.4	..
Czech Republic	3.3	..	..	21.0	5.1	−2.4	−4.4	38.3	3.3	77.3
Denmark	0.6	..	..	23.6	15.7	5.9	−2.0	50.6	2.4	74.6
Djibouti	3.5	..	..	..	..	..	..	..	3.7	..
Dominica	3.2	1.1	1.7	10.8	..	−11.5	−11.9	..	1.4	97.4
Dominican Republic	5.6	2.5	3.9	9.2	..	−6.8	−2.9	..	3.7	34.3
Ecuador	4.4	4.0	4.1	26.9	6.1	−0.2	..	..	5.1	31.6
Egypt, Arab Rep.	4.9	1.8	2.3	13.0	0.0	−2.7	−10.6	..	7.1	74.1
El Salvador	2.0	1.9	2.3	8.9	6.6	−5.3	−2.2	47.8	1.7	44.6
Equatorial Guinea	10.9	..	..	..	..	..	..	..	6.1	18.7
Eritrea	0.9	6.0	3.5	..	..	..	..	..	..	114.7
Estonia[b]	3.7	..	..	25.0	12.5	−1.8	1.0	6.9	3.9	59.6
Ethiopia	8.9	7.0	7.2	28.8	6.1	−7.2	−1.4	..	22.8	..
Faeroe Islands	..	..	..	..	..	..	..	..	..	..
Fiji	1.2	2.4	2.1	..	..	−1.4	..	..	3.4	68.8
Finland[b]	1.7	..	..	18.1	7.6	−1.5	−0.5	48.0	2.8	..
France[b]	1.1	..	..	17.5	9.9	−2.2	−5.1	93.7	2.0	..
French Polynesia	..	..	..	..	..	..	..	..	..	..
Gabon	2.4	4.2	4.2	..	..	..	..	..	2.7	20.8
Gambia, The	3.4	6.5	7.5	17.1	0.9	6.4	..	..	4.3	53.6
Georgia	6.5[d]	2.5[d]	6.3[d]	18.3[d]	7.0[d]	−11.7	−0.5	32.6	−0.9	30.2
Germany[b]	1.1	..	..	24.2	15.8	7.0	−0.4	55.3	2.0	..
Ghana	6.6	7.4	7.4	21.5	2.7	−11.7	−3.9	..	9.2	31.3
Greece[b]	1.1	..	..	9.8	−4.3	−2.5	−9.8	106.5	1.5	..
Greenland	1.7	..	..	..	..	..	..	..	..	..
Grenada	1.9	1.1	1.1	−10.2	..	−28.0	−5.8	..	2.4	95.4
Guam	..	..	..	..	..	..	..	..	..	..
Guatemala	3.5	3.3	3.4	12.0	−2.3	−2.6	−2.3	24.4	3.8	46.2
Guinea	2.6	4.0	4.7	−6.2	−42.8	−18.4	..	..	15.2	36.4
Guinea-Bissau	2.3	3.0	2.7	1.5	−22.4	−8.5	..	..	2.1	38.8
Guyana	1.7	4.4	3.9	11.1	−11.8	−13.9	..	..	2.4	67.0
Haiti	0.8	3.4	4.2	25.6	12.7	−4.4	..	..	6.3	45.8
Honduras	4.3	2.9	3.4	16.5	11.4	−8.6	−3.2	..	5.2	51.0
Hungary	1.6	0.7	1.7	23.4	12.4	0.9	3.7	82.4	5.7	60.9
Iceland	2.4	..	..	9.3	..	−5.5	−5.3	119.1	5.2	89.8
India	7.7	4.8	6.2	30.3	14.8	−4.9	−3.8	49.7	9.3	75.6
Indonesia	5.5	5.6	5.3	32.0	24.1	−2.7	−1.1	26.2	4.3	40.1
Iran, Islamic Rep.	4.8	−1.5	1.0	..	..	..	..	..	27.3	19.7
Iraq	5.1	4.2	6.5	26.7	..	13.7	..	..	5.8	30.7
Ireland[b]	2.2	..	..	16.0	10.9	4.4	−13.0	102.0	1.7	..
Isle of Man	6.2	..	..	..	..	..	..	..	..	..
Israel	3.7	..	..	14.8	6.0	1.3	−5.4	..	1.7	..

4 Economy

	Gross domestic product			Gross savings	Adjusted net savings	Current account balance	Central government cash surplus or deficit	Central government debt	Consumer price index	Broad money
	average annual % growth	Estimate	Forecast	% of GDP	% of GNI	% of GDP	% of GDP	% of GDP	% growth	% of GDP
	2000–12	2012–13	2013–14	2012	2012	2012	2012	2012	2012	2012
Italy[b]	0.2	..	..	17.4	3.3	−0.4	−3.5	110.8	3.0	..
Jamaica	..	..	..	8.3	3.5	−12.9	−4.2	..	6.9	47.1
Japan	0.7	..	..	21.5	1.5	1.0	−8.3	189.8	0.0	241.2
Jordan	6.2	3.0	3.1	8.5	−0.7	−18.4	−8.3	66.8	4.8	118.4
Kazakhstan	7.7	6.0	5.8	26.2	−8.0	3.8	7.7	9.9	5.1	34.7
Kenya	4.4	5.0	5.1	9.4	4.7	−10.4	−4.8	..	9.4	50.6
Kiribati	1.4	1.8	1.8	..	..	..	−7.2	..	..	..
Korea, Dem. People's Rep.	..	..	..	..	..	..	..	..	..	..
Korea, Rep.	4.0	..	..	30.9	18.1	3.8	1.8	..	2.2	144.3
Kosovo	5.2	..	..	18.3	..	−7.5	..	..	2.5	40.6
Kuwait	5.1	..	..	59.5	11.2	43.2	27.9	..	2.8	57.6
Kyrgyz Republic	4.2	7.8	6.5	29.6	12.1	−22.1	−6.6	..	2.7	..
Lao PDR	7.4	8.0	7.7	15.7	−11.6	−4.4	−0.8	..	4.3	35.9
Latvia	3.6	..	..	25.7	11.0	−2.5	−2.8	42.1	2.3	44.1
Lebanon	5.0	0.7	2.0	13.6	−2.2	−3.9	−8.8	..	4.0	241.7
Lesotho	4.1	4.6	5.1	18.1	11.5	−24.0	..	..	6.1	35.6
Liberia	6.6	7.9	7.5	31.4	−6.0	−49.1	−2.6	32.7	6.8	34.9
Libya	5.4	−6.0	23.0	..	..	..	..	..	6.1	..
Liechtenstein	2.5	..	..	..	..	..	..	..	..	..
Lithuania	4.3	..	..	17.1	9.1	−0.2	−5.1	43.5	3.1	47.4
Luxembourg[b]	2.5	..	..	16.4	8.3	6.5	−0.4	17.2	2.7	..
Macedonia, FYR	3.2	2.5	3.0	25.5	6.0	−3.1	−4.0	..	3.3	58.3
Madagascar	3.0	4.1	4.8	..	..	..	−1.7	..	6.4	24.4
Malawi	3.7	4.4	4.8	12.5	−2.7	−18.8	..	..	21.3	36.4
Malaysia	4.9	4.5	4.8	31.9	16.1	6.1	−4.5	53.3	1.7	141.2
Maldives	7.2	4.3	4.2	..	..	−27.0	−8.8	73.8	13.1	58.6
Mali	5.2	4.0	5.2	8.5	−10.8	−12.6	−2.5	..	5.4	32.3
Malta[b]	1.8	..	..	11.7	..	2.1	−2.7	84.0	2.4	..
Marshall Islands	1.4	5.0	5.0	..	..	..	..	..	..	..
Mauritania	5.6	5.7	4.6	..	..	..	..	..	4.9	33.3
Mauritius	3.9	3.7	4.1	15.1	4.5	−11.2	−1.1	36.4	3.9	100.5
Mexico	2.2	1.4	3.4	21.5	5.8	−1.2	..	..	4.1	32.0
Micronesia, Fed. Sts.	0.0	1.4	1.4	..	..	..	..	..	..	41.3
Moldova	4.8[e]	4.2[e]	3.8[e]	12.8[e]	6.2[e]	−6.8	−1.8	23.7	4.7	56.4
Monaco	4.2	..	..	..	..	..	..	..	..	..
Mongolia	7.7	12.5	10.3	33.3	13.8	−32.7	−8.5	..	15.0	54.6
Montenegro	4.0	1.8	2.5	−0.2	..	−17.6	..	..	3.2	50.5
Morocco	4.8[f]	4.5[f]	3.6[f]	25.8[f]	14.7[f]	−10.0	−4.2	56.8	1.3	113.9
Mozambique	7.5	7.0	8.5	12.4	0.4	−44.2	−2.8	..	2.1	46.0
Myanmar	..	..	..	..	..	..	..	..	1.5	..
Namibia	4.8	4.2	4.3	18.2	12.0	−1.2	..	..	6.5	57.1
Nepal	4.0	3.6	3.8	40.8	30.0	3.0	−0.6	33.9	9.5	77.5
Netherlands[b]	1.3	..	..	24.8	16.9	9.4	−3.9	66.4	2.4	..
New Caledonia	..	..	..	..	..	..	..	..	..	..
New Zealand	2.3	..	..	14.6	8.0	−4.1	−7.2	62.5	0.9	94.7
Nicaragua	3.4	3.8	4.2	17.3	3.7	−13.0	0.5	..	7.2	33.6
Niger	4.5	5.6	6.2	20.1	10.0	−19.9	..	..	0.5	23.1

 Front User guide  World view People Environment

	Gross domestic product			Gross savings	Adjusted net savings	Current account balance	Central government cash surplus or deficit	Central government debt	Consumer price index	Broad money
	average annual % growth	Estimate	Forecast	% of GDP	% of GNI	% of GDP	% of GDP	% of GDP	% growth	% of GDP
	2000–12	2012–13	2013–14	2012	2012	2012	2012	2012	2012	2012
Nigeria	6.8	6.7	6.7	40.6	8.2	7.8	..	..	12.2	36.5
Northern Mariana Islands	..	..	..				..	..	..	..
Norway	1.5		..	39.1	21.7	14.5	14.6	20.9	0.7	..
Oman	5.0	..		..	..	10.6	10.6	5.0	2.9	36.3
Pakistan	4.4	6.1	3.4	20.3	3.7	−0.9	−8.0	..	9.7	39.9
Palau	−0.1	5.8	5.8	..	..	..	..	..	..	..
Panama	7.5	7.9	7.3	26.7	23.3	−9.0	..	..	5.7	80.6
Papua New Guinea	4.7	4.0	8.5	..	..	−6.7	..	..	2.2	52.0
Paraguay	3.7	14.1	4.6	12.4	6.1	0.5	1.6	..	3.7	44.6
Peru	6.3	4.9	5.5	25.4	7.7	−3.4	1.2	19.1	3.7	36.8
Philippines	4.9	6.9	6.5	23.9	9.4	2.8	−1.9	51.5	3.2	58.9
Poland	4.2	..	..	17.5	7.9	−3.7	−4.3	..	3.6	57.9
Portugal[b]	0.4	..	..	15.9	8.7	−2.1	−4.0	92.5	2.8	..
Puerto Rico	−0.4	..	..	..	..	..	..	..	..	..
Qatar	14.0	..	..	66.2	46.1	32.0	2.9	..	1.9	54.4
Romania	4.2	2.5	2.5	22.2	7.0	−4.4	−5.1	..	3.3	37.8
Russian Federation	4.8	..	..	29.6	15.3	3.6	3.3	9.3	5.1	51.5
Rwanda	7.9	7.0	7.5	11.5	−3.7	−11.6	−0.9	..	6.3	..
Samoa	2.4	2.1	2.1	..	..	−5.2	0.0	..	2.0	44.6
San Marino	3.2	..	..	..	..	..	..	..	2.8	..
São Tomé and Príncipe	4.5	5.5	4.9	..	..	−37.8	−12.6	..	10.4	36.9
Saudi Arabia	6.1	..	..	50.5	10.0	23.2	..	..	2.9	54.1
Senegal	4.0	4.0	4.5	21.8	15.9	−7.9	−6.2	..	1.4	40.4
Serbia	3.3	2.0	1.0	18.0	..	−10.7	−4.5	..	7.3	49.8
Seychelles	3.1	3.5	3.9	..	..	−24.7	4.8	73.3	7.1	48.0
Sierra Leone	6.9	17.0	14.1	10.2	−22.7	−29.0	−5.2	..	12.9	20.5
Singapore	5.9	..	..	45.6	31.9	18.7	9.0	115.1	4.5	137.6
Sint Maarten	..	..	..	..	..	..	..	..	..	..
Slovak Republic[b]	4.8	..	..	22.0	6.1	2.2	−4.9	45.6	3.6	..
Slovenia[b]	2.5	..	..	21.4	9.5	3.3	−5.9	..	2.6	..
Solomon Islands	5.1	4.0	3.5	..	..	0.2	..	..	7.3	41.3
Somalia	..	..	..	..	..	..	..	..	..	..
South Africa	3.6	1.9	2.7	13.2	0.4	−5.2	−4.4	..	5.4	75.2
South Sudan	..	33.9	17.0	..	..	..	..	..	47.3	..
Spain[b]	1.7	..	..	18.9	5.9	−1.1	−3.6	56.1	2.4	..
Sri Lanka	5.9	7.0	7.4	24.1	19.7	−6.7	−6.1	79.1	7.5	38.6
St. Kitts and Nevis	2.4	..	..	18.3	..	−9.2	10.7	..	1.4	140.7
St. Lucia	2.7	0.7	1.5	13.0	4.5	−14.9	−6.8	..	4.2	95.8
St. Martin	..	..	..	..	..	..	..	..	..	..
St. Vincent & the Grenadines	2.8	2.1	2.7	−6.7	..	−30.3	−2.0	..	2.6	68.6
Sudan	5.2[g]	2.9[h]	2.9[h]	9.9[h]	−6.7[h]	−10.8	..	..	37.4	27.9[h]
Suriname	4.9	3.9	4.1	..	..	4.7	−0.7	..	5.0	49.1
Swaziland	2.2	0.0	0.0	7.7	1.4	4.1	..	..	8.9	31.4
Sweden	2.2	..	..	25.4	17.8	6.1	−0.4	36.6	0.9	85.2
Switzerland	1.9	..	..	32.8	18.9	8.5	0.6	26.7	−0.7	188.0
Syrian Arab Republic	5.0	−22.5	−8.6	16.8	..	..	..	..	36.7	73.9
Tajikistan	7.8	7.0	6.0	17.9	9.0	−3.2	..	..	5.8	15.5

4 Economy

	Gross domestic product			Gross savings	Adjusted net savings	Current account balance	Central government cash surplus or deficit	Central government debt	Consumer price index	Broad money
	average annual % growth	Estimate	Forecast	% of GDP	% of GNI	% of GDP	% of GDP	% of GDP	% growth	% of GDP
	2000–12	2012–13	2013–14	2012	2012	2012	2012	2012	2012	2012
Tanzania[i]	7.0	7.1	7.4	23.5	8.7	–12.9	–7.2	..	16.0	32.8
Thailand	4.1	3.2	4.5	30.2	16.7	–0.4	–1.2	30.2	3.0	131.1
Timor-Leste	5.8	..	..	326.7	..	211.9	..	..	11.8	31.5
Togo	2.8	5.0	4.5	0.0	–21.3	–6.3	–6.3	..	2.6	46.4
Tonga	1.1	1.2	1.2	5.9	..	–20.2	..	..	1.2	40.5
Trinidad and Tobago	5.1	..	..	..	..	12.3	–1.6	..	9.3	62.0
Tunisia	4.2	2.6	2.5	14.5	–3.1	–8.3	–5.0	44.1	5.5	66.7
Turkey	4.6	4.3	3.5	14.5	3.4	–6.1	–1.1	47.2	8.9	55.4
Turkmenistan	9.0	10.1	10.7	..	..	..	..	..	..	..
Turks and Caicos Islands	..	..	..	..	..	..	..	..	..	..
Tuvalu	1.3	1.0	1.0	..	..	..	..	..	..	..
Uganda	7.5	6.2	6.7	12.8	–11.2	–11.1	–3.9	42.7	14.0	24.2
Ukraine	3.8	–1.1	2.0	9.3	–3.7	–8.4	–2.3	27.4	0.6	54.9
United Arab Emirates	4.2	..	..	..	..	..	0.1	..	0.9	61.2
United Kingdom	1.5	..	..	10.9	3.0	–3.7	–7.6	99.8	2.8	161.6
United States	1.7	..	..	16.5	7.3	–2.7	–7.5	93.8	2.1	87.4
Uruguay	4.2	..	..	15.0	1.6	–5.3	–2.1	44.6	8.1	43.6
Uzbekistan	7.4	7.4	7.0	..	..	..	..	..	..	..
Vanuatu	3.8	1.7	2.2	19.3	..	–6.4	–2.3	..	1.4	78.1
Venezuela, RB	4.3	0.7	0.5	25.6	6.8	2.9	..	..	21.1	47.5
Vietnam	6.6	5.3	5.4	31.6	12.7	5.8	..	..	9.1	106.5
Virgin Islands (U.S.)	..	..	..	..	..	..	..	..	..	..
West Bank and Gaza	..	..	..	..	..	..	..	..	..	..
Yemen, Rep.	3.1	3.0	3.4	8.1	–10.8	–3.2	..	..	17.3	34.6
Zambia	5.9	6.0	6.5	24.7	1.8	0.0	5.0	..	6.6	24.2
Zimbabwe	–4.1	2.2	3.3	..	..	..	..	..	..	..
World	**2.7 w**	**2.4 w**	**3.2 w**	**21.6 w**	**11.3 w**					
Low income	5.6	6.2	6.3	23.8	7.1					
Middle income	6.3	4.9	5.6	30.9	18.6					
Lower middle income	6.2	4.5	5.9	26.9	12.5					
Upper middle income	6.3	5.0	5.5	32.2	20.2					
Low & middle income	6.3	4.8	5.3	30.9	18.4					
East Asia & Pacific	9.2	7.2	7.2	46.0	31.8					
Europe & Central Asia	4.7	3.4	3.5	16.9	2.8					
Latin America & Carib.	3.6	2.5	2.9	19.2	5.1					
Middle East & N. Africa	4.6	–0.1	2.8	..	5.3					
South Asia	7.2	4.6	5.7	29.5	13.9					
Sub-Saharan Africa	5.0	4.7	5.3	19.8	–0.4					
High income	1.8	1.3	2.2	19.6	8.2					
Euro area	1.1	–0.4	1.1	20.1	10.2					

a. Data for Argentina are officially reported by the National Statistics and Censuses Institute of Argentina. The International Monetary Fund has, however, issued a declaration of censure and called on Argentina to adopt remedial measures to address the quality of official GDP and consumer price index data. Alternative data sources have shown significantly lower real growth and higher inflation than the official data since 2008. In this context, the World Bank is also using alternative data sources and estimates for the surveillance of macroeconomic developments in Argentina. b. As members of the European Monetary Union, these countries share a single currency, the euro. c. Refers to the area controlled by the government of Cyprus. d. Excludes Abkhazia and South Ossetia. e. Excludes Transnistria. f. Includes Former Spanish Sahara. g. Excludes South Sudan after July 9, 2011. h. Excludes South Sudan. i. Covers mainland Tanzania only.

 Front | ? User guide | World view | People | Environment

Economic data are organized by several different accounting conventions: the system of national accounts, the balance of payments, government finance statistics, and international finance statistics. There has been progress in unifying the concepts in the system of national accounts, balance of payments, and government finance statistics, but there are many national variations in the implementation of these standards. For example, even though the United Nations recommends using the 2008 System of National Accounts (2008 SNA) methodology in compiling national accounts, many are still using earlier versions, some as old as 1968. The International Monetary Fund (IMF) has recently published a new balance of payments methodology (BPM6), but many countries are still using the previous version. Similarly, the standards and definitions for government finance statistics were updated in 2001, but several countries still report using the 1986 version. For individual country information about methodology used, refer to *Primary data documentation*.

Economic growth

An economy's growth is measured by the change in the volume of its output or in the real incomes of its residents. The 2008 SNA offers three plausible indicators for calculating growth: the volume of gross domestic product (GDP), real gross domestic income, and real gross national income. Only growth in GDP is reported here.

Growth rates of GDP and its components are calculated using the least squares method and constant price data in the local currency for countries and using constant price U.S. dollar series for regional and income groups. Local currency series are converted to constant U.S. dollars using an exchange rate in the common reference year. The growth rates are average annual and compound growth rates. Methods of computing growth are described in *Statistical methods*. Forecasts of growth rates come from World Bank (2014).

Rebasing national accounts

Rebasing of national accounts can alter the measured growth rate of an economy and lead to breaks in series that affect the consistency of data over time. When countries rebase their national accounts, they update the weights assigned to various components to better reflect current patterns of production or uses of output. The new base year should represent normal operation of the economy—it should be a year without major shocks or distortions. Some developing countries have not rebased their national accounts for many years. Using an old base year can be misleading because implicit price and volume weights become progressively less relevant and useful.

To obtain comparable series of constant price data for computing aggregates, the World Bank rescales GDP and value added by industrial origin to a common reference year. This year's *World Development Indicators* switches the reference year to 2005. Because rescaling changes the implicit weights used in forming regional and income group aggregates, aggregate growth rates in this year's

edition are not comparable with those from earlier editions with different base years.

Rescaling may result in a discrepancy between the rescaled GDP and the sum of the rescaled components. To avoid distortions in the growth rates, the discrepancy is left unallocated. As a result, the weighted average of the growth rates of the components generally does not equal the GDP growth rate.

Adjusted net savings

Adjusted net savings measure the change in a country's real wealth after accounting for the depreciation and depletion of a full range of assets in the economy. If a country's adjusted net savings are positive and the accounting includes a sufficiently broad range of assets, economic theory suggests that the present value of social welfare is increasing. Conversely, persistently negative adjusted net savings indicate that the present value of social welfare is decreasing, suggesting that an economy is on an unsustainable path.

Adjusted net savings are derived from standard national accounting measures of gross savings by making four adjustments. First, estimates of fixed capital consumption of produced assets are deducted to obtain net savings. Second, current public expenditures on education are added to net savings (in standard national accounting these expenditures are treated as consumption). Third, estimates of the depletion of a variety of natural resources are deducted to reflect the decline in asset values associated with their extraction and harvest. And fourth, deductions are made for damages from carbon dioxide emissions and local pollution. By accounting for the depletion of natural resources and the degradation of the environment, adjusted net savings go beyond the definition of savings or net savings in the SNA.

Balance of payments

The balance of payments records an economy's transactions with the rest of the world. Balance of payments accounts are divided into two groups: the current account, which records transactions in goods, services, primary income, and secondary income, and the capital and financial account, which records capital transfers, acquisition or disposal of nonproduced, nonfinancial assets, and transactions in financial assets and liabilities. The current account balance is one of the most analytically useful indicators of an external imbalance.

A primary purpose of the balance of payments accounts is to indicate the need to adjust an external imbalance. Where to draw the line for analytical purposes requires a judgment concerning the imbalance that best indicates the need for adjustment. There are a number of definitions in common use for this and related analytical purposes. The trade balance is the difference between exports and imports of goods. From an analytical view it is arbitrary to distinguish goods from services. For example, a unit of foreign exchange earned by a freight company strengthens the balance of payments to the same extent as the foreign exchange earned by a goods exporter.

4 Economy

Even so, the trade balance is useful because it is often the most timely indicator of trends in the current account balance. Customs authorities are typically able to provide data on trade in goods long before data on trade in services are available.

Beginning in August 2012, the International Monetary Fund implemented the Balance of Payments Manual 6 (BPM6) framework in its major statistical publications. The World Bank implemented BPM6 in its online databases and publications from April 2013. Balance of payments data for 2005 onward will be presented in accord with the BPM6. The historical BPM5 data series will end with data for 2008, which can be accessed through the *World Development Indicators* archives.

The complete balance of payments methodology can be accessed through the International Monetary Fund website (www.imf.org /external/np/sta/bop/bop.htm).

Government finance

Central government cash surplus or deficit, a summary measure of the ongoing sustainability of government operations, is comparable to the national accounting concept of savings plus net capital transfers receivable, or net operating balance in the 2001 update of the IMF's *Government Finance Statistics Manual.*

The 2001 manual, harmonized with the 1993 SNA, recommends an accrual accounting method, focusing on all economic events affecting assets, liabilities, revenues, and expenses, not just those represented by cash transactions. It accounts for all changes in stocks, so stock data at the end of an accounting period equal stock data at the beginning of the period plus flows over the period. The 1986 manual considered only debt stocks.

For most countries central government finance data have been consolidated into one account, but for others only budgetary central government accounts are available. Countries reporting budgetary data are noted in *Primary data documentation.* Because budgetary accounts may not include all central government units (such as social security funds), they usually provide an incomplete picture. In federal states the central government accounts provide an incomplete view of total public finance.

Data on government revenue and expense are collected by the IMF through questionnaires to member countries and by the Organisation for Economic Co-operation and Development (OECD). Despite IMF efforts to standardize data collection, statistics are often incomplete, untimely, and not comparable across countries.

Government finance statistics are reported in local currency. The indicators here are shown as percentages of GDP. Many countries report government finance data by fiscal year; see *Primary data documentation* for information on fiscal year end by country.

Financial accounts

Money and the financial accounts that record the supply of money lie at the heart of a country's financial system. There are several commonly used definitions of the money supply. The narrowest, M1, encompasses currency held by the public and demand deposits with banks. M2 includes M1 plus time and savings deposits with banks that require prior notice for withdrawal. M3 includes M2 as well as various money market instruments, such as certificates of deposit issued by banks, bank deposits denominated in foreign currency, and deposits with financial institutions other than banks. However defined, money is a liability of the banking system, distinguished from other bank liabilities by the special role it plays as a medium of exchange, a unit of account, and a store of value.

A general and continuing increase in an economy's price level is called inflation. The increase in the average prices of goods and services in the economy should be distinguished from a change in the relative prices of individual goods and services. Generally accompanying an overall increase in the price level is a change in the structure of relative prices, but it is only the average increase, not the relative price changes, that constitutes inflation. A commonly used measure of inflation is the consumer price index, which measures the prices of a representative basket of goods and services purchased by a typical household. The consumer price index is usually calculated on the basis of periodic surveys of consumer prices. Other price indices are derived implicitly from indexes of current and constant price series.

Consumer price indexes are produced more frequently and so are more current. They are constructed explicitly, using surveys of the cost of a defined basket of consumer goods and services. Nevertheless, consumer price indexes should be interpreted with caution. The definition of a household, the basket of goods, and the geographic (urban or rural) and income group coverage of consumer price surveys can vary widely by country. In addition, weights are derived from household expenditure surveys, which, for budgetary reasons, tend to be conducted infrequently in developing countries, impairing comparability over time. Although useful for measuring consumer price inflation within a country, consumer price indexes are of less value in comparing countries.

Definitions

• **Gross domestic product (GDP)** at purchaser prices is the sum of gross value added by all resident producers in the economy plus any product taxes (less subsidies) not included in the valuation of output. It is calculated without deducting for depreciation of fabricated capital assets or for depletion and degradation of natural resources. Value added is the net output of an industry after adding up all outputs and subtracting intermediate inputs. • **Gross savings** are the difference between gross national income and public and private consumption, plus net current transfers. • **Adjusted net savings** measure the change in value of a specified set of assets, excluding capital gains. Adjusted net savings are net savings plus education expenditure minus energy depletion, mineral depletion, net forest depletion, and carbon dioxide and particulate emissions damage. • **Current account balance** is the sum of net exports of goods and services, net primary income, and net secondary income. • **Central**

 Front User guide World view People Environment

government cash surplus or deficit is revenue (including grants) minus expense, minus net acquisition of nonfinancial assets. In editions before 2005 nonfinancial assets were included under revenue and expenditure in gross terms. This cash surplus or deficit is close to the earlier overall budget balance (still missing is lending minus repayments, which are included as a financing item under net acquisition of financial assets). • **Central government debt** is the entire stock of direct government fixed-term contractual obligations to others outstanding on a particular date. It includes domestic and foreign liabilities such as currency and money deposits, securities other than shares, and loans. It is the gross amount of government liabilities reduced by the amount of equity and financial derivatives held by the government. Because debt is a stock rather than a flow, it is measured as of a given date, usually the last day of the fiscal year. • **Consumer price index** reflects changes in the cost to the average consumer of acquiring a basket of goods and services that may be fixed or may change at specified intervals, such as yearly. The Laspeyres formula is generally used. • **Broad money** (IFS line 35L..ZK) is the sum of currency outside banks; demand deposits other than those of the central government; the time, savings, and foreign currency deposits of resident sectors other than the central government; bank and traveler's checks; and other securities such as certificates of deposit and commercial paper.

Data sources

Data on GDP for most countries are collected from national statistical organizations and central banks by visiting and resident World Bank missions; data for selected high-income economies are from the OECD. Estimates of GDP growth for 2012–13 and projections for 2013–14 are from the World Bank's Global Economic Prospects database. Data on gross savings are from World Bank national accounts data files. Data on adjusted net savings are based on a conceptual underpinning by Hamilton and Clemens (1999) and calculated using data on consumption of fixed capital from the United Nations Statistics Division's *National Accounts Statistics: Main Aggregates and Detailed Tables,* extrapolated to 2010; data on education expenditure from the United Nations Educational, Scientific, and Cultural Organization Institute for Statistics online database, with missing data estimated by World Bank staff; data on forest, energy, and mineral depletion based on sources and methods in World Bank (2011); estimates of damages from carbon dioxide emissions following the method of Fankhauser (1994) and using emissions data published by the International Energy Agency (2013); and predicted concentrations of local air pollution following the method of Pandey and others (2006) and using monitoring data for air quality available online in the World Health Organization's Global Health Observatory database, the Clean Air Asia's Cities-ACT database, the European Environment Agency's database, and the database of the U.S. Environmental Protection Agency. Data on

current account balance are from the IMF's *Balance of Payments Statistics Yearbook* and *International Financial Statistics.* Data on central government finances are from the IMF's Government Finance Statistics database. Data on the consumer price index are from the IMF's *International Financial Statistics.* Data on broad money are from the IMF's monthly *International Financial Statistics* and annual *International Financial Statistics Yearbook.*

References

Asian Development Bank. 2012. *Asian Development Outlook 2012 Update: Services and Asia's Future Growth.* Manila.

De la Torre, Augusto, Eduardo Levy Yeyati, Samuel Pienknagura. 2013. *Latin America's Deceleration and the Exchange Rate Buffer.* Semiannual Report, Office of the Chief Economist. Washington, DC: World Bank.

Fankhauser, Samuel. 1994. "The Social Costs of Greenhouse Gas Emissions: An Expected Value Approach." *Energy Journal* 15 (2): 157–84.

Hamilton, Kirk, and Michael Clemens. 1999. "Genuine Savings Rates in Developing Countries." *World Bank Economic Review* 13 (2): 333–56.

IMF (International Monetary Fund). 2001. *Government Finance Statistics Manual.* Washington, DC.

International Energy Agency. 2013. IEA CO2 Emissions from Fuel Combustion Statistics database. [http://dx.doi.org/10.1787/data-00430-en]. Paris.

Pandey, Kiran D., Katharine Bolt, Uwe Deichmann, Kirk Hamilton, Bart Ostro, and David Wheeler. 2006. "The Human Cost of Air Pollution: New Estimates for Developing Countries." World Bank, Development Research Group and Environment Department, Washington, DC.

United Nations Statistics Division. Various years. *National Accounts Statistics: Main Aggregates and Detailed Tables. Parts 1 and 2.* New York: United Nations.

World Bank. 2011. *The Changing Wealth of Nations: Measuring Sustainable Development for the New Millennium.* Washington, DC.

———. 2013a. *East Asia and Pacific Economic Update 2013: Rebuilding Policy Buffers, Reinvigorating Growth.* Washington, DC.

———. 2013b. *South Asia Economic Focus—Regaining Momentum.* Washington, DC.

———. 2013c. *Africa's Pulse: An Analysis of Issues Shaping Africa's Economic Future.* Volume 8, October. Washington, DC.

———. 2013d. EU11 *Regular Economic Report.* Issue 26, January. Washington, DC.

———. 2013e. EU11 *Regular Economic Report.* Issue 27, June. Washington, DC.

———. 2013f. *Global Economic Prospects, Volume 7, June 13: Assuring Growth over the Medium Term.* Washington, DC.

———. 2014. *Global Economic Prospects: Coping with Policy Normalization in High-income Countries.* Volume 8, January 14. Washington, DC.

———. Various years. *World Development Indicators.* Washington, DC.

4 Economy

Online tables and indicators

To access the World Development Indicators online tables, use the URL http://wdi.worldbank.org/table/ and the table number (for example, http://wdi.worldbank.org/table/4.1). To view a specific indicator online, use the URL http://data.worldbank.org/indicator/ and the indicator code (for example, http://data.worldbank.org /indicator/NY.GDP.MKTP.KD.ZG).

4.1 Growth of output

Gross domestic product	NY.GDP.MKTP.KD.ZG
Agriculture	NV.AGR.TOTL.KD.ZG
Industry	NV.IND.TOTL.KD.ZG
Manufacturing	NV.IND.MANF.KD.ZG
Services	NV.SRV.TETC.KD.ZG

4.2 Structure of output

Gross domestic product	NY.GDP.MKTP.CD
Agriculture	NV.AGR.TOTL.ZS
Industry	NV.IND.TOTL.ZS
Manufacturing	NV.IND.MANF.ZS
Services	NV.SRV.TETC.ZS

4.3 Structure of manufacturing

Manufacturing value added	NV.IND.MANF.CD
Food, beverages and tobacco	NV.MNF.FBTO.ZS.UN
Textiles and clothing	NV.MNF.TXTL.ZS.UN
Machinery and transport equipment	NV.MNF.MTRN.ZS.UN
Chemicals	NV.MNF.CHEM.ZS.UN
Other manufacturing	NV.MNF.OTHR.ZS.UN

4.4 Structure of merchandise exports

Merchandise exports	TX.VAL.MRCH.CD.WT
Food	TX.VAL.FOOD.ZS.UN
Agricultural raw materials	TX.VAL.AGRI.ZS.UN
Fuels	TX.VAL.FUEL.ZS.UN
Ores and metals	TX.VAL.MMTL.ZS.UN
Manufactures	TX.VAL.MANF.ZS.UN

4.5 Structure of merchandise imports

Merchandise imports	TM.VAL.MRCH.CD.WT
Food	TM.VAL.FOOD.ZS.UN
Agricultural raw materials	TM.VAL.AGRI.ZS.UN
Fuels	TM.VAL.FUEL.ZS.UN
Ores and metals	TM.VAL.MMTL.ZS.UN
Manufactures	TM.VAL.MANF.ZS.UN

4.6 Structure of service exports

Commercial service exports	TX.VAL.SERV.CD.WT
Transport	TX.VAL.TRAN.ZS.WT
Travel	TX.VAL.TRVL.ZS.WT
Insurance and financial services	TX.VAL.INSF.ZS.WT
Computer, information, communications, and other commercial services	TX.VAL.OTHR.ZS.WT

4.7 Structure of service imports

Commercial service imports	TM.VAL.SERV.CD.WT
Transport	TM.VAL.TRAN.ZS.WT
Travel	TM.VAL.TRVL.ZS.WT
Insurance and financial services	TM.VAL.INSF.ZS.WT
Computer, information, communications, and other commercial services	TM.VAL.OTHR.ZS.WT

4.8 Structure of demand

Household final consumption expenditure	NE.CON.PETC.ZS
General government final consumption expenditure	NE.CON.GOVT.ZS
Gross capital formation	NE.GDI.TOTL.ZS
Exports of goods and services	NE.EXP.GNFS.ZS
Imports of goods and services	NE.IMP.GNFS.ZS
Gross savings	NY.GNS.ICTR.ZS

4.9 Growth of consumption and investment

Household final consumption expenditure	NE.CON.PRVT.KD.ZG
Household final consumption expenditure, Per capita	NE.CON.PRVT.PC.KD.ZG
General government final consumption expenditure	NE.CON.GOVT.KD.ZG
Gross capital formation	NE.GDI.TOTL.KD.ZG
Exports of goods and services	NE.EXP.GNFS.KD.ZG
Imports of goods and services	NE.IMP.GNFS.KD.ZG

4.10 Toward a broader measure of national income

Gross domestic product, $	NY.GDP.MKTP.CD
Gross national income, $	NY.GNP.MKTP.CD
Consumption of fixed capital	NY.ADJ.DKAP.GN.ZS
Natural resource depletion	NY.ADJ.DRES.GN.ZS
Adjusted net national income	NY.ADJ.NNTY.CD
Gross domestic product, % growth	NY.GDP.MKTP.KD.ZG
Gross national income, % growth	NY.GNP.MKTP.KD.ZG
Adjusted net national income	NY.ADJ.NNTY.KD.ZG

4.11 Toward a broader measure of savings

Gross savings	NY.ADJ.ICTR.GN.ZS
Consumption of fixed capital	NY.ADJ.DKAP.GN.ZS
Education expenditure	NY.ADJ.AEDU.GN.ZS
Net forest depletion	NY.ADJ.DFOR.GN.ZS
Energy depletion	NY.ADJ.DNGY.GN.ZS
Mineral depletion	NY.ADJ.DMIN.GN.ZS
Carbon dioxide damage	NY.ADJ.DCO2.GN.ZS
Local pollution damage	NY.ADJ.DPEM.GN.ZS
Adjusted net savings	NY.ADJ.SVNG.GN.ZS

4.12 Central government finances

Revenue	GC.REV.XGRT.GD.ZS
Expense	GC.XPN.TOTL.GD.ZS
Cash surplus or deficit	GC.BAL.CASH.GD.ZS
Net incurrence of liabilities, Domestic	GC.FIN.DOMS.GD.ZS
Net incurrence of liabilities, Foreign	GC.FIN.FRGN.GD.ZS
Debt and interest payments, Total debt	GC.DOD.TOTL.GD.ZS
Debt and interest payments, Interest	GC.XPN.INTP.RV.ZS

4.13 Central government expenditure

Goods and services	GC.XPN.GSRV.ZS
Compensation of employees	GC.XPN.COMP.ZS
Interest payments	GC.XPN.INTP.ZS
Subsidies and other transfers	GC.XPN.TRFT.ZS
Other expense	GC.XPN.OTHR.ZS

4.14 Central government revenues

Taxes on income, profits and capital gains	GC.TAX.YPKG.RV.ZS
Taxes on goods and services	GC.TAX.GSRV.RV.ZS
Taxes on international trade	GC.TAX.INTT.RV.ZS
Other taxes	GC.TAX.OTHR.RV.ZS
Social contributions	GC.REV.SOCL.ZS
Grants and other revenue	GC.REV.GOTR.ZS

4.15 Monetary indicators

Broad money	FM.LBL.BMNY.ZG
Claims on domestic economy	FM.AST.DOMO.ZG.M3
Claims on central governments	FM.AST.CGOV.ZG.M3
Interest rate, Deposit	FR.INR.DPST
Interest rate, Lending	FR.INR.LEND
Interest rate, Real	FR.INR.RINR

4.16 Exchange rates and price

Official exchange rate	PA.NUS.FCRF
Purchasing power parity (PPP) conversion factor	PA.NUS.PPP
Ratio of PPP conversion factor to market exchange rate	PA.NUS.PPPC.RF
Real effective exchange rate	PX.REX.REER
GDP implicit deflator	NY.GDP.DEFL.KD.ZG
Consumer price index	FP.CPI.TOTL.ZG
Wholesale price index	FP.WPI.TOTL

4.17 Balance of payments current account

Goods and services, Exports	BX.GSR.GNFS.CD
Goods and services, Imports	BM.GSR.GNFS.CD
Balance on primary income	BN.GSR.FCTY.CD
Balance on secondary income	BN.TRF.CURR.CD
Current account balance	BN.CAB.XOKA.CD
Total reserves	FI.RES.TOTL.CD

STATES AND MARKETS

States and markets includes indicators of private investment and performance, the role of the public sector in nurturing investment and growth, and the quality and availability of infrastructure essential for growth and development. These indicators measure the business environment, the functions of government, financial system development, infrastructure, information and communication technology, science and technology, performance of governments and their policies, and conditions in fragile countries with weak institutions.

Data on the access to finance, availability of credit, and cost of service improve understanding of the state of financial development. Credit is an important link in money transmission; it finances production, consumption, and capital formation, which in turn affect economic activity. The availability of credit to households, private companies, and public entities shows the depth of banking and financial sector development in the economy. In 2012 East Asia and Pacific provided more credit to the private sector, 122 percent of GDP, than did other developing regions.

In previous years we have presented both data for total domestic credit and credit to the private sector as a percentage of GDP. Data for the numerator come from the International Monetary Fund (IMF)'s *International Financial Statistics* database. In 2009 the IMF began publishing a new presentation of monetary statistics for countries that report data in accord with the IMF's *Monetary and Financial Statistics Manual 2000* and its *Monetary and Financial Statistics Compilation Guide 2008*. The new presentation aligns the reporting of monetary and financial statistics with the financial account of the *1993 System of National Accounts*. In this edition we have revised the indicator name to make the definition clearer. And more significantly we are adding a new indicator, domestic credit to the private sector by banks, to capture the resources that domestic banks provide to private firms.

The data on domestic credit provided by financial sector (previously domestic credit provided by banking sector) are from the financial corporation survey or, when unavailable, from the depository corporations survey. Similarly, data for domestic credit to the private sector capture the claims on the private sector by financial corporation or, when unavailable, by depository corporations. The financial corporations survey includes all resident corporations or quasi-corporations principally engaged in financial intermediation or in related auxiliary financial activities. It combines the data for depository corporations (central banks and other depository corporations) and other financial corporations, such as finance and leasing companies, money lenders, insurance corporations, pension funds, and foreign exchange companies. The newly reported data generally start only in December 2001 and in most cases are slightly higher than the values previously reported in the World Development Indicators database.

The IMF is planning soon to issue a combined *Monetary and Financial Statistics Manual* and *Monetary and Financial Statistics Compilation Guide* aligned to the *2008 System of National Accounts* and the sixth edition of the *Balance of Payments and International Investment Position Manual*. The latest information, manual, and guidelines can be viewed at the IMF website (http://www.imf.org/external/data.htm#guide).

Highlights

Major economies are requiring higher capital to asset ratios in banks

Average bank capital to asset ratio (%)

Source: Online table 5.5.

The ratio of capital to assets measures bank solvency and resiliency—and the extent to which banks can deal with unexpected losses. With banks under stress in the global financial crisis, the likelihood and cost of bank failures led countries to review their banking regulations. Many major economies have required higher minimum capital ratios to ensure bank capacity to cover liabilities and protect depositors and other lenders. In the United States the average ratio of capital to assets rose to 11.2 percent in 2011, up from 9.3 percent in 2008. Also maintaining higher ratios were euro area countries (6.7 percent) and the United Kingdom (5.1 percent). Japan and Germany, by contrast, kept rates below 5 percent because of their banking conditions.

A rising proportion of high-technology exports from developing countries

High-technology exports (% of manufactured exports)

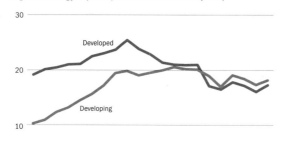

Source: Online table 5.13.

Exports are an engine of industrial competitiveness and economic growth. And the share of high-technology goods in manufactured exports is a common indicator of the innovation in an economy. In the early 1990s the proportion of high-technology manufactured exports from developed countries was twice the proportion from developing countries. Since then, exports from developing countries have grown rapidly and diversified, moving away from traditional resource- and labor-intensive products toward high-technology manufacturing. In 2004 the gap between developed and developing countries closed, with both around 21 percent. Shares have since fallen slightly, to 18 percent in developing countries and 17 percent in developed countries in 2012.

Large differences in fixed-broadband Internet penetration across regions

Fixed-broadband Internet subscriptions (% of population)

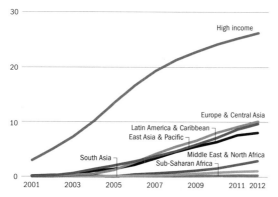

Source: International Telecommunication Union's World Telecommunication/ICT indicators database; online table 5.12.

After more than a decade of growth, there were about 640 million fixed broadband subscriptions in the world at the end of 2012—a global penetration rate of 9 percent. More than 340 million of the subscriptions were in high-income countries—a 26 percent penetration rate. The nearly 300 million subscriptions in low- and middle-income countries indicate very low penetration—about 5 percent. And the differences across regions are large. The lowest rates are in South Asia (1.1 percent) and Sub-Saharan Africa (0.2 percent), and the highest rate in Europe and Central Asia (over 10 percent), followed closely by East Asia and Pacific (9.7 percent) and Latin America and the Caribbean (8 percent). The Middle East and North Africa remains farther behind, at 3 percent.

 Front User guide World view People Environment

Electricity consumption up dramatically in middle-income countries

Between 1991 and 2011 electricity consumption increased 82 percent globally and 69 percent in low-income countries. But the share of global electricity consumed by low-income countries remained fairly constant, despite a 60 percent increase in their population, while the share consumed by high-income countries dropped from 76 percent to 56 percent. The share consumed by middle-income countries rose from 24 percent to 43 percent, with China accounting for more than half of that. Middle-income countries also saw per capita consumption increase—by 152 percent, from 721 kilowatt-hours in 1991 to 1,816 in 2011.

Electric power consumption (trillions of kilowatt-hours)

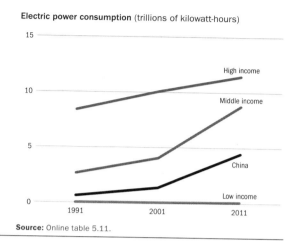

Source: Online table 5.11.

Business tax rates fall in developing countries

Taxes fund a range of social and economic programs such as financing public goods and services and redistributing income to the elderly and unemployed. According to the Doing Business report, high corporate tax rates are negatively associated with corporate investment and entrepreneurship. Between 2004 and 2012 countries in East Asia and Pacific reduced their total tax rates 5 percentage points, leaving them with the lowest average rate, 36 percent in 2012. The largest reductions were in Europe and Central Asia (18 percentage points) and Sub-Saharan Africa (19 percentage points). The average rate in the Middle East and North Africa fell from 56 percent in 2004 to 43 percent in 2005 but has since dropped only 3 percentage points. South Asia saw an increase in 2009 and 2010, but the average rate fell to 41 percent in 2012. The average rate in Latin America and the Caribbean has changed little.

Average total corporate tax rate (% of commercial profits)

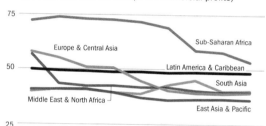

Source: Online table 5.3.

Air carriers from East Asia and Pacific countries take flight

From 2002 to 2012 global air passenger transport grew 76 percent, to 2.8 billion passengers. While the total number of passengers carried increased in all regions, the rise for carriers registered in East Asia and the Pacific was by far the highest. In 2002 the share of global air passenger transport by carriers registered in North America was 38 percent, followed by Europe and Central Asia at 26 percent and East Asia and the Pacific with 23 percent. By 2012 North America and East Asia and Pacific each had 28 percent, with Europe and Central Asia remaining steady at 26 percent. The increase in passenger traffic by carriers registered in countries in East Asia and the Pacific has been rapid: from around 425 million in 2002 to 810 million in 2012.

Passengers carried by air (millions)

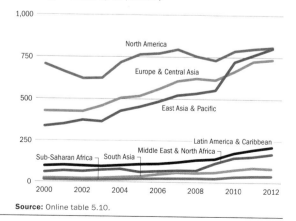

Source: Online table 5.10.

	Business entry density per 1,000 people ages 15–64 2012	Time required to start a business days June 2013	Stock market capitalization % of GDP 2012	Domestic credit provided by financial sector % of GDP 2012	Tax revenue collected by central government % of GDP 2012	Military expenditures % of GDP 2012	Electric power consumption per capita kilowatt-hours 2011	Mobile cellular subscriptions[a] per 100 people 2012	Individuals using the Internet[a] % of population 2012	High-technology exports % of manufactured exports 2012
Afghanistan	0.15	5	..	−4.0	7.5[b]	3.6	..	60	5	..
Albania	0.88	5	..	66.5	..	1.5	2,022	111	55	0.4
Algeria	0.53	25	..	−2.1	*37.4*	4.6	1,091	98	15	0.1
American Samoa	..	..	..	..	..	..	..	..	..	..
Andorra	..	..	..	..	..	..	..	82	86	..
Angola	..	66	..	15.9	19.0[b]	3.6	248	47	17	..
Antigua and Barbuda	..	21	..	98.0	19.7[b]	..	..	143	59	0.0
Argentina	0.47	25	7.2	37.3	..	0.9	2,967	152	56	7.7
Armenia	1.55	4	1.3	44.2	18.7[b]	3.9	1,755	112	39	2.6
Aruba	..	..	..	*56.0*	..	..	..	132	74	10.2
Australia	12.16	3	83.9	154.2	21.6	1.7	10,712	106	82	12.7
Austria	0.50	25	26.9	135.0	18.9	0.8	8,374	161	81	12.8
Azerbaijan	0.70	7	..	24.7	13.0[b]	4.6	1,705	109	54	7.3
Bahamas, The	..	24	..	105.0	15.7[b]	..	..	81	72	0.0
Bahrain	..	9	52.9	73.1	*1.1*	3.1	10,018	161	88	0.2
Bangladesh	0.09	11	15.0	69.0	10.0[b]	1.3	259	63	6	..
Barbados	..	18	106.4	..	*25.2*	..	..	123	73	12.0
Belarus	1.14	9	..	32.2	15.2[b]	1.2	3,628	114	47	2.9
Belgium	2.48	4	62.1	116.7	25.7	1.1	8,021	111	82	11.4
Belize	4.31	44	..	63.0	22.6[b]	0.9	..	53	25	4.8
Benin	..	15	..	19.7	15.5	1.0	..	84	4	0.5
Bermuda	..	..	27.2	..	..	..	..	140	91	7.3
Bhutan	0.20	32	..	50.4	..	..	..	76	25	*0.0*
Bolivia	0.56	49	16.4	48.7	..	1.5	623	90	34	9.2
Bosnia and Herzegovina	0.70	37	..	67.9	20.9	1.4	3,189	88	65	2.5
Botswana	12.30	60	31.6	14.9	27.2[b]	2.3	1,603	154	12	1.2
Brazil	2.17	108	54.6	110.5	15.4[b]	1.5	2,438	125	50	10.5
Brunei Darussalam	..	101	..	13.5	..	2.4	8,507	114	60	12.8
Bulgaria	9.03	18	13.1	71.0	19.6[b]	1.5	4,864	148	55	7.7
Burkina Faso	0.15	13	..	19.3	16.3	1.4	..	61	4	5.9
Burundi	..	5	..	26.1	..	2.4	..	23	1	2.7
Cabo Verde	..	10	..	79.7	17.1[b]	*0.5*	..	86	35	*0.6*
Cambodia	..	104	..	33.9	11.6	1.5	164	129	5	0.1
Cameroon	..	15	..	15.0	..	1.4	256	60	6	3.7
Canada	1.07	5	113.3	..	11.9	1.3	16,473	80	87	12.4
Cayman Islands	..	..	..	..	..	..	..	172	74	..
Central African Republic	..	22	..	26.3	9.4	*2.6*	..	25	3	*0.0*
Chad	..	62	..	5.3	..	*2.0*	..	35	2	..
Channel Islands	..	..	..	..	..	..	..	..	..	..
Chile	5.69	6	116.1	108.0	18.9	2.0	3,568	138	61	4.6
China	..	33	44.9	155.1	*10.6[b]*	2.0[c]	3,298	81	42	26.3
Hong Kong SAR, China	28.12	3	420.9	200.6	*14.2*	..	5,949	229	73	16.2
Macao SAR, China	..	..	..	−13.0	36.5[b]	..	..	290	64	0.0
Colombia	2.00	15	70.9	72.9	13.3	3.3	1,123	103	49	5.2
Comoros	..	15	..	21.6	..	..	..	40	6	..
Congo, Dem. Rep.	0.02	31	..	11.1	*13.7[b]*	1.8	105	31	2	..
Congo, Rep.	..	101	..	−8.9	..	*1.1*	172	99	6	*3.7*

 Front ? User guide World view People Environment

	Business entry density per 1,000 people ages 15–64 2012	Time required to start a business days June 2013	Stock market capitalization % of GDP 2012	Domestic credit provided by financial sector % of GDP 2012	Tax revenue collected by central government % of GDP 2012	Military expenditures % of GDP 2012	Electric power consumption per capita kilowatt-hours 2011	Mobile cellular subscriptions[a] per 100 people 2012	Individuals using the Internet[a] % of population 2012	High-technology exports % of manufactured exports 2012
Costa Rica	3.55	24	4.5	53.4	13.7	..	1,844	112	48	39.6
Côte d'Ivoire	..	8	31.7	27.3	15.6	1.7	212	91	2	15.1
Croatia	2.82	8	36.4	96.3	19.6[b]	1.7	3,901	115	63	9.9
Cuba	..	..	..	..	..	3.3	1,327	15	26	..
Curaçao	..	..	..	..	..	..	..	..	..	..
Cyprus	22.51	8	8.8	347.3	25.5	2.1	4,271	98	61	13.0
Czech Republic	2.96	20	18.9	68.4	14.2[b]	1.1	6,289	127	75	16.1
Denmark	4.36	6	71.3	206.0	34.1	1.4	6,122	118	93	14.2
Djibouti	..	17	..	..	..	..	..	25	8	..
Dominica	3.30	12	..	62.4	23.4[b]	..	..	152	55	8.8
Dominican Republic	1.05	19	..	46.5	12.8	0.6	893	87	45	2.7
Ecuador	..	56	7.0	29.2	..	2.8	1,192	106	35	2.5
Egypt, Arab Rep.	..	8	22.1	77.7	13.2[b]	1.7	1,743	120	44	0.6
El Salvador	0.48	17	45.0	66.1	14.5	1.0	830	137	26	4.7
Equatorial Guinea	..	135	..	–3.5	..	..	..	68	14	..
Eritrea	..	84	..	104.0	..	..	49	5	1	..
Estonia	7.92	7	10.4	77.2	16.5	1.9	6,279	160	79	10.7
Ethiopia	0.03	15	..	..	9.4[b]	0.9	52	22	1	2.4
Faeroe Islands	..	..	..	..	..	..	..	119	85	..
Fiji	..	59	11.6	116.3	..	1.5	..	98	34	2.1
Finland	2.32	14	64.1	105.2	20.7	1.5	15,738	172	91	8.5
France	2.88	7	69.8	136.4	22.0	2.3	7,289	97	83	25.4
French Polynesia	..	..	..	..	..	..	..	83	53	2.5
Gabon	4.11	50	..	13.2	..	1.4	907	179	9	..
Gambia, The	..	27	..	44.4	..	..	..	85	12	3.3
Georgia	4.86	2	6.0	35.0	24.1[b]	2.9	1,918	108	46	2.4
Germany	1.29	15	43.4	122.5	11.9	1.3	7,081	112	84	15.8
Ghana	0.90	14	8.5	32.3	14.9[b]	0.3	344	101	17	7.3
Greece	0.77	14	17.9	135.5	22.5	2.6	5,380	120	56	9.2
Greenland	..	..	..	..	..	..	..	105	65	2.4
Grenada	..	15	..	95.2	19.5[b]	..	..	121	42	..
Guam	..	..	..	..	..	..	..	..	62	..
Guatemala	0.52	20	..	39.2	10.9[b]	0.4	539	138	16	4.7
Guinea	0.23	16	..	32.2	..	..	..	42	1	..
Guinea-Bissau	..	9	..	20.3	..	2.0	..	63	3	..
Guyana	..	20	21.4	50.6	..	1.1	..	69	33	0.1
Haiti	0.06	97	..	19.6	..	..	32	60	10	..
Honduras	..	14	..	55.9	14.7	1.1	708	93	18	..
Hungary	4.75	5	16.9	68.7	23.3	0.8	3,895	116	72	18.1
Iceland	8.17	5	20.8	143.9	23.2	0.1	52,374	108	96	14.3
India	0.12	27	68.0	75.9	10.7[b]	2.4	684	70	13	6.6
Indonesia	0.29	48	45.2	42.6	..	0.8	680	114	15	7.3
Iran, Islamic Rep.	..	16	25.5	..	18.0	..	2,649	76	26	4.1
Iraq	0.13	29	..	–1.8	..	2.8	1,343	82	7	..
Ireland	4.50	10	51.7	201.7	23.2	0.6	5,701	107	79	22.6
Isle of Man	45.27	..	..	..	..	..	..	..	..	..
Israel	2.96	14	56.1	..	22.1	5.7	6,926	121	73	15.8

	Business entry density	Time required to start a business	Stock market capitalization	Domestic credit provided by financial sector	Tax revenue collected by central government	Military expenditures	Electric power consumption per capita	Mobile cellular subscriptions[a]	Individuals using the Internet[a]	High-technology exports
	per 1,000 people ages 15–64	days	% of GDP	% of GDP	% of GDP	% of GDP	kilowatt-hours	per 100 people	% of population	% of manufactured exports
	2012	June 2013	2012	2012	2012	2012	2011	2012	2012	2012
Italy	1.91	6	23.8	167.5	23.2	1.7	5,393	160	58	7.1
Jamaica	1.11	6	43.3	51.8	27.1	0.9	1,553	96	47	0.6
Japan	1.15	22	61.8	346.1	10.1	1.0	7,848	111	79	17.4
Jordan	0.98	12	87.0	114.2	15.3	4.7	2,289	128	41	2.5
Kazakhstan	1.71	12	11.5	41.1	..	1.2	4,893	186	53	30.0
Kenya	0.84	32	36.3	52.3	19.7[b]	2.0	155	71	32	5.7
Kiribati	0.11	31	..	..	16.1[b]	..	..	16	11	38.5
Korea, Dem. People's Rep.	..	..	..	..	..	..	739	7	0	..
Korea, Rep.	2.03	6	104.5	168.7	15.6[b]	2.8	10,162	109	84	26.2
Kosovo	1.22	30	..	21.0	..	..	2,947	..	..	..
Kuwait	..	32	53.0	47.9	0.7[b]	3.3	16,122	157	79	..
Kyrgyz Republic	0.92	8	2.5	..	18.5[b]	3.7	1,642	124	22	4.6
Lao PDR	0.10	92	..	26.5	14.8[b]	0.2	..	65	11	..
Latvia	11.63	13	3.9	62.9	13.8[b]	0.9	3,264	112	74	9.8
Lebanon	..	9	24.0	176.4	15.6	4.0	3,499	81	61	2.0
Lesotho	1.49	29	..	3.2	..	1.9	..	75	5	..
Liberia	..	5	..	33.9	20.9[b]	0.8	..	57	4	..
Libya	..	35	..	..	..	..	3,926	156	14	..
Liechtenstein	25.11	..	..	..	..	..	..	97	89	..
Lithuania	4.71	7	9.4	52.0	13.4	1.0	3,530	165	68	10.4
Luxembourg	20.98	19	127.5	173.6	26.1	0.6	15,530	145	92	8.1
Macedonia, FYR	3.60	2	5.8	48.9	16.6[b]	1.4	3,881	106	63	3.9
Madagascar	0.05	8	..	12.9	10.1	0.7	..	39	2	0.4
Malawi	0.08	40	17.7	35.6	..	0.9	..	29	4	3.2
Malaysia	2.28	6	156.2	134.0	16.1[b]	1.5	4,246	141	66	43.7
Maldives	4.39	9	..	83.9	15.6[b]	..	..	166	39	..
Mali	..	11	..	19.7	14.6	1.4	..	98	2	1.2
Malta	13.61	40	41.6	154.2	27.5	0.6	4,689	127	70	45.7
Marshall Islands	..	17	..	..	..	..	..	..	10	..
Mauritania	..	19	..	36.8	..	..	..	106	5	..
Mauritius	7.40	6	67.6	113.7	19.0	0.2	..	120	41	0.9
Mexico	0.88	6	44.6	47.0	..	0.6	2,092	83	38	16.3
Micronesia, Fed. Sts.	..	16	..	−19.1	..	..	..	30	26	..
Moldova	1.63	7	..	42.2	18.7[b]	0.3	1,470	102	43	4.8
Monaco	..	..	..	..	..	..	..	88	87	..
Mongolia	..	11	12.6	30.8	18.3[b]	1.1	1,577	121	16	..
Montenegro	10.66	10	87.5	58.7	..	1.9	5,747	181	57	..
Morocco	1.26	11	54.8	115.4	24.5	3.5	826	120	55	6.4
Mozambique	..	13	..	29.1	21.8[b]	0.9	447	36	5	24.7
Myanmar	..	72	..	..	..	..	110	10	1	0.0
Namibia	0.85	66	10.0	49.5	14.9[b]	3.1	1,549	95	13	5.3
Nepal	0.66	17	21.9	67.9	13.8[b]	1.4	106	60	11	0.3
Netherlands	4.44	4	84.5	216.2	21.1	1.3	7,036	118	93	20.1
New Caledonia	..	..	..	..	..	..	..	91	58	10.6
New Zealand	15.07	1	46.6	154.0	29.3	1.1	9,399	110	90	9.7
Nicaragua	..	36	..	44.0	15.0[b]	0.6	522	86	14	4.8
Niger	..	17	..	13.2	..	1.0	..	31	1	6.0

 Front User guide World view People Environment

	Business entry density per 1,000 people ages 15–64 2012	Time required to start a business days June 2013	Stock market capitalization % of GDP 2012	Domestic credit provided by financial sector % of GDP 2012	Tax revenue collected by central government % of GDP 2012	Military expenditures % of GDP 2012	Electric power consumption per capita kilowatt-hours 2011	Mobile cellular subscriptions[a] per 100 people 2012	Individuals using the Internet[a] % of population 2012	High-technology exports % of manufactured exports 2012
Nigeria	0.91	28	21.5	35.6	2.7[b]	0.9	149	67	33	1.9
Northern Mariana Islands	..	..	..	..	..	..	..	..	..	..
Norway	7.83	7	50.6	..	27.3	1.4	23,174	117	95	18.8
Oman	..	8	25.7	35.4	2.6[b]	8.6	6,292	159	60	3.4
Pakistan	0.04	21	19.4	45.8	10.1[b]	3.1	449	67	10	1.7
Palau	..	28	..	..	..	..	..	83	..	..
Panama	14.10	6	34.6	89.0	..	..	1,829	178	45	35.4
Papua New Guinea	..	53	68.4	38.3	..	0.5	..	38	2	3.5
Paraguay	..	35	3.8	37.2	12.4[b]	1.7	1,228	102	27	6.9
Peru	3.83	25	47.5	17.4	15.6[b]	1.3	1,248	98	38	3.5
Philippines	0.27	35	105.6	50.9	12.9[b]	1.2	647	107	36	48.9
Poland	0.53	30	36.3	63.8	16.2	1.9	3,832	140	65	7.0
Portugal	3.62	3	30.9	198.9	20.9	1.8	4,848	116	64	4.1
Puerto Rico	..	6	..	..	..	..	..	83	51	..
Qatar	1.74	9	65.7	77.5	14.7[b]	1.5	15,755	127	88	0.0
Romania	4.12	9	9.4	54.3	18.8	1.3	2,639	105	50	6.4
Russian Federation	4.30	15	43.4	41.5	15.0	4.5	6,486	183	53	8.4
Rwanda	1.07	2	..	..	13.3[b]	1.1	..	50	8	2.5
Samoa	1.04	9	..	45.3	0.0[b]	..	..	..	13	0.1
San Marino	..	40	..	..	..	..	..	115	51	..
São Tomé and Príncipe	3.75	5	..	35.1	14.0	..	..	65	22	14.3
Saudi Arabia	..	21	52.5	−10.5	..	8.0	8,161	187	54	0.6
Senegal	0.27	6	..	31.3	19.2	1.5	187	84	19	0.7
Serbia	1.68	12	19.9	62.3	21.5[b]	2.2	4,474	118	48	..
Seychelles	..	39	..	35.5	28.5[b]	0.8	..	148	47	..
Sierra Leone	0.32	12	..	14.0	10.9[b]	0.7	..	37	1	..
Singapore	8.04	3	150.8	99.5	14.5[b]	3.5	8,404	152	74	45.3
Sint Maarten	..	..	..	..	..	..	..	..	..	..
Slovak Republic	5.11	19	5.1	..	12.4	1.1	5,348	112	80	9.3
Slovenia	4.36	6	14.3	93.8	17.9[b]	1.2	6,806	109	70	6.2
Solomon Islands	..	9	..	12.0	..	..	..	55	7	87.4
Somalia	..	..	..	..	..	..	..	23	1	..
South Africa	6.54	19	159.3	187.2	26.4	1.2	4,604	131	41	5.5
South Sudan	0.73	17	..	..	..	9.4	..	21	..	..
Spain	2.71	23	75.2	225.9	7.3	0.9	5,530	108	72	7.0
Sri Lanka	0.51	8	28.7	48.4	12.0[b]	2.4	490	92	18	0.9
St. Kitts and Nevis	5.69	19	85.6	105.6	19.3[b]	..	..	157	79	0.1
St. Lucia	3.00	15	..	129.0	24.2[b]	..	..	126	49	..
St. Martin	..	..	..	..	..	..	..	..	..	..
St. Vincent & the Grenadines	1.37	10	..	56.8	22.4[b]	..	..	124	48	0.1
Sudan	..	36	..	24.6	..	..	143	74[d]	21[d]	0.7
Suriname	1.63	208	..	25.4	19.4[b]	..	..	106	35	6.5
Swaziland	..	38	..	21.1	..	3.2	..	65	21	..
Sweden	6.41	16	107.0	145.3	21.5	1.2	14,030	125	94	13.4
Switzerland	2.53	18	171.0	192.9	10.3	0.8	7,928	130	85	25.8
Syrian Arab Republic	0.04	13	..	47.7	..	3.9	1,715	59	24	1.3
Tajikistan	0.26	33	..	13.1	..	..	1,714	82	15	..

5 States and markets

	Business entry density per 1,000 people ages 15–64 2012	Time required to start a business days June 2013	Stock market capitalization % of GDP 2012	Domestic credit provided by financial sector % of GDP 2012	Tax revenue collected by central government % of GDP 2012	Military expenditures % of GDP 2012	Electric power consumption per capita kilowatt-hours 2011	Mobile cellular subscriptions[a] per 100 people 2012	Individuals using the Internet[a] % of population 2012	High-technology exports % of manufactured exports 2012
Tanzania	..	26	6.4	24.7	16.1[b]	1.1	92	57	4	10.2
Thailand	0.86	28	104.7	169.6	16.5	1.5	2,316	127	27	20.5
Timor-Leste	2.76	94	..	−52.7	..	2.9	..	56	1	0.2
Togo	0.12	19	..	37.6	16.8	1.6	..	50	4	0.2
Tonga	1.91	16	..	27.3	..	..	..	53	35	6.5
Trinidad and Tobago	..	38	65.0	37.5	28.3[b]	..	6,332	141	60	0.1
Tunisia	1.52	11	19.5	82.3	20.8[b]	1.6	1,297	118	41	5.6
Turkey	0.79	6	39.1	71.9	20.4	2.3	2,709	91	45	1.8
Turkmenistan	..	..	..	..	..	..	2,444	76	7	..
Turks and Caicos Islands	..	..	..	..	..	..	..	..	..	1.9
Tuvalu	..	..	..	..	..	..	..	28	35	..
Uganda	1.17	32	36.7	16.3	13.0[b]	1.4	..	45	15	20.7
Ukraine	0.92	21	11.7	80.2	18.3[b]	2.8	3,662	130	34	6.3
United Arab Emirates	1.38	8	17.7	76.5	0.4	5.5	9,389	150	85	..
United Kingdom	11.04	12	122.0	206.7	26.7	2.4	5,472	135	87	21.7
United States	..	5	114.9	229.9	10.2	4.2	13,246	95	81	17.8
Uruguay	2.98	7	0.4	32.0	19.3[b]	1.9	2,810	147	55	9.3
Uzbekistan	0.64	9	..	..	..	..	1,626	71	37	..
Vanuatu	2.34	35	..	69.5	16.1[b]	..	..	59	11	54.0
Venezuela, RB	..	144	6.6	42.0	..	1.1	3,313	102	44	2.5
Vietnam	..	34	21.1	104.9	..	2.2	1,073	148	39	14.5
Virgin Islands (U.S.)	..	..	..	..	..	..	..	..	41	..
West Bank and Gaza	..	45	..	..	..	..	..	76	41	..
Yemen, Rep.	..	40	..	26.9	..	4.0	193	58	17	0.2
Zambia	1.36	7	14.6	18.6	19.7[b]	1.6	599	75	13	24.8
Zimbabwe	..	90	120.5	..	..	3.2	757	92	17	5.9
World	**3.83 u**	**25 u**	**75.3 w**	**169.0 w**	**14.5 w**	**2.9 w**	**3,044 w**	**89 w**	**36 w**	**17.6 w**
Low income	0.40	29	..	39.4	12.8	1.7	233	47	6	..
Middle income	2.25	28	48.9	104.7	13.3	3.3	1,816	88	30	18.2
Lower middle income	1.12	26	50.6	62.0	11.5	8.9	734	83	19	8.4
Upper middle income	3.01	30	48.4	116.8	14.0	1.8	2,932	92	42	20.8
Low & middle income	1.86	28	48.6	103.6	13.3	3.3	1,646	82	26	18.1
East Asia & Pacific	1.34	40[e]	51.5	141.5	11.2	1.9	2,582	89	36	26.5
Europe & Central Asia	2.19	12[e]	25.6	62.6	19.7	2.0	2,951	108	43	8.2
Latin America & Carib.	2.38	41[e]	43.3	73.6	..	1.3	1,985	108	43	11.7
Middle East & N. Africa	0.55	21[e]	28.9	37.4	..	..	1,696	95	31	2.2
South Asia	0.25	16[e]	59.1	71.1	10.6	2.4	605	69	12	6.2
Sub-Saharan Africa	2.09	27[e]	83.8	77.8	17.3	1.5	535	59	15	4.0
High income	7.47	17	86.8	197.8	14.4	2.7	8,896	123	75	17.3
Euro area	6.75	13	51.6	153.3	17.7	1.5	6,599	120	76	15.2

a. Data are from the International Telecommunication Union's (ITU) World Telecommunication/ICT Indicators database. Please cite ITU for third party use of these data. b. Data were reported on a cash basis and have been adjusted to the accrual framework of the International Monetary Fund's *Government Finance Statistics Manual 2001*. c. Differs from the official value published by the government of China (1.3 percent; see National Bureau of Statistics of China, www.stats.gov.cn). d. Excludes South Sudan. e. Differs from data reported on the Doing Business website because the regional aggregates on the Doing Business website include developed economies.

 Front | User guide |  World view | People | Environment

About the data

Entrepreneurial activity

The rate new businesses are added to an economy is a measure of its dynamism and entrepreneurial activity. Data on business entry density are from the World Bank's 2013 Entrepreneurship Database, which includes indicators for more than 150 countries for 2004–12. Survey data are used to analyze firm creation, its relationship to economic growth and poverty reduction, and the impact of regulatory and institutional reforms. Data on total registered businesses were collected from national registrars of companies. For cross-country comparability, only limited liability corporations that operate in the formal sector are included. For additional information on sources, methodology, calculation of entrepreneurship rates, and data limitations see www.doingbusiness.org/data/exploretopics/entrepreneurship.

Data on time required to start a business are from the Doing Business database, whose indicators measure business regulation, gauge regulatory outcomes, and measure the extent of legal protection of property, the flexibility of employment regulation, and the tax burden on businesses. The fundamental premise is that economic activity requires good rules and regulations that are efficient, accessible, and easy to implement. Some indicators give a higher score for more regulation, such as stricter disclosure requirements in related-party transactions, and others give a higher score for simplified regulations, such as a one-stop shop for completing business startup formalities. There are 11 sets of indicators covering starting a business, registering property, dealing with construction permits, getting electricity, enforcing contracts, getting credit, protecting investors, paying taxes, trading across borders, resolving insolvency, and employing workers. The indicators are available at www.doingbusiness.org.

Doing Business data are collected with a standardized survey that uses a simple business case to ensure comparability across economies and over time—with assumptions about the legal form of the business, its size, its location, and nature of its operation. Surveys in 189 countries are administered through more than 10,200 local experts, including lawyers, business consultants, accountants, freight forwarders, government officials, and other professionals who routinely administer or advise on legal and regulatory requirements.

The Doing Business methodology has limitations that should be considered when interpreting the data. First, the data collected refer to businesses in the economy's largest city and may not represent regulations in other locations of the economy. To address this limitation, subnational indicators are being collected for selected economies; they point to significant differences in the speed of reform and the ease of doing business across cities in the same economy. Second, the data often focus on a specific business form—generally a limited liability company of a specified size—and may not represent regulation for other types of businesses such as sole proprietorships. Third, transactions described in a standardized business case refer to a specific set of issues and may not represent all the issues a business encounters. Fourth, the time measures involve an element of judgment by the expert respondents. When sources indicate different estimates, the Doing Business time indicators represent the median values of several responses given under the assumptions of the standardized case. Fifth, the methodology assumes that a business has full information on what is required and does not waste time when completing procedures. In constructing the indicators, it is assumed that entrepreneurs know about all regulations and comply with them. In practice, entrepreneurs may not be aware of all required procedures or may avoid legally required procedures altogether.

Financial systems

Stock markets and banking systems both enhance growth, the main factor in poverty reduction. At low levels of economic development commercial banks tend to dominate the financial system, while at higher levels domestic stock markets become more active and efficient.

Open economies with sound macroeconomic policies, good legal systems, and shareholder protection attract capital and thus have larger financial markets. The table includes market capitalization as a share of gross domestic product (GDP) as a measure of stock market size. Market size can be measured in other ways that may produce a different ranking of countries. Recent research on stock market development shows that modern communications technology and increased financial integration have resulted in more cross-border capital flows, a stronger presence of financial firms around the world, and the migration of trading activities to international exchanges. Many firms in emerging markets now cross-list on international exchanges, which provides them with lower cost capital and more liquidity-traded shares. However, this also means that exchanges in emerging markets may not have enough financial activity to sustain them. Comparability across countries may be limited by conceptual and statistical weaknesses, such as inaccurate reporting and differences in accounting standards.

Standard & Poor's (S&P) Indices provides regular updates on 21 emerging stock markets and 36 frontier markets. The S&P Global Equity Indices, S&P Indices's leading emerging markets index, is designed to be sufficiently investable to support index tracking portfolios in emerging market stocks that are legally and practically open to foreign portfolio investment. The S&P Frontier Broad Market Index measures the performance of 36 smaller and less liquid markets. These indexes are widely used benchmarks for international portfolio management. See www.spindices.com for further information on the indexes.

Because markets included in S&P's emerging markets category vary widely in level of development, it is best to look at the entire category to identify the most significant market trends. And it is useful to remember that stock market trends may be distorted by currency conversions, especially when a currency has registered a significant devaluation (Demirgüç-Kunt and Levine 1996; Beck and Levine 2001; and Claessens, Klingebiel, and Schmukler 2002).

Domestic credit provided by the financial sector as a share of GDP measures banking sector depth and financial sector development in terms of size. Data are taken from the financial corporation survey of the International Monetary Fund's (IMF) *International Financial*

5 States and markets

Statistics or, when unavailable, from its deposit corporation survey. The financial corporation survey includes monetary authorities (the central bank), deposit money banks, and other banking institutions, such as finance companies, development banks, and savings and loan institutions. In a few countries governments may hold international reserves as deposits in the banking system rather than in the central bank. Claims on the central government are a net item (claims on the central government minus central government deposits) and thus may be negative, resulting in a negative value for domestic credit provided by the financial sector.

Tax revenues

Taxes are the main source of revenue for most governments. Tax revenue as a share of GDP provides a quick overview of the fiscal obligations and incentives facing the private sector across countries. The table shows only central government data, which may significantly understate the total tax burden, particularly in countries where provincial and municipal governments are large or have considerable tax authority.

Low ratios of tax revenue to GDP may reflect weak administration and large-scale tax avoidance or evasion. Low ratios may also reflect a sizable parallel economy with unrecorded and undisclosed incomes. Tax revenue ratios tend to rise with income, with higher income countries relying on taxes to finance a much broader range of social services and social security than lower income countries are able to.

Military expenditures

Although national defense is an important function of government, high expenditures for defense or civil conflicts burden the economy and may impede growth. Military expenditures as a share of GDP are a rough indicator of the portion of national resources used for military activities. As an "input" measure, military expenditures are not directly related to the "output" of military activities, capabilities, or security. Comparisons across countries should take into account many factors, including historical and cultural traditions, the length of borders that need defending, the quality of relations with neighbors, and the role of the armed forces in the body politic.

Data are from the Stockholm International Peace Research Institute (SIPRI), whose primary source of military expenditure data is official data provided by national governments. These data are derived from budget documents, defense white papers, and other public documents from official government agencies, including government responses to questionnaires sent by SIPRI, the United Nations Office for Disarmament Affairs, or the Organization for Security and Co-operation in Europe. Secondary sources include international statistics, such as those of the North Atlantic Treaty Organization (NATO) and the IMF's *Government Finance Statistics Yearbook.* Other secondary sources include country reports of the Economist Intelligence Unit, country reports by IMF staff, and specialist journals and newspapers.

In the many cases where SIPRI cannot make independent estimates, it uses country-provided data. Because of differences in definitions and the difficulty of verifying the accuracy and completeness of data, data are not always comparable across countries. However, SIPRI puts a high priority on ensuring that the data series for each country is comparable over time. More information on SIPRI's military expenditure project can be found at www.sipri.org /contents/milap/.

Infrastructure

The quality of an economy's infrastructure, including power and communications, is an important element in investment decisions and economic development. The International Energy Agency (IEA) collects data on electric power consumption from national energy agencies and adjusts the values to meet international definitions. Consumption by auxiliary stations, losses in transformers that are considered integral parts of those stations, and electricity produced by pumping installations are included. Where data are available, electricity generated by primary sources of energy—coal, oil, gas, nuclear, hydro, geothermal, wind, tide and wave, and combustible renewables—are included. Consumption data do not capture the reliability of supplies, including breakdowns, load factors, and frequency of outages.

The International Telecommunication Union (ITU) estimates that there were 6.3 billion mobile subscriptions globally in 2012. No technology has ever spread faster around the world. Mobile communications have a particularly important impact in rural areas. The mobility, ease of use, flexible deployment, and relatively low and declining rollout costs of wireless technologies enable them to reach rural populations with low levels of income and literacy. The next billion mobile subscribers will consist mainly of the rural poor.

Operating companies have traditionally been the main source of telecommunications data, so information on subscriptions has been widely available for most countries. This gives a general idea of access, but a more precise measure is the penetration rate—the share of households with access to telecommunications. During the past few years more information on information and communication technology use has become available from household and business surveys. Also important are data on actual use of telecommunications services. The quality of data varies among reporting countries as a result of differences in regulations covering data provision and availability.

High-technology exports

The method for determining high-technology exports was developed by the Organisation for Economic Co-operation and Development in collaboration with Eurostat. It takes a "product approach" (rather than a "sectoral approach") based on research and development intensity (expenditure divided by total sales) for groups of products from Germany, Italy, Japan, the Netherlands, Sweden, and the United States. Because industrial sectors specializing in a few high-technology products may also produce low-technology products, the product approach is more appropriate for international trade. The

 Front User guide World view People Environment

method takes only research and development intensity into account, but other characteristics of high technology are also important, such as knowhow, scientific personnel, and technology embodied in patents. Considering these characteristics would yield a different list (see Hatzichronoglou 1997).

Definitions

• **Business entry density** is the number of newly registered limited liability corporations per 1,000 people ages 15–64. • **Time required to start a business** is the number of calendar days to complete the procedures for legally operating a business using the fastest procedure, independent of cost. • **Stock market capitalization** (also known as market value) is the share price times the number of shares outstanding. • **Domestic credit provided by financial sector** is all credit to various sectors on a gross basis, except to the central government, which is net. The financial sector includes monetary authorities, deposit money banks, and other banking institutions for which data are available. • **Tax revenue collected by central government** is compulsory transfers to the central government for public purposes. Certain compulsory transfers such as fines, penalties, and most social security contributions are excluded. Refunds and corrections of erroneously collected tax revenue are treated as negative revenue. The analytic framework of the IMF's *Government Finance Statistics Manual 2001* (GFSM 2001) is based on accrual accounting and balance sheets. For countries still reporting government finance data on a cash basis, the IMF adjusts reported data to the GFSM 2001 accrual framework. These countries are footnoted in the table. • **Military expenditures** are SIPRI data derived from NATO's former definition (in use until 2002), which includes all current and capital expenditures on the armed forces, including peacekeeping forces; defense ministries and other government agencies engaged in defense projects; paramilitary forces, if judged to be trained and equipped for military operations; and military space activities. Such expenditures include military and civil personnel, including retirement pensions and social services for military personnel; operation and maintenance; procurement; military research and development; and military aid (in the military expenditures of the donor country). Excluded are civil defense and current expenditures for previous military activities, such as for veterans benefits, demobilization, and weapons conversion and destruction. This definition cannot be applied for all countries, however, since that would require more detailed information than is available about military budgets and off-budget military expenditures (for example, whether military budgets cover civil defense, reserves and auxiliary forces, police and paramilitary forces, and military pensions). • **Electric power consumption per capita** is the production of power plants and combined heat and power plants less transmission, distribution, and transformation losses and own use by heat and power plants, divided by midyear population. • **Mobile cellular subscriptions** are the number of subscriptions to a public mobile telephone service that provides access to the public switched telephone network using cellular technology. Postpaid subscriptions and active prepaid accounts (that is, accounts that have been used during the last three months) are included. The indicator applies to all mobile cellular subscriptions that offer voice communications and excludes subscriptions for data cards or USB modems, subscriptions to public mobile data services, private-trunked mobile radio, telepoint, radio paging, and telemetry services. • **Individuals using the Internet** are the percentage of individuals who have used the Internet (from any location) in the last 12 months. Internet can be used via a computer, mobile phone, personal digital assistant, games machine, digital television, or similar device. • **High-technology exports** are products with high research and development intensity, such as in aerospace, computers, pharmaceuticals, scientific instruments, and electrical machinery.

Data sources

Data on business entry density are from the World Bank's Entrepreneurship Database (www.doingbusiness.org/data/exploretopics/entrepreneurship). Data on time required to start a business are from the World Bank's Doing Business project (www.doingbusiness.org). Data on stock market capitalization are from Standard & Poor's (2012). Data on domestic credit are from the IMF's *International Financial Statistics*. Data on central government tax revenue are from the IMF's *Government Finance Statistics*. Data on military expenditures are from SIPRI's Military Expenditure Database (www.sipri.org/databases/milex). Data on electricity consumption are from the IEA's *Energy Statistics of Non-OECD Countries, Energy Balances of Non-OECD Countries,* and *Energy Statistics of OECD Countries* and from the United Nations Statistics Division's *Energy Statistics Yearbook*. Data on mobile cellular phone subscriptions and individuals using the Internet are from the ITU's World Telecommunication/ICT Indicators database. Data on high-technology exports are from the United Nations Statistics Division's Commodity Trade (Comtrade) database.

References

Beck, Thorsten, and Ross Levine. 2001. "Stock Markets, Banks, and Growth: Correlation or Causality?" Policy Research Working Paper 2670, World Bank, Washington, DC.

Claessens, Stijn, Daniela Klingebiel, and Sergio L. Schmukler. 2002. "Explaining the Migration of Stocks from Exchanges in Emerging Economies to International Centers." Policy Research Working Paper 2816, World Bank, Washington, DC.

Demirgüç-Kunt, Asli, and Ross Levine. 1996. "Stock Market Development and Financial Intermediaries: Stylized Facts." *World Bank Economic Review* 10 (2): 291–321.

Hatzichronoglou, Thomas. 1997. "Revision of the High-Technology Sector and Product Classification." STI Working Paper 1997/2. Organisation for Economic Co-operation and Development, Directorate for Science, Technology, and Industry, Paris.

Standard & Poors. 2012. *Global Stock Markets Factbook 2012*. New York.

5 States and markets

To access the World Development Indicators online tables, use the URL http://wdi.worldbank.org/table/ and the table number (for example, http://wdi.worldbank.org/table/5.1). To view a specific

indicator online, use the URL http://data.worldbank.org/indicator/ and the indicator code (for example, http://data.worldbank.org /indicator/IE.PPI.TELE.CD).

5.1 Private sector in the economy

Telecommunications investment	IE.PPI.TELE.CD
Energy investment	IE.PPI.ENGY.CD
Transport investment	IE.PPI.TRAN.CD
Water and sanitation investment	IE.PPI.WATR.CD
Domestic credit to private sector	FS.AST.PRVT.GD.ZS
Businesses registered, New	IC.BUS.NREG
Businesses registered, Entry density	IC.BUS.NDNS.ZS

5.2 Business environment: enterprise surveys

Time dealing with officials	IC.GOV.DURS.ZS
Number of visits or meetings with tax officials	IC.TAX.METG
Time required to obtain operating license	IC.FRM.DURS
Informal payments to public officials	IC.FRM.CORR.ZS
Losses due to theft, robbery, vandalism, and arson	IC.FRM.CRIM.ZS
Firms competing against unregistered firms	IC.FRM.CMPU.ZS
Firms with female top manager	IC.FRM.FEMM.ZS
Firms using banks to finance investment	IC.FRM.BNKS.ZS
Value lost due to electrical outages	IC.FRM.OUTG.ZS
Internationally recognized quality certification	IC.FRM.ISOC.ZS
Average time to clear exports through customs	IC.CUS.DURS.EX
Firms offering formal training	IC.FRM.TRNG.ZS

5.3 Business environment: Doing Business indicators

Number of procedures to start a business	IC.REG.PROC
Time required to start a business	IC.REG.DURS
Cost to start a business	IC.REG.COST.PC.ZS
Number of procedures to register property	IC.PRP.PROC
Time required to register property	IC.PRP.DURS
Number of procedures to build a warehouse	IC.WRH.PROC
Time required to build a warehouse	IC.WRH.DURS
Time required to get electricity	IC.ELC.TIME
Number of procedures to enforce a contract	IC.LGL.PROC
Time required to enforce a contract	IC.LGL.DURS
Business disclosure index	IC.BUS.DISC.XQ
Time required to resolve insolvency	IC.ISV.DURS

5.4 Stock markets

Market capitalization, $	CM.MKT.LCAP.CD
Market capitalization, % of GDP	CM.MKT.LCAP.GD.ZS
Value of shares traded	CM.MKT.TRAD.GD.ZS
Turnover ratio	CM.MKT.TRNR
Listed domestic companies	CM.MKT.LDOM.NO
S&P/Global Equity Indices	CM.MKT.INDX.ZG

5.5 Financial access, stability, and efficiency

Strength of legal rights index	IC.LGL.CRED.XQ
Depth of credit information index	IC.CRD.INFO.XQ
Depositors with commercial banks	FB.CBK.DPTR.P3
Borrowers from commercial banks	FB.CBK.BRWR.P3
Commercial bank branches	FB.CBK.BRCH.P5
Automated teller machines	FB.ATM.TOTL.P5
Bank capital to assets ratio	FB.BNK.CAPA.ZS
Ratio of bank non-performing loans to total gross loans	FB.AST.NPER.ZS
Domestic credit to private sector by banks (% of GDP)	FD.AST.PRVT.GD.ZS
Interest rate spread	FR.INR.LNDP
Risk premium on lending	FR.INR.RISK

5.6 Tax policies

Tax revenue collected by central government	GC.TAX.TOTL.GD.ZS
Number of tax payments by businesses	IC.TAX.PAYM
Time for businesses to prepare, file and pay taxes	IC.TAX.DURS
Business profit tax	IC.TAX.PRFT.CP.ZS
Business labor tax and contributions	IC.TAX.LABR.CP.ZS
Other business taxes	IC.TAX.OTHR.CP.ZS
Total business tax rate	IC.TAX.TOTL.CP.ZS

5.7 Military expenditures and arms transfers

Military expenditure, % of GDP	MS.MIL.XPND.GD.ZS
Military expenditure, % of central government expenditure	MS.MIL.XPND.ZS
Arm forces personnel	MS.MIL.TOTL.P1
Arm forces personnel, % of total labor force	MS.MIL.TOTL.TF.ZS
Arms transfers, Exports	MS.MIL.XPRT.KD
Arms transfers, Imports	MS.MIL.MPRT.KD

5.8 Fragile situations

International Development Association Resource Allocation Index	IQ.CPA.IRAI.XQ
Peacekeeping troops, police, and military observers	VC.PKP.TOTL.UN
Battle related deaths	VC.BTL.DETH
Intentional homicides	VC.IHR.PSRC.P5
Military expenditures	MS.MIL.XPND.GD.ZS
Losses due to theft, robbery, vandalism, and arson	IC.FRM.CRIM.ZS
Firms formally registered when operations started	IC.FRM.FREG.ZS

Front | ? User guide | World view | People | Environment

Children in employment ♀♂	SL.TLF.0714.ZS	Air freight	IS.AIR.GOOD.MT.K1
Refugees, By country of origin	SM.POP.REFG.OR		
Refugees, By country of asylum	SM.POP.REFG		

5.11 Power and communications

Internally displaced persons	VC.IDP.TOTL.HE
Access to an improved water source	SH.H2O.SAFE.ZS
Access to improved sanitation facilities	SH.STA.ACSN
Maternal mortality ratio, National estimate	SH.STA.MMRT.NE
Maternal mortality ratio, Modeled estimate	SH.STA.MMRT
Under-five mortality rate ♀♂	SH.DYN.MORT
Depth of food deficit	SN.ITK.DFCT
Primary gross enrollment ratio ♀♂	SE.PRM.ENRR

Electric power consumption per capita	EG.USE.ELEC.KH.PC
Electric power transmission and distribution losses	EG.ELC.LOSS.ZS
Fixed telephone subscriptions	IT.MLT.MAIN.P2
Mobile cellular subscriptions	IT.CEL.SETS.P2
Fixed telephone international voice traffic	..[a]
Mobile cellular network international voice traffic	..[a]
Population covered by mobile cellular network	..[a]
Fixed telephone sub-basket	..[a]
Mobile cellular sub-basket	..[a]
Telecommunications revenue	..[a]
Mobile cellular and fixed-line subscribers per employee	..[a]

5.9 Public policies and institutions

International Development Association Resource Allocation Index	IQ.CPA.IRAI.XQ
Macroeconomic management	IQ.CPA.MACR.XQ
Fiscal policy	IQ.CPA.FISP.XQ
Debt policy	IQ.CPA.DEBT.XQ
Economic management, Average	IQ.CPA.ECON.XQ
Trade	IQ.CPA.TRAD.XQ
Financial sector	IQ.CPA.FINS.XQ
Business regulatory environment	IQ.CPA.BREG.XQ
Structural policies, Average	IQ.CPA.STRC.XQ
Gender equality	IQ.CPA.GNDR.XQ
Equity of public resource use	IQ.CPA.PRES.XQ
Building human resources	IQ.CPA.HRES.XQ
Social protection and labor	IQ.CPA.PROT.XQ
Policies and institutions for environmental sustainability	IQ.CPA.ENVR.XQ
Policies for social inclusion and equity, Average	IQ.CPA.SOCI.XQ
Property rights and rule-based governance	IQ.CPA.PROP.XQ
Quality of budgetary and financial management	IQ.CPA.FINQ.XQ
Efficiency of revenue mobilization	IQ.CPA.REVN.XQ
Quality of public administration	IQ.CPA.PADM.XQ
Transparency, accountability, and corruption in the public sector	IQ.CPA.TRAN.XQ
Public sector management and institutions, Average	IQ.CPA.PUBS.XQ

5.12 The information age

Households with television	..[a]
Households with a computer	..[a]
Individuals using the Internet	..[a]
Fixed (wired) broadband Internet subscriptions	IT.NET.BBND.P2
International Internet bandwidth	..[a]
Fixed broadband sub-basket	..[a]
Secure Internet servers	IT.NET.SECR.P6
Information and communications technology goods, Exports	TX.VAL.ICTG.ZS.UN
Information and communications technology goods, Imports	TM.VAL.ICTG.ZS.UN
Information and communications technology services, Exports	BX.GSR.CCIS.ZS

5.13 Science and technology

Research and development (R&D), Researchers	SP.POP.SCIE.RD.P6
Research and development (R&D), Technicians	SP.POP.TECH.RD.P6
Scientific and technical journal articles	IP.JRN.ARTC.SC
Expenditures for R&D	GB.XPD.RSDV.GD.ZS
High-technology exports, $	TX.VAL.TECH.CD
High-technology exports, % of manufactured exports	TX.VAL.TECH.MF.ZS
Charges for the use of intellectual property, Receipts	BX.GSR.ROYL.CD
Charges for the use of intellectual property, Payments	BM.GSR.ROYL.CD
Patent applications filed, Residents	IP.PAT.RESD
Patent applications filed, Nonresidents	IP.PAT.NRES
Trademark applications filed, Total	IP.TMK.TOTL

5.10 Transport services

Total road network	IS.ROD.TOTL.KM
Paved roads	IS.ROD.PAVE.ZS
Road passengers carried	IS.ROD.PSGR.K6
Road goods hauled	IS.ROD.GOOD.MT.K6
Rail lines	IS.RRS.TOTL.KM
Railway passengers carried	IS.RRS.PASG.KM
Railway goods hauled	IS.RRS.GOOD.MT.K6
Port container traffic	IS.SHP.GOOD.TU
Registered air carrier departures worldwide	IS.AIR.DPRT
Air passengers carried	IS.AIR.PSGR

♀♂ Data disaggregated by sex are available in the World Development Indicators database.
a. Available online only as part of the table, not as an individual indicator.

GLOBAL
LINKS

The world economy is bound together by trade in goods and services, financial flows, and movements of people. As national economies develop, their links expand and grow more complex. The indicators in *Global links* measure the size and direction of these flows and document the effects of policy interventions, such as tariffs, trade facilitation, and aid flows, on the development of the world economy.

Volatility in international financial markets was still prevalent in 2012. Concerns about the sustainability of public finances, inherited from the financial crisis in the euro area, appear to have affected direct investment. Global foreign direct investment (FDI) inflows dropped 16 percent from 2011. FDI flows to high-income economies dropped 22 percent, with the euro area accounting for almost half the fall. But FDI flows to low- and middle-income economies showed a more moderate decline of only 6 percent. FDI flows to low- and middle-income economies were around $617 billion in 2012, accounting for an increase in the share of world inflows of 17 percentage points over the previous five years. Although more of these economies receive FDI, the flows remain highly concentrated among the 10 largest recipients, with Brazil, China, and India accounting for more than half.

Net debt flows to developing countries fell 9 percent in 2012, to $412 billion, and were characterized by important shifts in borrowing patterns and financing sources. Viewed from the borrower, net flows of public and publicly guaranteed debt drove the overall increase in long-term debt flows in 2012. They jumped 67 percent to $155 billion, in contrast to a 17 percent fall in net flows to private nonguaranteed borrowers, and a sharp 41 percent contraction in short-term debt flows.

Unlike debt and direct investment, global portfolio equity investment grew in 2012 at a faster pace than had been expected, resulting in equity inflows that were three times higher than in 2011. Inflows to high-income economies in 2012 were well above their 2011 level, attributable mainly to investors' switching from debt securities to equity. Flows of portfolio equity to low- and middle-income economies also rose considerably, as growth prospects remained good, with high expected returns.

The sovereign debt crisis in the euro area continued to restrain international trade. The slowdown of demand for goods from high-income economies, especially euro area economies, slowed the growth in merchandise imports from an annual 19.4 percent in 2011 to 0.4 percent in 2012. The growth of merchandise exports also dropped, by nearly 20 percentage points. But merchandise exports to low- and middle-income countries rose 4.4 percent from the previous year, while those to high-income countries fell 0.8 percent. Brazil, China, India, and the Russian Federation are among the top traders, with China accounting for almost 70 percent of the total merchandise trade in East Asia and Pacific.

Official development assistance—a stable source of development financing and buffer against the impact of several financial crises—was $133 billion in 2012, or 0.59 percent of developing countries' combined gross national income, down from 0.66 percent in 2011.

Highlights

Bond issuance rises

Bond issuance by developing country borrowers ($ billions)

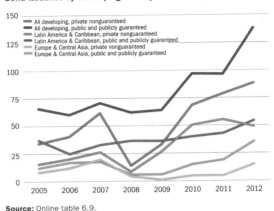

Legend:
- All developing, private nonguaranteed
- All developing, public and publicly guaranteed
- Latin America & Caribbean, private nonguaranteed
- Latin America & Caribbean, public and publicly guaranteed
- Europe & Central Asia, private nonguaranteed
- Europe & Central Asia, public and publicly guaranteed

Source: Online table 6.9.

Bond issuance from public and private borrowers in developing economies rose to a record $226 billion in 2012, up from $175 billion in 2011. The increase was driven mainly by new bond issuances from the public sector, which rose 30 percent in 2012 as emerging economies continued to diversify risk away from banks and pursue different sources of financing after the 2008 crisis. Influenced by purchases of Mexico's domestically issued sovereign bonds by nonresidents, Latin America and the Caribbean held the largest share, 39 percent, while Europe and Central Asia accounted for the second largest share, 25 percent. Private borrowers also saw an increase in bond issuances, but at a more moderate rate of 11 percent in 2012, to $88.1 billion. Private borrowers in Latin America and the Caribbean also claimed the largest share, with Mexico and Brazil dominant bond issuers.

Europe and Central Asia: remittances are more resilient than foreign direct investment

Inflows of remittances and foreign direct investment, Europe and Central Asia (% of GDP)

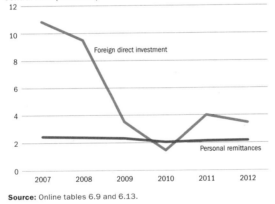

Source: Online tables 6.9 and 6.13.

Inflows of personal remittances yet again proved resilient to economic downturns in Europe and Central Asia, especially when compared with inflows of foreign direct investment (FDI). Personal remittances received as a percentage of GDP continued a slow but steady path of growth, up 1.5 percent in 2012. Despite signs of recovery in 2011, FDI inflows as a percentage of GDP fell 15 percent in 2012, showing that the region had not fully recovered from the financial crisis. The high volatility of FDI inflows is not evident in remittances, where flows have proven more resilient to economic shocks. The greater persistence in remittances has proven beneficial for countries in the region that rely heavily on inflows of remittances for economic stability, such as the Kyrgyz Republic, Moldova, and Tajikistan.

Capital equity investment in India turns around in 2012

Equity investment flows to India ($ billions)

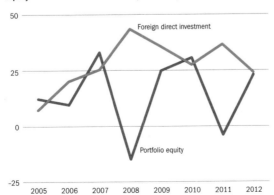

Source: Online table 6.9.

The Indian economy saw net capital equity inflows in 2012 rise 44 percent, or 2.7 percent of GDP (up from 1.7 percent in 2011). Direct investment inflows in 2012 reflected the country's slow economic growth and high inflation rate, which shook investor confidence. Even though foreign direct investment flows fell by a third in 2012 to $24 billion, the lowest since 2005, India remained the third most important developing country destination for investment flows, after China and Brazil. The downturn was partly offset by a considerable turnaround in portfolio equity flows. In January 2012 India began allowing qualified foreign investors to invest directly in the Indian stock market. Portfolio equity investment inflows shot up to a remarkable $23 billion from a depletion of $40 billion in 2011, thanks mainly to qualified foreign investor purchases of equities in the Indian stock market.

 Front | ? User guide | World view | People | Environment

Debt indicators improve in Europe and Central Asia

Europe and Central Asia, the most indebted region, recorded the highest external debt outstanding ratio to gross national income (GNI), 68.3 percent, in 2012—three times the comparable ratio for all developing countries combined. Similarly, external debt stock as a percentage of exports at the end of 2012, 144.7 percent, was twice the developing country average. But despite a mild deterioration in 2012, the ratio of external debt stock to GNI has declined 12 percentage points since 2009 while the ratio of external debt stock to exports declined 23 percentage points. The main drivers of growth and higher export earnings are the oil exporters, notably Kazakhstan and Turkey, followed by Hungary and Ukraine. Investment in Kazakhstan's hydrocarbon sector in 2012 tremendously increased production and exports.

Debt ratios for Europe and Central Asia (%)

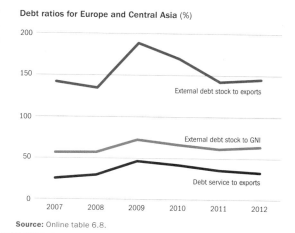

Source: Online table 6.8.

The Syrian refugee population continues to rise

The refugee population by country of origin has remained fairly steady since 2004 among developing countries. For over a decade five countries accounted for more than 50 percent of refugees from developing countries: Afghanistan, Somalia, Iraq, Sudan, and the Democratic Republic of Congo. But conflict in Middle East and North Africa has changed that. In 2011 the Syrian Arab Republic was ranked 32nd, with fewer than 20,000 refugees, but by 2012 the number of refugees fleeing the country had grown 35 times to almost 730,000, fourth highest among developing countries. And the increase is expected to continue. According to the Office of the UN High Commissioner for Refugees (2013), an estimated 1.3 million people from Syria sought refuge in surrounding countries in the first half of 2013.

Refugee population by origin, top five (millions)

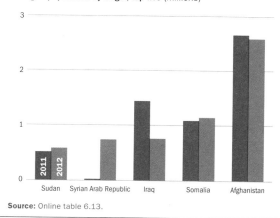

Source: Online table 6.13.

Commodity prices fall in 2013

Except for energy, commodity price indexes continued to fall in 2013. In real terms (2005) the biggest declines were in fertilizers (16 percent) and precious metals (16 percent), followed by agriculture (6 percent) and metals and minerals (4 percent). Even though fertilizer prices have more than doubled from a decade ago, the price index has declined 46 percent from its peak in 2008 (from 197 to 107). Energy and fertilizer prices typically move together because natural gas is a key input for fertilizer. But the correlation has reversed with U.S. natural gas trading at 80 percent below crude oil. Precious metals saw their first price decline in 11 years in 2013. The gold market, driven mainly by China and India, has fallen due to India's restrictions on gold imports. China, despite overtaking India as the world's largest gold consumer, is not expected to offset the weak physical demand from India (World Bank 2014).

Change in commodity price indices (%)

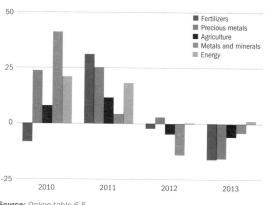

Source: Online table 6.5.

6 Global links

	Merchandise trade	Net barter terms of trade index	Inbound tourism expenditure	Net official development assistance	Net migration	Personal remittances, received	Foreign direct investment	Portfolio equity	Total external debt stock	Total debt service
							Net inflow	Net inflow		% of exports of goods, services, and primary income
	% of GDP	2000 = 100	% of exports	% of GNI	thousands	$ millions	$ millions	$ millions	$ millions	
	2012	2012	2012	2012	2010–15	2012	2012	2012	2012	2012
Afghanistan	32.0	139.1	3.2	32.8	−400	385	94	2	2,709	0.3
Albania	54.2	96.2	45.9	2.7	−50	1,027	1,265	13	6,934	7.1
Algeria	58.7	217.3	0.4	0.1	−50	213	1,602	..	5,643	1.1
American Samoa	..	129.0	..	..	..	..	..	..	..	..
Andorra	..	..	..	..	..	..	..	..	..	..
Angola	85.0	257.6	1.0	0.2	66	0	−6,898	..	22,171	5.9
Antigua and Barbuda	51.6	64.2	..	0.2	0	21	71	..	..	..
Argentina	31.5	130.3	5.9	0.0	−100	573	12,128	876	121,013	13.2
Armenia	57.2	117.6	20.1	2.6	−50	2,123	489	2	7,608	30.9
Aruba	..	122.0	44.9	..	1	5	−140	0	..	..
Australia	33.8	184.8	11.0	..	750	1,827	56,595	15,174	..	..
Austria	87.3	86.9	9.9	..	150	2,754	4,144	936	..	..
Azerbaijan	63.5	199.9	7.2	0.6	0	1,990	5,293	0	9,712	5.1
Bahamas, The	54.6	88.5	65.7	..	10	..	360	..	..	..
Bahrain	116.6	129.0	7.6	..	22	..	891	1,383	..	..
Bangladesh	50.9	59.2	0.4	1.7	−2,041	14,085	1,178	91	26,130	5.4
Barbados	55.4	107.6	..	..	2	..	356	..	..	..
Belarus	146.0	100.7	1.9	0.2	−10	1,053	1,464	−4	34,173	9.5
Belgium	182.3	94.2	3.1	..	150	10,123	−1,917	4,570	..	..
Belize	..	93.8	28.7	..	8	76	194	..	1,241	11.3
Benin	47.6	117.9	..	6.8	−10	..	159	..	2,055	..
Bermuda	16.8	62.1	32.6	..	..	1,191	133	−10	..	..
Bhutan	90.5	134.3	13.5	9.6	10	18	10	..	1,459	17.8
Bolivia	70.3	179.1	4.8	2.6	−125	1,111	1,060	..	6,909	5.3
Bosnia and Herzegovina	86.9	98.8	12.8	3.2	−5	1,849	350	..	10,577	18.4
Botswana	96.5	85.0	0.5	0.5	20	18	293	−9	2,488	0.8
Brazil	21.1	128.9	2.4	0.1	−190	2,583	76,111	5,600	440,478	15.5
Brunei Darussalam	100.0	226.5	..	..	2	..	850	..	..	..
Bulgaria	116.6	107.4	12.4	..	−50	1,449	2,095	5	50,750	13.0
Burkina Faso	51.3	126.9	..	10.8	−125	..	40	..	2,506	..
Burundi	36.8	149.1	1.2	21.2	−20	46	1	..	663	8.5
Cabo Verde	44.8	108.9	60.6	13.3	−17	167	74	..	1,261	4.6
Cambodia	136.8	75.2	23.4	6.1	−175	256	1,557	..	5,716	1.5
Cameroon	45.8	156.6	5.1	2.4	−50	210	526	0	3,672	3.1
Canada	52.2	118.5	3.8	..	1,100	1,206	43,085	949	..	..
Cayman Islands	..	82.9	..	..	..	..	4,234	..	..	..
Central African Republic	24.3	68.8	..	10.4	10	..	71	..	552	..
Chad	50.4	220.6	..	4.9	−120	..	323	..	1,831	..
Channel Islands	..	..	..	..	4	..	..	..	..	..
Chile	58.6	182.4	3.5	0.0	30	..	30,323	5,222	..	..
China	47.0	71.8	2.5	0.0	−1,500	39,221	253,475	29,903	754,009	3.3
Hong Kong SAR, China	397.9	96.0	6.7	..	150	368	74,584	25,006	..	..
Macao SAR, China	23.2	92.9	94.2	..	35	46	4,261	..	..	..
Colombia	32.3	151.1	4.9	0.2	−120	4,019	15,649	3,778	79,051	22.0
Comoros	54.5	80.3	..	11.5	−10	..	17	..	251	..
Congo, Dem. Rep.	72.1	143.1	..	17.8	−75	12	2,892	..	5,651	3.2
Congo, Rep.	118.4	221.0	..	1.3	−45	..	2,758	..	2,829	..

 Front User guide  World view People Environment

	Merchandise trade	Net barter terms of trade index	Inbound tourism expenditure	Net official development assistance	Net migration	Personal remittances, received	Foreign direct investment	Portfolio equity	Total external debt stock	Total debt service
	% of GDP	2000 = 100	% of exports	% of GNI	thousands	$ millions	Net inflow $ millions	Net inflow $ millions	$ millions	% of exports of goods, services, and primary income
	2012	2012	2012	2012	2010–15	2012	2012	2012	2012	2012
Costa Rica	64.2	77.7	20.0	0.1	64	562	2,636	..	14,458	17.6
Côte d'Ivoire	89.7	144.3	..	11.1	50	..	478	..	9,871	..
Croatia	55.9	98.1	36.2	..	−20	1,437	1,395	−174	..	..
Cuba	..	144.6	..	..	−140	..	..	..	..	..
Curaçao	..	..	..	..	14	30	57	..	..	..
Cyprus	39.8	94.2	27.8	..	35	112	1,247	742	..	..
Czech Republic	151.3	101.0	5.2	..	200	2,026	10,581	−148	..	..
Denmark	63.2	99.8	3.6	..	75	1,257	1,269	4,784	..	..
Djibouti	..	82.0	4.6	..	−16	33	110	..	808	8.8
Dominica	49.0	103.1	57.2	5.5	..	23	20	..	284	10.0
Dominican Republic	45.0	91.5	39.3	0.5	−140	3,615	3,857	..	16,851	14.0
Ecuador	58.5	134.7	3.9	0.2	−30	2,456	591	5	16,931	9.8
Egypt, Arab Rep.	37.7	156.2	22.3	0.7	−216	19,236	2,798	−983	40,000	6.6
El Salvador	65.4	90.2	14.7	1.0	−225	3,927	467	..	13,279	18.7
Equatorial Guinea	121.5	244.8	..	0.1	20	..	2,115	..	..	..
Eritrea	45.9	98.5	..	4.4	55	..	74	..	994	..
Estonia	150.9	93.9	7.9	..	0	401	1,648	−151	..	..
Ethiopia	36.1	130.6	33.0	7.9	−60	624	279	..	10,462	7.2
Faeroe Islands	..	104.0	..	..	..	..	..	..	..	..
Fiji	86.8	108.1	40.5	2.9	−29	191	267	..	732	..
Finland	60.1	87.1	5.3	..	50	866	4,332	3,097	..	..
France	47.6	88.8	8.3	..	650	21,676	28,122	36,077	..	..
French Polynesia	..	78.7	..	..	−1	..	87	..	..	..
Gabon	86.5	226.0	..	0.4	5	..	702	..	2,870	..
Gambia, The	52.9	92.1	29.6	15.9	−13	141	34	..	513	7.1
Georgia	64.9	134.2	26.0	4.2	−125	1,770	831	74	13,426	23.3
Germany	75.1	95.3	3.0	..	550	13,964	27,221	−3,746	..	..
Ghana	73.7	172.2	6.9	4.7	−100	138	3,295	..	12,436	4.2
Greece	37.9	87.2	21.0	..	50	681	1,663	−66	..	..
Greenland	..	79.0	..	..	..	..	..	..	..	..
Grenada	48.3	91.1	56.8	1.1	−4	29	30	..	591	7.7
Guam	..	81.1	..	..	0	..	..	..	..	..
Guatemala	54.0	87.7	11.3	0.6	−75	5,035	1,150	..	14,975	10.9
Guinea	65.7	103.7	0.1	6.5	−10	66	605	..	1,097	7.0
Guinea-Bissau	46.2	81.6	..	9.6	−10	..	16	..	279	..
Guyana	112.3	128.3	3.8	4.0	−33	469	276	..	1,974	8.7
Haiti	46.2	67.9	16.3	16.1	−175	1,612	179	..	1,154	0.3
Honduras	103.6	84.3	10.0	3.3	−50	2,909	1,068	..	4,987	13.8
Hungary	159.8	92.6	5.3	..	75	2,144	9,356	1,137	203,757	84.6
Iceland	72.4	87.3	10.7	..	5	19	1,086	−3	..	..
India	42.1	127.4	4.1	0.1	−2,294	68,821	23,996	22,809	379,099	6.8
Indonesia	43.1	129.2	4.5	0.0	−700	7,212	19,618	1,698	254,899	17.1
Iran, Islamic Rep.	27.5	194.5	..	..	−300	..	4,870	..	11,477	..
Iraq	70.1	227.1	1.7	0.6	450	271	3,400	7	..	..
Ireland	85.1	92.7	4.0	..	50	700	40,962	105,422	..	..
Isle of Man	..	..	..	..	..	..	..	..	..	..
Israel	..	97.6	6.7	..	−76	685	9,481	290	..	..

6 Global links

	Merchandise trade % of GDP 2012	Net barter terms of trade index 2000 = 100 2012	Inbound tourism expenditure % of exports 2012	Net official development assistance % of GNI 2012	Net migration thousands 2010–15	Personal remittances, received $ millions 2012	Foreign direct investment Net inflow $ millions 2012	Portfolio equity Net inflow $ millions 2012	Total external debt stock $ millions 2012	Total debt service % of exports of goods, services, and primary income 2012
Italy	48.9	94.8	7.4	..	900	7,326	6,686	20,835	..	..
Jamaica	56.3	87.1	46.8	0.1	−80	2,145	229	−1	14,333	38.2
Japan	28.3	60.5	1.8	..	350	2,540	2,525	34,941	..	..
Jordan	92.1	83.7	33.0	4.6	400	3,574	1,497	53	18,632	6.9
Kazakhstan	67.2	231.3	1.6	0.1	0	171	15,117	−418	137,014	23.5
Kenya	55.1	89.9	18.2	6.5	−50	1,214	259	26	11,569	5.1
Kiribati	62.9	96.6	..	25.0	−1	..	−2	..	..	..
Korea, Dem. People's Rep.	..	85.9	..	..	0	..	79	..	..	..
Korea, Rep.	94.5	61.8	3.0	..	300	8,474	4,999	16,925	..	..
Kosovo	..	..	..	8.9	..	1,059	293	1	2,002	8.8
Kuwait	80.2	227.8	0.6	..	300	8	1,851	−41	..	..
Kyrgyz Republic	112.2	108.2	23.8	7.8	−175	2,031	372	0	6,026	10.9
Lao PDR	54.2	109.4	16.2	4.6	−75	59	294	6	6,372	8.2
Latvia	109.2	102.9	6.3	..	−10	730	1,076	4	..	..
Lebanon	64.2	97.9	22.6	1.7	500	6,918	3,678	−239	28,950	14.2
Lesotho	151.2	77.7	4.4	10.3	−20	554	198	..	860	2.3
Liberia	88.0	138.6	..	36.1	−20	..	1,354	..	487	..
Libya	..	201.4	..	..	−239	..	..	..	..	..
Liechtenstein	..	..	..	..	..	..	..	..	..	..
Lithuania	145.6	93.2	4.0	..	−28	1,508	574	−51	..	..
Luxembourg	84.7	75.8	5.2	..	26	1,681	27,878	161,691	..	..
Macedonia, FYR	109.4	88.7	5.5	1.6	−5	394	283	−6	6,678	15.1
Madagascar	45.6	80.2	..	3.9	−5	..	895	..	2,896	..
Malawi	85.6	95.9	2.7	28.4	0	28	129	1	1,314	2.0
Malaysia	139.0	101.3	7.6	0.0	450	1,320	9,734	..	103,950	3.5
Maldives	84.1	102.0	79.9	3.1	0	3	284	0	1,027	3.8
Mali	49.1	172.1	..	10.2	−302	..	310	..	3,073	..
Malta	115.9	125.9	15.9	..	5	33	599	3	..	..
Marshall Islands	95.9	106.4	..	34.7	..	..	38	..	..	..
Mauritania	126.2	153.1	..	10.0	−20	..	1,204	..	3,348	4.9
Mauritius	74.9	70.9	29.2	1.7	0	1	361	6,840	4,459	2.4
Mexico	63.8	109.1	3.4	0.0	−1,200	23,366	15,453	10,038	354,897	17.7
Micronesia, Fed. Sts.	75.1	98.3	..	33.5	−8	..	1	..	..	..
Moldova	101.7	101.5	10.6	6.1	−103	1,786	185	14	6,135	15.1
Monaco	..	..	..	..	..	..	..	..	..	..
Mongolia	108.3	206.0	9.0	4.7	−15	320	4,452	15	5,080	4.5
Montenegro	64.2	..	50.3	2.3	−3	333	618	0	2,833	13.6
Morocco	68.3	145.4	26.3	1.6	−450	6,508	2,842	−108	33,816	11.2
Mozambique	76.5	100.2	5.8	14.8	−25	220	5,238	..	4,788	1.6
Myanmar	..	112.8	..	..	−100	..	2,243	..	2,563	..
Namibia	83.0	122.9	..	2.1	−3	..	357	..	..	..
Nepal	39.3	77.7	19.6	4.0	−401	4,793	92	..	3,818	10.3
Netherlands	161.8	93.1	3.2	..	50	1,617	6,684	3,674	..	..
New Caledonia	..	195.9	..	..	6	..	1,588	..	..	..
New Zealand	44.1	129.4	10.7	..	75	..	2,209	442	..	..
Nicaragua	81.2	82.4	8.5	5.2	−120	1,016	805	0	8,858	12.3
Niger	65.0	169.0	..	13.5	−28	..	793	..	2,340	..

 Front | User guide | World view | People | Environment

	Merchandise trade	Net barter terms of trade index	Inbound tourism expenditure	Net official development assistance	Net migration	Personal remittances, received	Foreign direct investment	Portfolio equity	Total external debt stock	Total debt service
	% of GDP	2000 = 100	% of exports	% of GNI	thousands	$ millions	Net inflow $ millions	Net inflow $ millions	$ millions	% of exports of goods, services, and primary income
	2012	2012	2012	2012	2010–15	2012	2012	2012	2012	2012
Nigeria	62.8	221.8	0.7	0.8	–300	20,633	7,101	10,003	10,077	0.3
Northern Mariana Islands	..	84.8	..	..	..		5		..	..
Norway	49.4	161.6	2.6	..	150	767	22,951	965	..	..
Oman	103.7	244.2	3.2	..	1,030	39	1,514	1,373	..	..
Pakistan	30.5	53.9	3.2	0.9	–1,634	14,007	854	178	..	..
Palau	64.4	105.3	..	7.3	..	..	5	..	61,867	14.9
Panama	108.7	86.2	13.6	0.2	29	402	3,383	..	..	..
Papua New Guinea	76.7	193.1	..	4.4	0	..	29	..	12,294	8.7
Paraguay	73.5	110.5	2.1	0.4	–40	634	363	..	23,128	..
Peru	43.3	163.7	6.5	0.2	–300	2,788	12,244	–32	6,331	6.3
Philippines	46.9	65.6	7.6	0.0	–700	24,641	2,797	1,728	54,148	12.5
Poland	77.5	97.1	5.2	..	–38	6,935	6,701	3,888	61,390	8.0
Portugal	61.4	91.3	17.6	..	100	3,904	13,377	–8,518	..	..
Puerto Rico	..	..	..	..	–104	..	..	..	..	..
Qatar	85.5	217.8	5.1	..	500	803	327	–925	..	..
Romania	75.5	110.7	3.0	..	–45	3,674	2,024	403	131,889	34.2
Russian Federation	42.9	248.9	3.0	..	1,100	5,788	50,661	1,162	..	..
Rwanda	34.8	214.9	33.2	12.5	–45	182	160	7	1,269	2.2
Samoa	61.7	81.1	61.1	18.6	–13	159	24	..	423	5.3
San Marino	..	..	..	..	..	..	..	..	..	..
São Tomé and Príncipe	57.3	106.8	50.4	18.7	–2	6	22	..	202	6.9
Saudi Arabia	74.6	215.5	2.1	..	300	246	12,182	..	..	..
Senegal	63.7	109.1	..	7.8	–100	..	338	..	4,900	..
Serbia	81.0	104.2	7.0	3.0	–100	2,763	355	–24	34,438	36.7
Seychelles	114.9	78.1	2.8	3.3	–2	1	12	..	2,024	64.3
Sierra Leone	63.2	58.1	3.1	11.7	–21	61	548	7	1,121	1.5
Singapore	286.9	80.6	3.5	..	400	..	56,651	2,851	..	..
Sint Maarten	..	..	..	..	..	13	14	..	..	..
Slovak Republic	174.7	92.3	2.7	..	15	1,928	1,527	0	..	..
Slovenia	141.3	94.2	8.3	..	22	644	–227	149	..	..
Solomon Islands	96.2	89.7	10.5	43.6	–12	17	68	..	228	4.5
Somalia	..	107.8	..	..	–150	..	107	..	3,055	..
South Africa	54.6	145.5	9.8	0.3	–100	1,085	4,644	–679	137,501	7.9
South Sudan	..	..	..	17.0	865	..	..	..	..	..
Spain	47.2	88.5	14.8	..	600	9,633	36,161	9,819	..	..
Sri Lanka	48.1	75.0	12.9	0.8	–317	6,000	898	305	25,382	13.3
St. Kitts and Nevis	35.9	71.4	37.5	3.0	..	45	100	..	..	..
St. Lucia	71.9	91.4	56.9	2.2	0	30	109	..	473	6.9
St. Martin	..	..	..	..	..	..	..	..	..	..
St. Vincent & the Grenadines	55.3	107.4	48.5	1.2	–5	30	125	..	267	16.6
Sudan	20.8	..	19.4	1.7[a]	–800[a]	401	2,488	2	21,840	8.9
Suriname	83.8	134.8	2.9	0.8	–5	8	66	..	..	..
Swaziland	102.8	110.2	..	2.6	–6	31	90	..	460	2.2
Sweden	63.9	92.3	5.0	..	200	812	4,039	3,968	..	..
Switzerland	67.1	80.3	4.8	..	320	3,039	2,748	14,554	..	..
Syrian Arab Republic	..	146.8	..	..	–1,500	..	..	..	4,736	..
Tajikistan	67.3	99.3	3.7	5.2	–100	3,626	198	..	3,648	25.5

6 Global links

	Merchandise trade	Net barter terms of trade index	Inbound tourism expenditure	Net official development assistance	Net migration	Personal remittances, received	Foreign direct investment	Portfolio equity	Total external debt stock	Total debt service
	% of GDP	2000 = 100	% of exports	% of GNI	thousands	$ millions	Net inflow $ millions	Net inflow $ millions	$ millions	% of exports of goods, services, and primary income
	2012	2012	2012	2012	2010–15	2012	2012	2012	2012	2012
Tanzania	58.8	145.2	18.8	10.1	−150	67	1,707	4	11,581	1.9
Thailand	130.4	93.2	13.7	0.0	100	4,713	10,689	2,663	134,223	4.1
Timor-Leste	29.5	..	20.5	5.8	−75	114	19	..	..	..
Togo	73.4	28.7	..	7.2	−10	..	166	..	754	..
Tonga	47.9	81.9	..	16.1	−8	60	8	..	197	7.8
Trinidad and Tobago	96.5	156.9	..	..	−15	..	2,527	..	..	..
Tunisia	90.8	97.1	13.2	2.3	−33	2,266	1,554	−15	25,475	11.5
Turkey	49.3	87.2	15.6	0.4	350	1,015	12,519	6,274	337,492	26.1
Turkmenistan	73.1	238.5	..	0.1	−25	..	3,159	..	492	..
Turks and Caicos Islands	..	68.4	..	..	..	..	..	..	..	..
Tuvalu	63.4	..	..	42.3	..	..	..	..	..	..
Uganda	41.6	110.0	23.4	8.5	−150	733	1,721	5	3,769	1.4
Ukraine	86.9	118.1	6.9	0.4	−40	8,449	7,833	516	135,067	31.5
United Arab Emirates	135.5	186.1	..	..	514	..	9,602	..	..	..
United Kingdom	46.4	99.4	6.0	..	900	1,776	56,136	−27,555	..	..
United States	23.9	94.7	9.0	..	5,000	6,285	203,790	232,063	..	..
Uruguay	40.8	104.2	16.7	0.0	−30	97	2,907	..	..	..
Uzbekistan	43.2	172.1	..	0.5	−200	..	1,094	..	8,853	..
Vanuatu	44.5	88.0	76.5	13.6	0	22	38	..	369	2.1
Venezuela, RB	41.3	262.1	0.9	0.0	40	118	2,199	−50	72,097	5.6
Vietnam	146.6	100.5	5.5	2.8	−200	..	8,368	1,887	59,133	4.4
Virgin Islands (U.S.)	..	..	..	..	−4	..	..	..	..	..
West Bank and Gaza	..	..	..	..	−44	..	..	..	..	..
Yemen, Rep.	57.5	167.7	..	2.1	−135	..	349	..	7,555	..
Zambia	80.4	183.6	1.6	4.9	−40	73	1,066	26	5,385	2.2
Zimbabwe	83.7	105.0	..	10.6	400	..	400	..	7,713	..
World	**50.8**	**..**	**5.8b**	**0.2c**	**0**	**478,461**	**1,509,565**	**776,000**	**..**	**..**
Low income	55.1	..	12.4	8.0	−3,647	30,184	24,291	142	134,345	4.8
Middle income	50.5	..	5.3	0.2	−13,345	320,209	592,608	104,290	4,695,263	9.9
Lower middle income	51.1	..	6.3	0.8	−11,030	199,670	103,112	38,172	3,421,974	10.0
Upper middle income	50.4	..	5.1	0.1	−2,314	120,539	489,495	66,118	4,829,608	9.8
Low & middle income	50.6	..	5.4	0.6	−16,991	350,393	616,899	104,432	1,273,289	9.7
East Asia & Pacific	54.2	..	4.4	0.1	−3,061	78,304	313,801	37,899	1,412,411	4.5
Europe & Central Asia	72.6	..	8.6	0.6	−661	38,706	65,194	7,988	1,149,505	32.9
Latin America & Carib.	38.2	..	4.7	0.2	−3,017	59,537	150,393	20,214	1,257,876	15.0
Middle East & N. Africa	47.5	..	11.0	..	−1,632	39,019	22,699	−1,286	177,092	3.9
South Asia	41.5	..	4.5	0.6	−7,076	108,112	27,405	23,386	501,491	7.3
Sub-Saharan Africa	61.6	..	6.6	3.8	−1,545	26,715	37,406	16,232	331,234	4.5
High income	50.9	..	5.9	0.0	16,941	128,067	892,666	671,568	..	..
Euro area	72.1	..	6.1	0.0	3,402	78,775	201,185	334,538	..	..

a. Excludes South Sudan. b. Calculated using the World Bank's weighted aggregation methodology (see *Statistical methods*) and thus may differ from data reported by the World Tourism Organization. c. Based on the World Bank classification of economies and thus may differ from data reported by the Organisation for Economic Co-operation and Development.

 Front | ? User guide | World view | People | Environment

About the data

Starting with *World Development Indicators 2013,* the World Bank changed its presentation of balance of payments data to conform to the International Monetary Fund's (IMF) Balance of Payments Manual, 6th edition (BPM6). The historical data series based on BPM5 ends with data for 2005. Balance of payments data from 2005 forward have been presented in accord with the BPM6 methodology, which can be accessed at www.imf.org/external/np/sta/bop/bop.htm.

Trade in goods

Data on merchandise trade are from customs reports of goods moving into or out of an economy or from reports of financial transactions related to merchandise trade recorded in the balance of payments. Because of differences in timing and definitions, trade flow estimates from customs reports and balance of payments may differ. Several international agencies process trade data, each correcting unreported or misreported data, leading to other differences. The most detailed source of data on international trade in goods is the United Nations Statistics Division's Commodity Trade Statistics (Comtrade) database. The IMF and the World Trade Organization also collect customs-based data on trade in goods.

The "terms of trade" index measures the relative prices of a country's exports and imports. The most common way to calculate terms of trade is the net barter (or commodity) terms of trade index, or the ratio of the export price index to the import price index. When a country's net barter terms of trade index increases, its exports have become more expensive or its imports cheaper.

Tourism

Tourism is defined as the activity of people traveling to and staying in places outside their usual environment for no more than one year for leisure, business, and other purposes not related to an activity remunerated from within the place visited. Data on inbound and outbound tourists refer to the number of arrivals and departures, not to the number of unique individuals. Thus a person who makes several trips to a country during a given period is counted each time as a new arrival. Data on inbound tourism show the arrivals of nonresident tourists (overnight visitors) at national borders. When data on international tourists are unavailable or incomplete, the table shows the arrivals of international visitors, which include tourists, same-day visitors, cruise passengers, and crew members. The aggregates are calculated using the World Bank's weighted aggregation methodology (see *Statistical methods*) and differ from the World Tourism Organization's aggregates.

For tourism expenditure, the World Tourism Organization uses balance of payments data from the IMF supplemented by data from individual countries. These data, shown in the table, include travel and passenger transport items as defined by the BPM6. When the IMF does not report data on passenger transport items, expenditure data for travel items are shown.

Official development assistance

Data on official development assistance received refer to aid to eligible countries from members of the Organisation of Economic Co-operation and Development's (OECD) Development Assistance Committee (DAC), multilateral organizations, and non-DAC donors. Data do not reflect aid given by recipient countries to other developing countries or distinguish among types of aid (program, project, or food aid; emergency assistance; or postconflict peacekeeping assistance), which may have different effects on the economy.

Ratios of aid to gross national income (GNI), gross capital formation, imports, and government spending measure a country's dependency on aid. Care must be taken in drawing policy conclusions. For foreign policy reasons some countries have traditionally received large amounts of aid. Thus aid dependency ratios may reveal as much about a donor's interests as about a recipient's needs. Increases in aid dependency ratios can reflect events affecting both the numerator (aid) and the denominator (GNI).

Data are based on information from donors and may not be consistent with information recorded by recipients in the balance of payments, which often excludes all or some technical assistance—particularly payments to expatriates made directly by the donor. Similarly, grant commodity aid may not always be recorded in trade data or in the balance of payments. DAC statistics exclude aid for military and antiterrorism purposes. The aggregates refer to World Bank classifications of economies and therefore may differ from those reported by the OECD.

Migration and personal remittances

The movement of people, most often through migration, is a significant part of global integration. Migrants contribute to the economies of both their host country and their country of origin. Yet reliable statistics on migration are difficult to collect and are often incomplete, making international comparisons a challenge.

Since data on emigrant stock is difficult for countries to collect, the United Nations Population Division provides data on net migration, taking into account the past migration history of a country or area, the migration policy of a country, and the influx of refugees in recent periods to derive estimates of net migration. The data to calculate these estimates come from various sources, including border statistics, administrative records, surveys, and censuses. When there are insufficient data, net migration is derived through the difference between the growth rate of a country's population over a certain period and the rate of natural increase of that population (itself being the difference between the birth rate and the death rate).

Migrants often send funds back to their home countries, which are recorded as personal transfers in the balance of payments. Personal transfers thus include all current transfers between resident and nonresident individuals, independent of the source of income of the sender (irrespective of whether the sender receives income from labor, entrepreneurial or property income, social benefits, or any other types of transfers or disposes of assets) and the relationship between the households (irrespective of whether they are related or unrelated individuals).

Compensation of employees refers to the income of border, seasonal, and other short-term workers who are employed in an economy where they are not resident and of residents employed by nonresident entities. Compensation of employees has three main components: wages and salaries in cash, wages and salaries in kind, and employers' social contributions. Personal remittances are the sum of personal transfers and compensation of employees.

Equity flows

Equity flows comprise foreign direct investment (FDI) and portfolio equity. The internationally accepted definition of FDI (from BPM6) includes the following components: equity investment, including investment associated with equity that gives rise to control or influence; investment in indirectly influenced or controlled enterprises; investment in fellow enterprises; debt (except selected debt); and reverse investment. The Framework for Direct Investment Relationships provides criteria for determining whether cross-border ownership results in a direct investment relationship, based on control and influence.

Direct investments may take the form of greenfield investment, where the investor starts a new venture in a foreign country by constructing new operational facilities; joint venture, where the investor enters into a partnership agreement with a company abroad to establish a new enterprise; or merger and acquisition, where the investor acquires an existing enterprise abroad. The IMF suggests that investments should account for at least 10 percent of voting stock to be counted as FDI. In practice many countries set a higher threshold. Many countries fail to report reinvested earnings, and the definition of long-term loans differs among countries.

Portfolio equity investment is defined as cross-border transactions and positions involving equity securities, other than those included in direct investment or reserve assets. Equity securities are equity instruments that are negotiable and designed to be traded, usually on organized exchanges or "over the counter." The negotiability of securities facilitates trading, allowing securities to be held by different parties during their lives. Negotiability allows investors to diversify their portfolios and to withdraw their investment readily. Included in portfolio investment are investment fund shares or units (that is, those issued by investment funds) that are evidenced by securities and that are not reserve assets or direct investment. Although they are negotiable instruments, exchange-traded financial derivatives are not included in portfolio investment because they are in their own category.

External debt

External indebtedness affects a country's creditworthiness and investor perceptions. Data on external debt are gathered through the World Bank's Debtor Reporting System (DRS). Indebtedness is calculated using loan-by-loan reports submitted by countries on long-term public and publicly guaranteed borrowing and using information on short-term debt collected by the countries, from creditors through the reporting systems of the Bank for International Settlements, or based on national data from the World Bank's *Quarterly External Debt Statistics*. These data are supplemented by information from major multilateral banks and official lending agencies in major creditor countries. Currently, 124 developing countries report to the DRS. Debt data are reported in the currency of repayment and compiled and published in U.S. dollars. End-of-period exchange rates are used for the compilation of stock figures (amount of debt outstanding), and projected debt service and annual average exchange rates are used for the flows. Exchange rates are taken from the IMF's *International Financial Statistics*. Debt repayable in multiple currencies, goods, or services and debt with a provision for maintenance of the value of the currency of repayment are shown at book value.

While data related to public and publicly guaranteed debt are reported to the DRS on a loan-by-loan basis, data on long-term private nonguaranteed debt are reported annually in aggregate by the country or estimated by World Bank staff for countries. Private nonguaranteed debt is estimated based on national data from the World Bank's *Quarterly External Debt Statistics*.

Total debt service as a share of exports of goods, services, and primary income provides a measure of a country's ability to service its debt out of export earnings.

 Front | ? User guide | World view | People | Environment

Definitions

• **Merchandise trade** includes all trade in goods and excludes trade in services. • **Net barter terms of trade index** is the percentage ratio of the export unit value indexes to the import unit value indexes, measured relative to the base year 2000. • **Inbound tourism expenditure** is expenditures by international inbound visitors, including payments to national carriers for international transport and any other prepayment made for goods or services received in the destination country. They may include receipts from same-day visitors, except when these are important enough to justify separate classification. Data include travel and passenger transport items as defined by BPM6. When passenger transport items are not reported, expenditure data for travel items are shown. Exports refer to all transactions between residents of a country and the rest of the world involving a change of ownership from residents to nonresidents of general merchandise, goods sent for processing and repairs, nonmonetary gold, and services. • **Net official development assistance** is flows (net of repayment of principal) that meet the DAC definition of official development assistance and are made to countries and territories on the DAC list of aid recipients, divided by World Bank estimates of GNI. • **Net migration** is the net total of migrants (immigrants less emigrants, including both citizens and noncitizens) during the period. Data are five-year estimates. • **Personal remittances, received,** are the sum of personal transfers (current transfers in cash or in kind made or received by resident households to or from nonresident households) and compensation of employees (remuneration for the labor input to the production process contributed by an individual in an employer-employee relationship with the enterprise). • **Foreign direct investment** is cross-border investment associated with a resident in one economy having control or a significant degree of influence on the management of an enterprise that is resident in another economy. • **Portfolio equity** is net inflows from equity securities other than those recorded as direct investment or reserve assets, including shares, stocks, depository receipts, and direct purchases of shares in local stock markets by foreign investors • **Total external debt stock** is debt owed to nonresident creditors and repayable in foreign currency, goods, or services by public and private entities in the country. It is the sum of long-term external debt, short-term debt, and use of IMF credit. • **Total debt service** is the sum of principal repayments and interest actually paid in foreign currency, goods, or services on long-term debt; interest paid on short-term debt; and repayments (repurchases and charges) to the IMF. Exports of goods and services and primary income are the total value of exports of goods and services, receipts of compensation of nonresident workers, and primary investment income from abroad.

Data sources

Data on merchandise trade are from the World Trade Organization. Data on trade indexes are from the United Nations Conference on Trade and Development's (UNCTAD) annual *Handbook of Statistics*. Data on tourism expenditure are from the World Tourism Organization's *Yearbook of Tourism Statistics* and World Tourism Organization (2013) and updated from its electronic files. Data on net official development assistance are compiled by the OECD (http://stats.oecd.org). Data on net migration are from United Nations Population Division (2013). Data on personal remittances are from the IMF's *Balance of Payments Statistics Yearbook* supplemented by World Bank staff estimates. Data on FDI are World Bank staff estimates based on IMF balance of payments statistics and UNCTAD data (http://unctadstat.unctad.org/ReportFolders/reportFolders.aspx). Data on portfolio equity are from the IMF's *Balance of Payments Statistics Yearbook*. Data on external debt are mainly from reports to the World Bank through its DRS from member countries that have received International Bank for Reconstruction and Development loans or International Development Assistance credits, with additional information from the files of the World Bank, the IMF, the African Development Bank and African Development Fund, the Asian Development Bank and Asian Development Fund, and the Inter-American Development Bank. Summary tables of the external debt of developing countries are published annually in the World Bank's *International Debt Statistics* and International Debt Statistics database.

References

IMF (International Monetary Fund). Various issues. *International Financial Statistics.* Washington, DC.

————. Various years. *Balance of Payments Statistics Yearbook. Parts 1 and 2.* Washington, DC.

UNCTAD (United Nations Conference on Trade and Development). Various years. *Handbook of Statistics.* New York and Geneva.

UNHCR (Office of the UN High Commissioner for Refugees). 2013. *UNHCR Mid-Year Trends 2013.* Geneva.

United Nations Population Division. 2013. *World Population Prospects: The 2012 Revision.* New York: United Nations, Department of Economic and Social Affairs.

World Bank. 2014. *Global Economic Prospects: Commodity Market Outlook.* January 2014. Washington, DC.

————. Various years. *International Debt Statistics.* Washington, DC.

World Tourism Organization. 2013. *Compendium of Tourism Statistics 2013.* Madrid.

————. Various years. *Yearbook of Tourism Statistics. Vols. 1 and 2.* Madrid.

6 Global links

To access the World Development Indicators online tables, use the URL http://wdi.worldbank.org/table/ and the table number (for example, http://wdi.worldbank.org/table/6.1). To view a specific indicator online, use the URL http://data.worldbank.org/indicator/ and the indicator code (for example, http://data.worldbank.org/indicator/TX.QTY.MRCH.XD.WD).

6.1 Growth of merchandise trade

Export volume	TX.QTY.MRCH.XD.WD
Import volume	TM.QTY.MRCH.XD.WD
Export value	TX.VAL.MRCH.XD.WD
Import value	TM.VAL.MRCH.XD.WD
Net barter terms of trade index	TT.PRI.MRCH.XD.WD

6.2 Direction and growth of merchandise trade

This table provides estimates of the flow of trade in goods between groups of economies. ..a

6.3 High-income economy trade with low- and middle-income economies

This table illustrates the importance of developing economies in the global trading system. ..a

6.4 Direction of trade of developing economies

Exports to developing economies within region	TX.VAL.MRCH.WR.ZS
Exports to developing economies outside region	TX.VAL.MRCH.OR.ZS
Exports to high-income economies	TX.VAL.MRCH.HI.ZS
Imports from developing economies within region	TM.VAL.MRCH.WR.ZS
Imports from developing economies outside region	TM.VAL.MRCH.OR.ZS
Imports from high-income economies	TM.VAL.MRCH.HI.ZS

6.5 Primary commodity prices

This table provides historical commodity price data. ..a

6.6 Tariff barriers

All products, Binding coverage	TM.TAX.MRCH.BC.ZS
Simple mean bound rate	TM.TAX.MRCH.BR.ZS
Simple mean tariff	TM.TAX.MRCH.SM.AR.ZS
Weighted mean tariff	TM.TAX.MRCH.WM.AR.ZS
Share of tariff lines with international peaks	TM.TAX.MRCH.IP.ZS
Share of tariff lines with specific rates	TM.TAX.MRCH.SR.ZS
Primary products, Simple mean tariff	TM.TAX.TCOM.SM.AR.ZS
Primary products, Weighted mean tariff	TM.TAX.TCOM.WM.AR.ZS
Manufactured products, Simple mean tariff	TM.TAX.MANF.SM.AR.ZS
Manufactured products, Weighted mean tariff	TM.TAX.MANF.WM.AR.ZS

6.7 Trade facilitation

Logistics performance index	LP.LPI.OVRL.XQ
Burden of customs procedures	IQ.WEF.CUST.XQ

Lead time to export	LP.EXP.DURS.MD
Lead time to import	LP.IMP.DURS.MD
Documents to export	IC.EXP.DOCS
Documents to import	IC.IMP.DOCS
Liner shipping connectivity index	IS.SHP.GCNW.XQ
Quality of port infrastructure	IQ.WEF.PORT.XQ

6.8 External debt

Total external debt, $	DT.DOD.DECT.CD
Total external debt, % of GNI	DT.DOD.DECT.GN.ZS
Long-term debt, Public and publicly guaranteed	DT.DOD.DPPG.CD
Long-term debt, Private nonguaranteed	DT.DOD.DPNG.CD
Short-term debt, $	DT.DOD.DSTC.CD
Short-term debt, % of total debt	DT.DOD.DSTC.ZS
Short-term debt, % of total reserves	DT.DOD.DSTC.IR.ZS
Total debt service	DT.TDS.DECT.EX.ZS
Present value of debt, % of GNI	DT.DOD.PVLX.GN.ZS
Present value of debt, % of exports of goods, services and primary income	DT.DOD.PVLX.EX.ZS

6.9 Global private financial flows

Foreign direct investment net inflows, $	BX.KLT.DINV.CD.WD
Foreign direct investment net inflows, % of GDP	BX.KLT.DINV.WD.GD.ZS
Portfolio equity	BX.PEF.TOTL.CD.WD
Bonds	DT.NFL.BOND.CD
Commercial banks and other lendings	DT.NFL.PCBO.CD

6.10 Net official financial flows

Net financial flows from bilateral sources	DT.NFL.BLAT.CD
Net financial flows from multilateral sources	DT.NFL.MLAT.CD
World Bank, IDA	DT.NFL.MIDA.CD
World Bank, IBRD	DT.NFL.MIBR.CD
IMF, Concessional	DT.NFL.IMFC.CD
IMF, Non concessional	DT.NFL.IMFN.CD
Regional development banks, Concessional	DT.NFL.RDBC.CD
Regional development banks, Nonconcessional	DT.NFL.RDBN.CD
Regional development banks, Other institutions	DT.NFL.MOTH.CD

6.11 Aid dependency

Net official development assistance (ODA)	DT.ODA.ODAT.CD
Net ODA per capita	DT.ODA.ODAT.PC.ZS

Grants, excluding technical cooperation	BX.GRT.EXTA.CD.WD
Technical cooperation grants	BX.GRT.TECH.CD.WD
Net ODA, % of GNI	DT.ODA.ODAT.GN.ZS
Net ODA, % of gross capital formation	DT.ODA.ODAT.GI.ZS
Net ODA, % of imports of goods and services and income	DT.ODA.ODAT.MP.ZS
Net ODA, % of central government expenditure	DT.ODA.ODAT.XP.ZS

6.12 Distribution of net aid by Development Assistance Committee members

Net bilateral aid flows from DAC donors	DC.DAC.TOTL.CD
United States	DC.DAC.USAL.CD
EU institutions	DC.DAC.CECL.CD
Germany	DC.DAC.DEUL.CD
France	DC.DAC.FRAL.CD
United Kingdom	DC.DAC.GBRL.CD
Japan	DC.DAC.JPNL.CD
Netherlands	DC.DAC.NLDL.CD
Australia	DC.DAC.AUSL.CD
Canada	DC.DAC.CANL.CD
Sweden	DC.DAC.SWEL.CD
Other DAC donors	..a,b

6.13 Movement of people

Net migration	SM.POP.NETM
International migrant stock	SM.POP.TOTL
Emigration rate of tertiary educated to OECD countries	SM.EMI.TERT.ZS
Refugees by country of origin	SM.POP.REFG.OR
Refugees by country of asylum	SM.POP.REFG
Personal remittances, Received	BX.TRF.PWKR.CD.DT
Personal remittances, Paid	BM.TRF.PWKR.CD.DT

6.14 Travel and tourism

International inbound tourists	ST.INT.ARVL
International outbound tourists	ST.INT.DPRT
Inbound tourism expenditure, $	ST.INT.RCPT.CD
Inbound tourism expenditure, % of exports	ST.INT.RCPT.XP.ZS
Outbound tourism expenditure, $	ST.INT.XPND.CD
Outbound tourism expenditure, % of imports	ST.INT.XPND.MP.ZS

a. Available online only as part of the table, not as an individual indicator.
b. Derived from data elsewhere in the World Development Indicators database.

Primary data documentation

As a major user of development data, the World Bank recognizes the importance of data documentation to inform users of the methods and conventions used by primary data collectors—usually national statistical agencies, central banks, and customs services—and by international organizations, which compile the statistics that appear in the World Development Indicators database.

This section provides information on sources, methods, and reporting standards of the principal demographic, economic, and environmental indicators in *World Development Indicators.* Additional documentation is available online in the World Development Indicators database and from the World Bank's Bulletin Board on Statistical Capacity at http://data.worldbank.org.

The demand for good-quality statistical data is ever increasing. Statistics provide the evidence needed to improve decisionmaking, document results, and heighten public accountability. However, differences among data collectors may give rise to large discrepancies over time, both within and across countries. Data relevant at the national level may not be suitable for standardized international use due to methodological concerns or the lack of clear documentation. Delays in reporting data and the use of old surveys as the base for current estimates may further compromise the quality of data reported.

To meet these challenges and improve the quality of data disseminated, the World Bank works closely with other international agencies, regional development banks, donors, and other partners to

· Develop appropriate frameworks, guidance, and standards of good practice for statistics.

· Build consensus and define internationally agreed indicators, such as those for the Millennium Development Goals and the post-2015 development agenda.

· Establish data exchange processes and methods.

· Help countries improve their statistical capacity.

More information on these activities and other data programs is available at http://data worldbank.org.

Primary data documentation

	Currency	Base year	Reference year	System of National Accounts	SNA price valuation	Alternative conversion factor	PPP survey year	Balance of Payments Manual in use	External debt	System of trade	Accounting concept	IMF data dissemination standard
Afghanistan	Afghan afghani	2002/03		1993	B				A	G	C	G
Albania	Albanian lek	[a]	1996	1993	B		Rolling	6	A	G	B	G
Algeria	Algerian dinar	1980		1968	B			6	A	S	B	G
American Samoa	U.S. dollar			1968						S		
Andorra	Euro	1990		1968						S		
Angola	Angolan kwanza	2002		1993	P	1991–96	2005	6	A	S	B	G
Antigua and Barbuda	East Caribbean dollar	2006		1968	B			6		G	B	G
Argentina	Argentine peso	1993		1993	B	1971–84	2005	6	A	S	C	S
Armenia	Armenian dram	[a]	1996	1993	B	1990–95	2005	6	A	S	C	S
Aruba	Aruban florin	2000		1993	B			6		S		
Australia	Australian dollar	[a]	2011	2008	B		2011	6		S	C	S
Austria	Euro	2005		1993	B		Rolling	6		S	C	S
Azerbaijan	New Azeri manat	2000		1993	B	1992–95	2005	6	A	G	C	G
Bahamas, The	Bahamian dollar	2006		1993	B			6		G	B	G
Bahrain	Bahraini dinar	1985		1968	P		2005	6		G	B	G
Bangladesh	Bangladeshi taka	1995/96		1993	B		2005	6	A	G	C	G
Barbados	Barbados dollar	1974		1968	B			6		G	B	G
Belarus	Belarusian rubel	[a]	2000	1993	B	1990–95	2005	6	A	G	C	S
Belgium	Euro	2005		1993	B		Rolling	6		S	C	S
Belize	Belize dollar	2000		1993	B			6	A	G	B	G
Benin	CFA franc	1985		1968	P	1992	2005	6	A	S	B	G
Bermuda	Bermuda dollar	2006		1993	B			6		G		
Bhutan	Bhutanese ngultrum	2000		1993	B		2005	6	A	G	C	G
Bolivia	Bolivian Boliviano	1990		1968	B	1960–85	2005	6	A	G	C	G
Bosnia and Herzegovina	Bosnia and Herzegovina convertible mark	[a]	1996	1993	B		Rolling	6	A	S	C	G
Botswana	Botswana pula	2006		1993	B		2005	6	A	G	B	G
Brazil	Brazilian real	2000		1993	B		2005	6	A	G	C	S
Brunei Darussalam	Brunei dollar	2000		1993	P		2005			S		G
Bulgaria	Bulgarian lev	[a]	2002	1993	B	1978–89, 1991–92	Rolling	6	A	S	C	S
Burkina Faso	CFA franc	1999		1993	B	1992–93	2005	6	A	G	B	G
Burundi	Burundi franc	2005		1993	B		2005	6	A	S	C	G
Cabo Verde	Cabo Verde escudo	2007		1993	P		2005	6	A	G	B	G
Cambodia	Cambodian riel	2000		1993	B		2005	6	A	S	B	G
Cameroon	CFA franc	2000		1993	B		2005	6	A	S	B	G
Canada	Canadian dollar	2005		2008	B		2011	6		G	C	S
Cayman Islands	Cayman Islands dollar	2007		1993						G		
Central African Republic	CFA franc	2000		1968	B		2005	6	A	S	B	
Chad	CFA franc	2005		1993	B		2005	6	P	S		G
Channel Islands	Pound sterling	2003	2007	1968	B							
Chile	Chilean peso	2008		1993	B		2011	6		S	C	S
China	Chinese yuan	2000		1993	P	1978–93	2005	6	P	S	C	G
Hong Kong SAR, China	Hong Kong dollar	[a]	2011	2008	B		2005	6		G	C	S
Macao SAR, China	Macao pataca	2011		1993	B		2005	6		G	C	S
Colombia	Colombian peso	2005		1993	B	1992–94	2005	6	A	G	C	S
Comoros	Comorian franc	1990		1968	P		2005		A	S		G
Congo, Dem. Rep.	Congolese franc	2000		1968	B	1999–2001	2005	6	A	S	C	G
Congo, Rep.	CFA franc	1990		1968	P	1993	2005	6	P	S	C	G
Costa Rica	Costa Rican colon	1991		1993	B			6	A	S	C	G
Côte d'Ivoire	CFA franc	1996		1968	P		2005	6	E	S	B	G
Croatia	Croatian kuna	[a]	2005	1993	B		Rolling	6		G	C	S
Cuba	Cuban peso	2005		1993	B					S		
Curaçao	Netherlands Antilles guilder			1993								
Cyprus	Euro	[a]	2000	1993	B		Rolling	6		G	C	S
Czech Republic	Czech koruna	2005		1993	B		Rolling	6		S	C	S

○ Front | ? User guide | ◉ World view | 🗣 People | Environment

Economy	Latest population census	Latest demographic, education, or health household survey	Source of most recent income and expenditure data	Vital registration complete	Latest agricultural census	Latest industrial data	Latest trade data	Latest water withdrawal data
Afghanistan	1979	MICS, 2010/11	IHS, 2008		2013/14		2012	2000
Albania	2011	DHS, 2008/09	LSMS, 2012	Yes	2012	2010	2012	2006
Algeria	2008	MICS, 2012	IHS, 1995				2012	2001
American Samoa	2010			Yes	2007			
Andorra	2011b			Yes			2006	
Angola	1970	MIS, 2011	IHS, 2008		2015			2005
Antigua and Barbuda	2011			Yes	2007		2012	2005
Argentina	2010	MICS, 2011/12	IHS, 2012	Yes	2013	2002	2012	2005
Armenia	2011	DHS, 2010	IHS, 2012	Yes	2013/14		2012	2000
Aruba	2010			Yes			2012	2007
Australia	2011		ES/BS, 1994	Yes	2011	2010	2012	2000
Austria	2011b		IS, 2000	Yes	2010	2009	2012	2002
Azerbaijan	2009	DHS, 2006	ES/BS, 2012	Yes	2015	2010	2012	2005
Bahamas, The	2010						2012	
Bahrain	2010			Yes			2011	2003
Bangladesh	2011	DHS, 2011	IHS, 2010		2008		2007	2008
Barbados	2010	MICS, 2012		Yes	2010c		2012	2005
Belarus	2009	MICS, 2012	ES/BS, 2012	Yes		2009	2012	2000
Belgium	2011		IHS, 2000	Yes	2010	2009	2012	2007
Belize	2010	MICS, 2011	ES/BS, 2011				2012	2000
Benin	2013	DHS, 2011/12	CWIQ, 2011		2011/12		2010	2001
Bermuda	2010			Yes			2012	
Bhutan	2005	MICS, 2010	IHS, 2012		2009		2011	2008
Bolivia	2012	DHS, 2008	IHS, 2009		2013	2001	2012	2000
Bosnia and Herzegovina	2013	MICS, 2011/12	LSMS, 2007	Yes			2012	2009
Botswana	2011	DHS, 1988	ES/BS, 2009/10		2011c	2010	2012	2000
Brazil	2010	WHS, 2003	IHS, 2012		2006	2010	2012	2006
Brunei Darussalam	2011			Yes			2012	1994
Bulgaria	2011	LSMS, 2007	ES/BS, 2007	Yes	2010	2010	2012	2009
Burkina Faso	2006	DHS, 2010	CWIQ, 2009		2010		2011	2001
Burundi	2008	MIS, 2012	CWIQ, 2006				2012	2000
Cabo Verde	2010	DHS, 2005	ES/BS, 2007	Yes	2014		2012	2001
Cambodia	2008	DHS, 2010	IHS, 2011		2013	2000	2012	2006
Cameroon	2005	DHS, 2011	PS, 2007			2002	2012	2000
Canada	2011		LFS, 2000	Yes	2011	2010	2012	1986
Cayman Islands	2010			Yes				
Central African Republic	2003	MICS, 2010	PS, 2008				2011	2005
Chad	2009	MICS, 2010	PS, 2002/03		2010/11		1995	2005
Channel Islands	2009/11d			Yese				
Chile	2012		IHS, 2011	Yes	2007	2008	2012	2007
China	2010	NSS, 2007	IHS, 2008		2007	2007	2012	2005
Hong Kong SAR, China	2011f			Yes		2010	2012	
Macao SAR, China	2011			Yes		2010	2012	
Colombia	2006	DHS, 2010	IHS, 2012		2013	2010	2012	2000
Comoros	2003	DHS, 2012	IHS, 2004				2009	1999
Congo, Dem. Rep.	1984	DHS, 2013	1-2-3, 2004/05					2005
Congo, Rep.	2007	DHS, 2011/12	CWIQ/PS, 2011		2013	2009	2010	2002
Costa Rica	2011	MICS, 2011	IHS, 2012	Yes	2014	2010	2012	1997
Côte d'Ivoire	1998	DHS, 2011/12	IHS, 2008		2014		2012	2005
Croatia	2011	WHS, 2003	ES/BS, 2008	Yes	2010		2012	2010
Cuba	2012	MICS, 2010/11		Yes			2006	2007
Curaçao								
Cyprus	2011			Yes	2010	2010	2012	2009
Czech Republic	2011	WHS, 2003	IS, 1996	Yes	2010	2007	2012	2007

Primary data documentation

	Currency	Base year	Reference year	System of National Accounts	SNA price valuation	Alternative conversion factor	PPP survey year	Balance of Payments Manual in use	External debt	System of trade	Accounting concept	IMF data dissemination standard
Denmark	Danish krone	2005		1993	B		Rolling	6		S	C	S
Djibouti	Djibouti franc	1990		1968	B		2005	6	A	G		G
Dominica	East Caribbean dollar	2006		1993	B			6	A	S	B	G
Dominican Republic	Dominican peso	1991		1993	B			6	A	G	C	G
Ecuador	U.S. dollar	2007		2008	B		2005	6	A	G	B	S
Egypt, Arab Rep.	Egyptian pound	1991/92		1993	B		2005	6	A	G	C	S
El Salvador	U.S. dollar	1990		1968	B			6	A	S	C	S
Equatorial Guinea	CFA franc	2000		1968	B	1965–84	2005			G	B	
Eritrea	Eritrean nakfa	2000		1968	B			6	E			
Estonia	Euro	2005		1993	B	1987–95	Rolling	6		S	C	S
Ethiopia	Ethiopian birr	2011		1993	B		2005	6	A	G	B	G
Faeroe Islands	Danish krone			1993	B			6		G		
Fiji	Fijian dollar	2005		1993	B		2005	6	A	G	B	S
Finland	Euro	2005		1993	B		Rolling	6		S	C	S
France	Euro		2005[a]	1993	B		Rolling	6		S	C	S
French Polynesia	CFP franc	1990/91		1993						S		
Gabon	CFA franc	1991		1993	P	1993	2005	6	A	S		G
Gambia, The	Gambian dalasi	2004		1993	P		2005	6	A	G	B	G
Georgia	Georgian lari		1996[a]	1993	B	1990–95	2005	6	A	G	C	S
Germany	Euro	2005		1993	B		Rolling	6		S	C	S
Ghana	New Ghanaian cedi	2006		1993	B	1973–87	2005	6	P	G	B	G
Greece	Euro		2005[a]	1993	B		Rolling	6		S	C	S
Greenland	Danish krone	1990		1993						G		
Grenada	East Caribbean dollar	2006		1968	B			6	A	S	B	G
Guam	U.S. dollar			1993						G		
Guatemala	Guatemalan quetzal	2001		1993	B			6	E	S	B	G
Guinea	Guinean franc	2003		1993	B		2005	6	E	S	B	G
Guinea-Bissau	CFA franc	2005		1993	B		2005	6	E	G		G
Guyana	Guyana dollar	2006		1993	B			6	A	S		G
Haiti	Haitian gourde	1986/87		1968	B	1991		6	A	G		G
Honduras	Honduran lempira	2000		1993	B	1988–89		6	A	S	C	G
Hungary	Hungarian forint		2005[a]	1993	B		Rolling	6	A	S	C	S
Iceland	Iceland krona	2005		1993	B		Rolling	6		G	C	S
India	Indian rupee	2004/05		1993	B		2005	6	A	G	C	S
Indonesia	Indonesian rupiah	2000		1993	P		2005	6	A	S	B	S
Iran, Islamic Rep.	Iranian rial	1997/98		1993	B	1980–2002	2005	6	A	S	C	G
Iraq	Iraqi dinar	1988		1968	P	1997, 2004	2005	6				G
Ireland	Euro	2005		1993	B		Rolling	6		G	C	S
Isle of Man	Pound sterling	2003		1968								
Israel	Israeli new shekel	2005		1993	P		2011	6		S	C	S
Italy	Euro	2005		1993	B		Rolling	6		S	C	S
Jamaica	Jamaican dollar	2007		1993	B			6	A	G	C	G
Japan	Japanese yen	2005		1993	B		2011	6		G	C	S
Jordan	Jordanian dinar	1994		1968	B		2005	6	A	G		S
Kazakhstan	Kazakh tenge		2000[a]	1993	B	1987–95	2005	6	A	G	C	S
Kenya	Kenyan shilling	2001		1993	B		2005	6	A	G	B	G
Kiribati	Australian dollar	2006		1993	B			6		G	B	G
Korea, Dem. People's Rep.	Democratic People's Republic of Korean won			1968				6				
Korea, Rep.	Korean won	2005		1993	B		2011	6		G	C	S
Kosovo	Euro	2008		1993	B				A			G
Kuwait	Kuwaiti dinar	1995		1968	P		2005	6		S	B	G
Kyrgyz Republic	Kyrgyz som		1995[a]	1993	B	1990–95	2005	6	A	S	B	S
Lao PDR	Lao kip	2002		1993	B		2005	6	P	S	B	
Latvia	Latvian lats	2000		1993	B	1987–95	Rolling	6		S	C	S
Lebanon	Lebanese pound	1997		1993	B		2005	6	A	G	B	G
Lesotho	Lesotho loti	2004		1993	B		2005	6	A	G	C	G

 Front User guide World view People | Environment

	Latest population census	Latest demographic, education, or health household survey	Source of most recent income and expenditure data	Vital registration complete	Latest agricultural census	Latest industrial data	Latest trade data	Latest water withdrawal data
Denmark	2011		ITR, 1997	Yes	2010	2009	2012	2009
Djibouti	2009	MICS, 2006	PS, 2002				2009	2000
Dominica	2011			Yes			2012	2004
Dominican Republic	2010	DHS, 2013	IHS, 2012		2012/13		2012	2005
Ecuador	2010	RHS, 2004	IHS, 2012		2013/15	2008	2012	2005
Egypt, Arab Rep.	2006	DHS, 2008	ES/BS, 2011	Yes	2009/10	2010	2012	2000
El Salvador	2007	RHS, 2008	IHS, 2012	Yes	2007/08		2012	2007
Equatorial Guinea	2002	DHS, 2011	PS, 2006					2000
Eritrea	1984	DHS, 2002	PS, 1993				2003	2004
Estonia	2012	WHS, 2003	ES/BS, 2004	Yes	2010	2010	2012	2007
Ethiopia	2007	DHS, 2011	ES/BS, 2010/11			2009	2012	2002
Faeroe Islands	2011			Yes			2009	
Fiji	2007		ES/BS, 2009	Yes	2009	2009	2012	2000
Finland	2010		IS, 2000	Yes	2010	2009	2012	2005
France	2006^g		ES/BS, 1994/95	Yes	2010	2009	2012	2007
French Polynesia	2007			Yes			2012	
Gabon	2013	DHS, 2012	CWIQ/IHS, 2005				2009	2005
Gambia, The	2013	DHS, 2013	IHS, 2010			2004	2011	2000
Georgia	2002	MICS, 2005; RHS, 2005	IHS, 2011	Yes		2010	2012	2005
Germany	2011		IHS, 2000	Yes	2010	2009	2012	2007
Ghana	2010	MICS, 2011	LSMS, 2005/06		2013/14	2003	2012	2000
Greece	2011		IHS, 2000	Yes	2009	2007	2012	2007
Greenland	2010			Yes			2012	
Grenada	2011	RHS, 1985		Yes	2012		2009	2005
Guam	2010			Yes	2007			
Guatemala	2002	RHS, 2008/09	LSMS, 2011	Yes	2013		2012	2006
Guinea	1996	DHS, 2012	CWIQ, 2012				2008	2001
Guinea-Bissau	2009	MICS, 2010	CWIQ, 2010				2005	2000
Guyana	2012	DHS, 2009	IHS, 1998				2012	2000
Haiti	2003	HIV/MCH SPA, 2013	IHS, 2001		2008/09		1997	2000
Honduras	2013	DHS, 2011/12	IHS, 2010		2013		2012	2006
Hungary	2011	WHS, 2003	ES/BS, 2007	Yes	2010	2009	2012	2007
Iceland	2011			Yes	2010	2005	2012	2005
India	2011	DHS, 2005/06	IHS, 2012		2011	2009	2012	2010
Indonesia	2010	DHS, 2012	IHS, 2013		2013	2009	2012	2000
Iran, Islamic Rep.	2011	DHS, 2000	ES/BS, 2005	Yes	2013	2009	2011	2004
Iraq	1997	MICS, 2011	IHS, 2007		2011/12			2000
Ireland	2011		IHS, 2000	Yes	2010	2009	2012	1979
Isle of Man	2011			Yes				
Israel	2009		ES/BS, 2001	Yes		2009	2012	2004
Italy	2012		ES/BS, 2000	Yes	2010	2009	2012	2000
Jamaica	2011	MICS, 2011	LSMS, 2010		2007		2012	1993
Japan	2010		IS, 1993	Yes	2010	2010	2012	2001
Jordan	2004	DHS, 2012	ES/BS, 2010		2007	2010	2012	2005
Kazakhstan	2009	MICS, 2010/11	ES/BS, 2012	Yes			2012	2010
Kenya	2009	MIS, 2010; HIV/MCH SPA, 2010	IHS, 2005/06		2009^c	2010	2010	2003
Kiribati	2010						2012	
Korea, Dem. People's Rep.	2008	MICS, 2009						2005
Korea, Rep.	2010		ES/BS, 1998	Yes	2010	2008	2012	2002
Kosovo	2011		IHS, 2011					
Kuwait	2011	FHS, 1996		Yes		2010	2009	2002
Kyrgyz Republic	2009	DHS, 2012	ES/BS, 2012	Yes	2014	2010	2012	2006
Lao PDR	2005	MICS, 2011/12	ES/BS, 2008		2010/11			2005
Latvia	2011	WHS, 2003	IHS, 2008	Yes	2010	2010	2012	2002
Lebanon	1970	MICS, 2000		Yes	2011	2007	2012	2005
Lesotho	2006	DHS, 2009	ES/BS, 2002/03		2010		2009	2000

Primary data documentation

	Currency	Base year	Reference year	System of National Accounts	SNA price valuation	Alternative conversion factor	PPP survey year	Balance of Payments Manual in use	External debt	System of trade	Accounting concept	IMF data dissemination standard
Liberia	Liberian dollar	2000		1968	P		2005	6	A	S	B	G
Libya	Libyan dinar	1999		1993	B	1986		6		G		G
Liechtenstein	Swiss franc	1990		1993	B					S		
Lithuania	Lithuanian litas	2000		1993	B	1990–95	Rolling	6		G	C	S
Luxembourg	Euro		a 2005	1993	B		Rolling	6		S	C	S
Macedonia, FYR	Macedonian denar	1995		1993	B		Rolling	6	A	S	C	S
Madagascar	Malagasy ariary	1984		1968	B		2005	6	A	S	C	G
Malawi	Malawi kwacha	2009		1993	B		2005	6	A	G		G
Malaysia	Malaysian ringgit	2005		1993	P		2005	6	E	G	B	S
Maldives	Maldivian rufiyaa	2003		1993	B		2005	6	A	G	C	G
Mali	CFA franc	1987		1968	B		2005	6	A	S	B	G
Malta	Euro	2005		1993	B		Rolling	6		G	C	S
Marshall Islands	U.S. dollar	2004		1968	B					G		
Mauritania	Mauritanian ouguiya	2004		1993	B		2005	6	A	S		G
Mauritius	Mauritian rupee	2006		1993	B		2005	6	A	G		S
Mexico	Mexican peso	2008		2008	B		2011	6	A	G	C	S
Micronesia, Fed. Sts.	U.S. dollar	2004		1993	B					G		
Moldova	Moldovan leu		a 1996	1993	B	1990–95	2005	6	A	G	C	S
Monaco	Euro	1990		1993						S		
Mongolia	Mongolian tugrik	2005		1993	B		2005	6	A	G	C	G
Montenegro	Euro	2000		1993	B		Rolling	6	A	S		G
Morocco	Moroccan dirham	1998		1993	B		2005	6	A	S	C	S
Mozambique	New Mozambican metical	2003		1993	B	1992–95	2005	6	A	S	B	G
Myanmar	Myanmar kyat	2005/06		1968	P			6	E	G	C	G
Namibia	Namibian dollar	2004/05		1993	B		2005	6		G	B	G
Nepal	Nepalese rupee	2000/01		1993	B		2005	6	A	G	B	G
Netherlands	Euro		a 2005	1993	B		Rolling	6		S	C	S
New Caledonia	CFP franc	1990		1993						S		
New Zealand	New Zealand dollar	2005/06		1993	B		2011	6		G	C	
Nicaragua	Nicaraguan gold cordoba	2006		1993	B	1965–95		6	A	G	B	G
Niger	CFA franc	2006		1993	P	1993	2005	6	A	S	B	G
Nigeria	Nigerian naira	1990		1993	B	1971–98	2005	6	A	G	B	G
Northern Mariana Islands	U.S. dollar			1968								
Norway	Norwegian krone		a 2005	1993	B		Rolling	6		G	C	S
Oman	Rial Omani	1988		1993	P		2005	6		G	B	G
Pakistan	Pakistani rupee	2005/06		1993	B		2005	6	A	G	B	G
Palau	U.S. dollar	2005		1993	B					S		G
Panama	Panamanian balboa	1996		1993	B			6	A	S	C	G
Papua New Guinea	Papua New Guinea kina	1998		1993	B	1989		6	A	G	B	G
Paraguay	Paraguayan guarani	1994		1993	B		2005	6	A	S	C	G
Peru	Peruvian new sol	1994		1993	B	1985–90	2005	6	A	S	C	S
Philippines	Philippine peso	2000		1993	P		2005	6	A	G	B	S
Poland	Polish zloty		a 2005	1993	B		Rolling	6		S	C	S
Portugal	Euro	2005		1993	B		Rolling	6		S	C	S
Puerto Rico	U.S. dollar	1954		1968	P					G		
Qatar	Qatari riyal	2001		1993	P		2005			S	B	G
Romania	New Romanian leu	2000		1993	B	1987–89, 1992	Rolling	6	A	S	C	S
Russian Federation	Russian ruble	2000		1993	B	1987–95	2011	6		G	C	S
Rwanda	Rwandan franc	2006		1993	P	1994	2005	6	A	G	B	S
Samoa	Samoan tala	2002		1993	B			6	A	S	B	G
San Marino	Euro	1995	2000	1993	B						C	G
São Tomé and Príncipe	São Tomé and Principe dobra	2001		1993	P		2005	6	A	S	B	G
Saudi Arabia	Saudi Arabian riyal	1999		1993	P		2005	6		S		G
Senegal	CFA franc	1999	1987	1993	B		2005	6	A	G	B	G
Serbia	New Serbian dinar		a 2002	1993	B		Rolling	6	A	S	C	G

	Latest population census	Latest demographic, education, or health household survey	Source of most recent income and expenditure data	Vital registration complete	Latest agricultural census	Latest industrial data	Latest trade data	Latest water withdrawal data
Liberia	2008	DHS, 2013	CWIQ, 2007		2008[c]			2000
Libya	2006				2013/14		2010	2000
Liechtenstein	2010			Yes			2010	2000
Lithuania	2011		ES/BS, 2008	Yes	2010	2010	2012	2007
Luxembourg	2011			Yes	2010	2009	2012	1999
Macedonia, FYR	2002	MICS, 2011	ES/BS, 2009	Yes	2007	2010	2012	2007
Madagascar	1993	MIS, 2013	PS, 2010			2006	2012	2000
Malawi	2008	HIV/MCH SPA, 2013	IHS, 2010/11		2006/07	2009	2011	2005
Malaysia	2010	WHS, 2003	ES/BS, 2012	Yes	2015	2010	2012	2005
Maldives	2006	DHS, 2009	IHS, 2010	Yes			2012	2008
Mali	2009	DHS, 2012/13	IHS, 2009/10				2012	2000
Malta	2011			Yes			2012	2000
Marshall Islands	2011				2010	2008	2012	2002
Mauritania	2013	MICS, 2011	IHS, 2008		2011[c]			
Mauritius	2011	RHS, 1991					2012	2005
Mexico	2010	ENADID, 2009	IHS, 2012	Yes	2013/14	2010	2012	2003
Micronesia, Fed. Sts.	2010		IHS, 2000		2007	2010	2012	2009
Moldova	2004	MICS, 2012	ES/BS, 2012	Yes	2011	2010	2012	2007
Monaco	2008			Yes				2009
Mongolia	2010	MICS, 2010	LSMS, 2012	Yes	2012	2008	2007	2009
Montenegro	2011	MICS, 2005/06	ES/BS, 2011	Yes	2010		2012	2010
Morocco	2004	MICS/PAPFAM, 2006	ES/BS, 2007				2012	2010
Mozambique	2007	DHS, 2011	ES/BS, 2008/09		2009/10		2012	2001
Myanmar	1983	MICS, 2009/10			2010	2003	2010	2000
Namibia	2011	DHS, 2013	ES/BS, 2009/10		2014		2012	2002
Nepal	2011	DHS, 2011	LSMS, 2011		2011/12	2008	2011	2006
Netherlands	2011		IHS, 1999	Yes	2010	2008	2012	2008
New Caledonia	2009			Yes			2012	
New Zealand	2013		IS, 1997	Yes	2012	2009	2012	2002
Nicaragua	2005	RHS, 2006/2007	LSMS, 2009		2011		2012	2001
Niger	2012	DHS, 2012	CWIQ/PS, 2007		2004-08	2002	2012	2005
Nigeria	2006	DHS, 2013	IHS, 2010		2013		2012	2005
Northern Mariana Islands	2010				2007			
Norway	2011		IS, 2000	Yes	2010	2008	2012	2006
Oman	2010	MICS, 2012			2012/13	2010	2012	2003
Pakistan	1998	DHS, 2012/13	IHS, 2008		2010	2006	2012	2008
Palau	2010			Yes			2012	
Panama	2010	LSMS, 2008	IHS, 2011		2011	2001	2011	2000
Papua New Guinea	2011	LSMS, 1996	IHS, 2009/10				2012	2005
Paraguay	2012	RHS, 2008	IHS, 2011		2008	2002	2012	2000
Peru	2007	Continuous DHS, 2013	IHS, 2012		2012	2010	2012	2000
Philippines	2010	DHS, 2013	ES/BS, 2012	Yes	2012	2008	2012	2009
Poland	2011		ES/BS, 2010	Yes	2010	2009	2012	2009
Portugal	2011		IS, 1997	Yes	2009	2009	2012	2002
Puerto Rico	2010	RHS, 1995/96		Yes	2007	2006		2005
Qatar	2010	MICS, 2012		Yes		2010	2012	2005
Romania	2011	RHS, 1999	LFS, 2010	Yes	2010	2010	2012	2009
Russian Federation	2010	WHS, 2003	IHS, 2012	Yes	2014	2010	2012	2001
Rwanda	2012	MIS, 2013	IHS, 2011		2008		2012	2000
Samoa	2011	DHS, 2009			2009		2012	
San Marino	2010			Yes				
São Tomé and Príncipe	2012	DHS, 2008/09	PS, 2009/10		2011/12		2012	1993
Saudi Arabia	2010	Demographic survey, 2007			2010	2006	2011	2006
Senegal	2013	Continuous DHS, 2013/14; HIV/MCH SPA, 2013/14	PS, 2010/11		2013	2010	2012	2002
Serbia	2011	MICS, 2010	IHS, 2010	Yes	2012	2010		2009

	Currency	Base year	Reference year	System of National Accounts	SNA price valuation	Alternative conversion factor	PPP survey year	Balance of Payments Manual in use	External debt	System of trade	Accounting concept	IMF data dissemination standard
Seychelles	Seychelles rupee	2006		1993	P			6	A	G	C	G
Sierra Leone	Sierra Leonean leone	2006		1993	B		2005	6	A	S	B	G
Singapore	Singapore dollar	2005		2008	B		2005	6		G	C	S
Sint Maarten	Netherlands Antilles guilder			1993								
Slovak Republic	Euro	2005		1993	B		Rolling	6		S	C	S
Slovenia	Euro	a	2005	1993	B		Rolling	6		S	C	S
Solomon Islands	Solomon Islands dollar	2004		1993	B			6	A	S		G
Somalia	Somali shilling	1985		1968	B	1977–90			E			
South Africa	South African rand	2005		1993	B		2005	6	P	G	C	S
South Sudan	South Sudanese pound	2009		1993								
Spain	Euro	2005		1993	B		Rolling	6		S	C	S
Sri Lanka	Sri Lankan rupee	2002		1993	P		2005	6	A	G	B	G
St. Kitts and Nevis	East Caribbean dollar	2006		1993	B			6		S	B	G
St. Lucia	East Caribbean dollar	2006		1968	B			6	A	S	B	G
St. Martin	Euro			1993								
St. Vincent and the Grenadines	East Caribbean dollar	2006		1993	B			6	A	S	B	G
Sudan	Sudanese pound	1981/82h	1996	1968	B		2005	6	A	G	B	G
Suriname	Suriname dollar	2007		1993	B			6		G	B	G
Swaziland	Swaziland lilangeni	2000		1993	B		2005	6	A	G	C	G
Sweden	Swedish krona	a	2005	1993	B		Rolling	6		G	C	S
Switzerland	Swiss franc	2005		1993	B		Rolling	6		S	C	S
Syrian Arab Republic	Syrian pound	2000		1968	B	1970–2010	2005	6	E	S	B	G
Tajikistan	Tajik somoni	a	2000	1993	B	1990–95	2005	6	A	G	C	G
Tanzania	Tanzanian shilling	a	2001	1993	B		2005	6	A	G	B	G
Thailand	Thai baht	1988		1993	P		2005	6	A	S	C	S
Timor-Leste	U.S. dollar	2010		2008	B					S		G
Togo	CFA franc	2000		1968	P		2005	6	A	S	B	G
Tonga	Tongan pa'anga	2010/11		1993	B			6	A	G		G
Trinidad and Tobago	Trinidad and Tobago dollar	2000		1993	B			6		S	C	G
Tunisia	Tunisian dinar	1990		1993	B		2005	6	A	G	C	S
Turkey	New Turkish lira	1998		1993	B		Rolling	6	A	S	C	S
Turkmenistan	New Turkmen manat	2005		1993	B	1987–95, 1997–2007		6	E	G		
Turks and Caicos Islands	U.S. dollar			1993						G		
Tuvalu	Australian dollar	2005		1968	B					G		G
Uganda	Ugandan shilling	2001/02		1968	B	1987–95	2005	6	A	G	B	G
Ukraine	Ukrainian hryvnia	a	2003	1993	B		2005	6	A	G	C	S
United Arab Emirates	U.A.E. dirham	2007		1993	P			6		G	C	S
United Kingdom	Pound sterling	2005		1993	B		Rolling	6		G	C	S
United States	U.S. dollar	a	2005	2008	B		2011	6		G	C	S
Uruguay	Uruguayan peso	2005		1993	B		2005	6		G	C	S
Uzbekistan	Uzbek sum	a	1997	1993	B	1990–95		6	A	G		
Vanuatu	Vanuatu vatu	2006		1993	B			6	E	G	B	G
Venezuela, RB	Venezuelan bolivar fuerte	1997		1993	B		2005	6	A	G	C	G
Vietnam	Vietnamese dong	2010		1993	P	1991	2005	6	A	G		G
Virgin Islands (U.S.)	U.S. dollar	1982		1968						G		
West Bank and Gaza	Israeli new shekel	1997		1968	B			6		S	B	S
Yemen, Rep.	Yemeni rial	1990		1993	P	1990–96	2005	6	A	S	B	G
Zambia	New Zambian kwacha	1994		1968	B	1990–92	2005	6	A	S	B	G
Zimbabwe	U.S. dollar	2009		1993	B	1991, 1998	2005	6	A	G	C	G

	Latest population census	Latest demographic, education, or health household survey	Source of most recent income and expenditure data	Vital registration complete	Latest agricultural census	Latest industrial data	Latest trade data	Latest water withdrawal data
Seychelles	2010		BS, 2006/07	Yes	2011		2008	2005
Sierra Leone	2004	DHS, 2013; MIS, 2013	IHS, 2011				2002	2005
Singapore	2010	NHS, 2010		Yes		2010	2012	1975
Sint Maarten	2011			Yes				
Slovak Republic	2011	WHS, 2003	IS, 2009	Yes	2010	2009	2012	2007
Slovenia	2011[b]	WHS, 2003	ES/BS, 2004	Yes	2010	2010	2012	2009
Solomon Islands	2009		IHS, 2005/06		2012/13		2012	
Somalia	1987	MICS, 2006						2003
South Africa	2011	DHS, 2003; WHS, 2003	ES/BS, 2010		2007	2010	2012	2000
South Sudan	2008		ES/BS, 2009					
Spain	2011		IHS, 2000	Yes	2010	2009	2012	2008
Sri Lanka	2012	DHS, 2006/07	ES/BS, 2010	Yes	2013/14	2010	2012	2005
St. Kitts and Nevis	2011			Yes			2011	
St. Lucia	2010	MICS, 2012	IHS, 1995	Yes	2007		2008	2005
St. Martin								
St. Vincent and the Grenadines	2011			Yes			2012	1995
Sudan	2008	SHHS, 2010	ES/BS, 2009		2013/14	2001	2011	2005[i]
Suriname	2012	MICS, 2010	ES/BS, 1999	Yes	2008		2011	2000
Swaziland	2007	MICS, 2010	ES/BS, 2009/10		2007[c]		2007	2000
Sweden	2011		IS, 2000	Yes	2010	2009	2012	2007
Switzerland	2010		ES/BS, 2000	Yes	2008	2007	2012	2000
Syrian Arab Republic	2004	MICS, 2006	ES/BS, 2004		2014		2010	2005
Tajikistan	2010	DHS, 2012	LSMS, 2009		2013		2000	2006
Tanzania	2012	HIV/MCH SPA, 2013/14	ES/BS, 2011/12		2007/08	2007	2012	2002
Thailand	2010	MICS, 2012	IHS, 2011		2013	2006	2012	2007
Timor-Leste	2010	DHS, 2009/10	LSMS, 2007		2010[c]		2005	2004
Togo	2010	DHS, 2013	CWIQ, 2011		2011/12		2012	2002
Tonga	2006						2012	
Trinidad and Tobago	2011	MICS, 2011	IHS, 1992	Yes		2006	2010	2000
Tunisia	2004	MICS, 2011/12	IHS, 2010		2014/15	2006	2011	2001
Turkey	2011	DHS, 2003; WHS, 2003	LFS, 2009			2009	2012	2003
Turkmenistan	2012	MICS, 2011	LSMS, 1998	Yes			2000	2004
Turks and Caicos Islands	2012			Yes			2012	
Tuvalu	2012						2008	
Uganda	2002	AIS, 2011; DHS, 2011	PS, 2009/10		2008/09	2000	2012	2002
Ukraine	2001	MICS, 2012	ES/BS, 2009	Yes	2012/13		2012	2005
United Arab Emirates	2010				2012		2011	2005
United Kingdom	2011		IS, 1999	Yes	2010	2009	2011	2005
United States	2010		LFS, 2000	Yes	2010	2009	2012	2007
Uruguay	2011	MICS, 2012	IHS, 2012	Yes	2012	2008	2012	2005
Uzbekistan	1989	MICS, 2006	ES/BS, 2011	Yes	2011	2008	2012	2000
Vanuatu	2009	MICS, 2007						2005
Venezuela, RB	2011	MICS, 2000	IHS, 2012	Yes	2007		2011	2000
Vietnam	2009	MICS, 2010/11	IHS, 2010	Yes	2011/12	2010	2011	2005
Virgin Islands (U.S.)	2010			Yes	2007			
West Bank and Gaza	2007	MICS, 2010	IHS, 2009			2010		2005
Yemen, Rep.	2004	DHS, 2013	ES/BS, 2005			2006	2012	2005
Zambia	2010	DHS, 2013	IHS, 2010		2010[c]		2011	2002
Zimbabwe	2012	DHS, 2010/11	IHS, 2011/12				2012	2002

Note: For explanation of the abbreviations used in the table, see notes following the table.
a. Original chained constant price data are rescaled. b. Population data compiled from administrative registers. c. Population and Housing Census. d. Latest population census: Guernsey, 2009; Jersey, 2011 e. Vital registration for Guernsey and Jersey. f. The population censuses for 1986 and 1996 were based on a one-in-seven sample of the population, while that for 2006 was based on a one-in-ten sample of the population. g. Rolling census based on continuous sample survey. h. Reporting period switch from fiscal year to calendar year from 1996. Pre-1996 data converted to calendar year. i. Includes South Sudan.

• **Base year** is the base or pricing period used for constant price calculations in the country's national accounts. Price indexes derived from national accounts aggregates, such as the implicit deflator for gross domestic product (GDP), express the price level relative to base year prices. • **Reference year** is the year in which the local currency constant price series of a country is valued. The reference year is usually the same as the base year used to report the constant price series. However, when the constant price data are chain linked, the base year is changed annually, so the data are rescaled to a specific reference year to provide a consistent time series. When the country has not rescaled following a change in base year, World Bank staff rescale the data to maintain a longer historical series. To allow for cross-country comparison and data aggregation, constant price data reported in *World Development Indicators* are rescaled to a common reference year (2000) and currency (U.S. dollars). • **System of National Accounts** identifies whether a country uses the 1968, 1993, or 2008 System of National Accounts (SNA). • **SNA price valuation** shows whether value added in the national accounts is reported at basic prices (B) or producer prices (P). Producer prices include taxes paid by producers and thus tend to overstate the actual value added in production. However, value added can be higher at basic prices than at producer prices in countries with high agricultural subsidies. • **Alternative conversion factor** identifies the countries and years for which a World Bank–estimated conversion factor has been used in place of the official exchange rate (line rf in the International Monetary Fund's [IMF] *International Financial Statistics*). See *Statistical methods* for further discussion of alternative conversion factors. • **Purchasing power parity (PPP) survey year** is the latest available survey year for the International Comparison Program's estimates of PPPs. • **Balance of Payments Manual in use** refers to the classification system used to compile and report data on balance of payments. 6 refers to the 6th edition of the IMF's *Balance of Payments Manual* (2009). • **External debt** shows debt reporting status for 2012 data. *A* indicates that data are as reported, *P* that data are based on reported or collected information but include an element of staff estimation, and *E* that data are World Bank staff estimates. • **System of trade** refers to the United Nations general trade system (G) or special trade system (S). Under the general trade system goods entering directly for domestic consumption and goods entered into customs storage are recorded as imports at arrival. Under the special trade system goods are recorded as imports when declared for domestic consumption whether at time of entry or on withdrawal from customs storage. Exports under the

general system comprise outward-moving goods: (a) national goods wholly or partly produced in the country; (b) foreign goods, neither transformed nor declared for domestic consumption in the country, that move outward from customs storage; and (c) nationalized goods that have been declared for domestic consumption and move outward without being transformed. Under the special system of trade, exports are categories a and c. In some compilations categories b and c are classified as re-exports. Direct transit trade—goods entering or leaving for transport only—is excluded from both import and export statistics. • **Government finance accounting concept** is the accounting basis for reporting central government financial data. For most countries government finance data have been consolidated (C) into one set of accounts capturing all central government fiscal activities. Budgetary central government accounts (B) exclude some central government units. • **IMF data dissemination standard** shows the countries that subscribe to the IMF's Special Data Dissemination Standard (SDDS) or General Data Dissemination System (GDDS). S refers to countries that subscribe to the SDDS and have posted data on the Dissemination Standards Bulletin Board at http://dsbb.imf.org. G refers to countries that subscribe to the GDDS. The SDDS was established for member countries that have or might seek access to international capital markets to guide them in providing their economic and financial data to the public. The GDDS helps countries disseminate comprehensive, timely, accessible, and reliable economic, financial, and sociodemographic statistics. IMF member countries elect to participate in either the SDDS or the GDDS. Both standards enhance the availability of timely and comprehensive data and therefore contribute to the pursuit of sound macroeconomic policies. The SDDS is also expected to improve the functioning of financial markets. • **Latest population census** shows the most recent year in which a census was conducted and in which at least preliminary results have been released. The preliminary results from the very recent censuses could be reflected in timely revisions if basic data are available, such as population by age and sex, as well as the detailed definition of counting, coverage, and completeness. Countries that hold register-based censuses produce similar census tables every 5 or 10 years. Germany's 2001 census is a register-based test census using a sample of 1.2 percent of the population. A rare case, France conducts a rolling census every year; the 1999 general population census was the last to cover the entire population simultaneously. • **Latest demographic, education, or health household survey** indicates the household surveys used to compile the demographic, education, and health data in section 2. AIS is

HIV/AIDS Indicator Survey, DHS is Demographic and Health Survey, ENADID is National Survey of Demographic Dynamics, FHS is Family Health Survey, HIV/MCH is HIV/Maternal and Child Health, LSMS is Living Standards Measurement Study Survey, MICS is Multiple Indicator Cluster Survey, MIS is Malaria Indicator Survey, NHS is National Health Survey, NSS is National Sample Survey on Population Change, PAPFAM is Pan Arab Project for Family Health, RHS is Reproductive Health Survey, SHHS is Sudan Household Health Survey, SPA is Service Provision Assessments, and WHS is World Health Survey. Detailed information for AIS, DHS, MIS, and SPA are available at www.measuredhs.com; for MICS at www.childinfo.org; for RHS at www.cdc.gov/reproductivehealth; and for WHS at www.who.int/healthinfo/survey/en. • **Source of most recent income and expenditure data** shows household surveys that collect income and expenditure data. Names and detailed information on household surveys can be found on the website of the International Household Survey Network (www.surveynetwork.org). Core Welfare Indicator Questionnaire Surveys (CWIQ), developed by the World Bank, measure changes in key social indicators for different population groups—specifically indicators of access, utilization, and satisfaction with core social and economic services. Expenditure survey/budget surveys (ES/BS) collect detailed information on household consumption as well as on general demographic, social, and economic characteristics. Integrated household surveys (IHS) collect detailed information on a wide variety of topics, including health, education, economic activities, housing, and utilities. Income surveys (IS) collect information on the income and wealth of households as well as various social and economic characteristics. Income tax registers (ITR) provide information on a population's income and allowance, such as gross income, taxable income, and taxes by socioeconomic group. Labor force surveys (LFS) collect information on employment, unemployment, hours of work, income, and wages. Living Standards Measurement Study Surveys (LSMS), developed by the World Bank, provide a comprehensive picture of household welfare and the factors that affect it; they typically incorporate data collection at the individual, household, and community levels. Priority surveys (PS) are a light monitoring survey, designed by the World Bank, that collect data from a large number of households cost-effectively and quickly. 1-2-3 (1-2-3) surveys are implemented in three phases and collect sociodemographic and employment data, data on the informal sector, and information on living conditions and household consumption. • **Vital registration complete** identifies countries that report at least 90 percent complete registries of vital (birth and death)

statistics to the United Nations Statistics Division and are reported in its *Population and Vital Statistics Reports*. Countries with complete vital statistics registries may have more accurate and more timely demographic indicators than other countries. • **Latest agricultural census** shows the most recent year in which an agricultural census was conducted or planned to be conducted, as reported to the Food and Agriculture Organization of the United Nations. • **Latest industrial data** show the most recent year for which manufacturing value added data at the three-digit level of the International Standard Industrial Classification (revision 2 or 3) are available in the United Nations Industrial Development Organization database. • **Latest trade data** show the most recent year for which structure of merchandise trade data from the United Nations Statistics Division's Commodity Trade (Comtrade) database are available. • **Latest water withdrawal data** show the most recent year for which data on freshwater withdrawals have been compiled from a variety of sources.

Exceptional reporting periods

In most economies the fiscal year is concurrent with the calendar year. Exceptions are shown in the table at right. The ending date reported here is for the fiscal year of the central government. Fiscal years for other levels of government and reporting years for statistical surveys may differ.

The **reporting period for national accounts data** is designated as either calendar year basis (CY) or fiscal year basis (FY). Most economies report their national accounts and balance of payments data using calendar years, but some use fiscal years. In *World Development Indicators* fiscal year data are assigned to the calendar year that contains the larger share of the fiscal year. If a country's fiscal year ends before June 30, data are shown in the first year of the fiscal period; if the fiscal year ends on or after June 30, data are shown in the second year of the period. Balance of payments data are reported in *World Development Indicators* by calendar year.

Revisions to national accounts data

National accounts data are revised by national statistical offices when methodologies change or data sources improve. National accounts data in *World Development Indicators* are also revised when data sources change. The following notes, while not comprehensive, provide information on revisions from previous data. • **Australia.** Value added current series updated by the Australian Bureau of Statistics; data have been revised from 1990 onward; Australia reports using SNA 2008. • **Botswana.** Based on official government statistics, national

accounts data have been revised from 2006 onward; the new base year is 2006. Data before 2006 were reported on a fiscal year basis. • **Cabo Verde.** Based on official government statistics and IMF data, national accounts data have been revised from 1990 onward; the new base year is 2007. • **Chad.** Based on IMF data, national accounts data have been revised from 2005 onward; the new base year is 2005. • **Canada.** Canada reports using SNA 2008. • **China.** Based on data from the National Bureau of Statistics, the methodology used to calculate exports and imports of goods and services in constant prices has been revised from 2000 onward. • **Ecuador.** Based on official government data, national accounts have been revised from 1965 onward; the new base year is 2007. Ecuador reports using SNA 2008. • **Ethiopia.** Based on IMF data, national accounts data have been revised from 2000 onward; the new base

Economies with exceptional reporting periods

Economy	Fiscal year end	Reporting period for national accounts data
Afghanistan	Mar. 20	FY
Australia	Jun. 30	FY
Bangladesh	Jun. 30	FY
Botswana	Mar. 31	CY
Canada	Mar. 31	CY
Egypt, Arab Rep.	Jun. 30	FY
Ethiopia	Jul. 7	FY
Gambia, The	Jun. 30	CY
Haiti	Sep. 30	FY
India	Mar. 31	FY
Indonesia	Mar. 31	CY
Iran, Islamic Rep.	Mar. 20	FY
Japan	Mar. 31	CY
Kenya	Jun. 30	CY
Kuwait	Jun. 30	CY
Lesotho	Mar. 31	CY
Malawi	Mar. 31	CY
Marshall Islands	Sep. 30	FY
Micronesia, Fed. Sts.	Sep. 30	FY
Myanmar	Mar. 31	FY
Namibia	Mar. 31	CY
Nepal	Jul. 14	FY
New Zealand	Mar. 31	FY
Pakistan	Jun. 30	FY
Palau	Sep. 30	FY
Puerto Rico	Jun. 30	FY
Samoa	Jun. 30	FY
Sierra Leone	Jun. 30	CY
Singapore	Mar. 31	CY
South Africa	Mar. 31	CY
Swaziland	Mar. 31	CY
Sweden	Jun. 30	CY
Thailand	Sep. 30	CY
Tonga	Jun. 30	FY
Uganda	Jun. 30	FY
United States	Sep. 30	CY
Zimbabwe	Jun. 30	CY

year is 2011. • **Fiji.** Based on data from the Bureau of Statistics, national accounts data on the expenditure side have been revised from 2005 onward; the new base year is 2005. • **Hong Kong SAR, China.** Hong Kong SAR, China, reports using SNA 2008. • **Iraq.** Based on official government data, national accounts have been revised from 2000 onward; the new base year is 1988. • **Kiribati.** Based on IMF, Asian Development Bank, and World Bank data, national accounts data have been revised from 2000 onward. • **Malawi.** Based on IMF data, national accounts data have been revised from 2000 onward; the new base year is 2009. • **Malaysia.** Based on official government statistics, value added services in constant and current prices have been revised from 1990 onward. National accounts data in constant prices have been linked back to 1960; the new base year is 2005. • **Mexico.** The base year has changed to 2008; Mexico reports using SNA 2008. • **Micronesia, Fed. Sts.** Based on the Pacific and Virgin Islands Training Initiative, national accounts data have been revised from 2009 onward. • **Niger.** Based on official government statistics, national accounts data have been revised from 2006 onward; the new base year is 2006. • **Nigeria.** Based on official government statistics, national accounts data have been revised from 1981 onward while preserving historical growth rates for constant GDP at market prices through 2006. • **Paraguay.** National accounts data have been revised from 1960 onward. The output of two hydroelectric plants (shared with neighboring countries) were added, raising GDP from previous estimates • **Romania.** Based on data from the National Statistical Institute, national accounts data have been revised; the new base year is 2000. • **Singapore.** Singapore reports using a blend of SNA 1993 and SNA 2008. • **Timor-Leste.** Based on official government statistics, national accounts data have been revised, and value added is measured at basic prices; the new base year is 2010. Timor-Leste reports using SNA 2008. • **Tuvalu.** Based on data from the IMF, World Bank, and official government statistics, national accounts data have been revised from 2006 onward. Value added is measured at producer prices through 1999 and at basic prices from 2000 onward. • **United States.** The United States reports using SNA 2008. • **Vanuatu.** Based on official government statistics, value added is measured at producer prices through 1997 and at basic prices from 1998 onward. • **Vietnam.** Based on data from the Vietnam Statistics Office, national accounts data have been revised from 2000 onward; the new base year is 2010. • **Zambia.** National accounts data have rebased to reflect the January 1, 2013, introduction of the new Zambian kwacha at a rate of 1,000 old kwacha = 1 new kwacha.

Statistical methods

This section describes some of the statistical procedures used in preparing *World Development Indicators*. It covers the methods employed for calculating regional and income group aggregates and for calculating growth rates, and it describes the *World Bank Atlas* method for deriving the conversion factor used to estimate gross national income (GNI) and GNI per capita in U.S. dollars. Other statistical procedures and calculations are described in the *About the data* sections following each table.

Aggregation rules

Aggregates based on the World Bank's regional and income classifications of economies appear at the end of the tables, including most of those available online. The 214 economies included in these classifications are shown on the flaps on the front and back covers of the book. Aggregates also contain data for Taiwan, China. Most tables also include the aggregate for the euro area, which includes the member states of the Economic and Monetary Union (EMU) of the European Union that have adopted the euro as their currency: Austria, Belgium, Cyprus, Estonia, Finland, France, Germany, Greece, Ireland, Italy, Latvia, Luxembourg, Malta, Netherlands, Portugal, Slovak Republic, Slovenia, and Spain. Other classifications, such as the European Union, are documented in *About the data* for the online tables in which they appear.

Because of missing data, aggregates for groups of economies should be treated as approximations of unknown totals or average values. The aggregation rules are intended to yield estimates for a consistent set of economies from one period to the next and for all indicators. Small differences between sums of subgroup aggregates and overall totals and averages may occur because of the approximations used. In addition, compilation errors and data reporting practices may cause discrepancies in theoretically identical aggregates such as world exports and world imports.

Five methods of aggregation are used in *World Development Indicators:*

- For group and world totals denoted in the tables by a *t*, missing data are imputed based on the relationship of the sum of available data to the total in the year of the previous estimate. The imputation process works forward and backward from 2005. Missing values in 2005 are imputed using one of several proxy variables for which complete data are available in that year. The imputed value is calculated so that it (or its proxy) bears the same relationship to the total of available data. Imputed values are usually not calculated if missing data account for more than a third of the total in the benchmark year. The variables used as proxies are GNI in U.S. dollars; total population; exports and imports of goods and services in U.S. dollars; and value added in agriculture, industry, manufacturing, and services in U.S. dollars.

- Aggregates marked by an *s* are sums of available data. Missing values are not imputed. Sums are not computed if more than a third of the observations in the series or a proxy for the series are missing in a given year.

- Aggregates of ratios are denoted by a *w* when calculated as weighted averages of the ratios (using the value of the denominator or, in some cases, another indicator as a weight) and denoted by a *u* when calculated as unweighted averages. The aggregate ratios are based on available data. Missing values are assumed to have the same average value as the available data. No aggregate is calculated if missing data account for more than a third of the value of weights in the benchmark year. In a few cases the aggregate ratio may be computed as the ratio of group totals after imputing values for missing data according to the above rules for computing totals.

- Aggregate growth rates are denoted by a *w* when calculated as a weighted average of growth rates. In a few cases growth rates may be computed from time series of group totals. Growth rates are not calculated if more than half the observations in a period are missing. For further discussion of methods of computing growth rates see below.

- Aggregates denoted by an *m* are medians of the values shown in the table. No value is shown if more than half the observations for countries with a population of more than 1 million are missing.

Exceptions to the rules may occur. Depending on the judgment of World Bank analysts, the aggregates may be based on as little as 50 percent of the available data. In other cases, where missing or excluded values are judged to be small or irrelevant, aggregates are based only on the data shown in the tables.

Growth rates

Growth rates are calculated as annual averages and represented as percentages. Except where noted, growth rates of values are computed from constant price series. Three principal methods are used to calculate growth rates: least squares, exponential endpoint, and geometric endpoint. Rates of change from one period to the next are calculated as proportional changes from the earlier period.

Least squares growth rate. Least squares growth rates are used wherever there is a sufficiently long time series to permit a reliable calculation. No growth rate is calculated if more than half the observations in a period are missing. The least squares growth rate, r, is estimated by fitting a linear regression trend line to the logarithmic annual values of the variable in the relevant period. The regression equation takes the form

$$\ln X_t = a + bt$$

which is the logarithmic transformation of the compound growth equation,

$$X_t = X_o (1 + r)^t.$$

In this equation X is the variable, t is time, and $a = \ln X_o$ and $b = \ln (1 + r)$ are parameters to be estimated. If b^* is the least squares estimate of b, then the average annual growth rate, r, is obtained as $[\exp(b^*) - 1]$ and is multiplied by 100 for expression as a percentage. The calculated growth rate is an average rate that is representative of the available observations over the entire period. It does not necessarily match the actual growth rate between any two periods.

Exponential growth rate. The growth rate between two points in time for certain demographic indicators, notably labor force and population, is calculated from the equation

$$r = \ln(p_n/p_0)/n$$

where p_n and p_0 are the last and first observations in the period, n is the number of years in the period, and ln is the natural logarithm operator. This growth rate is based on a model of continuous, exponential growth between two points in time. It does not take into account the intermediate values of the series. Nor does it correspond to the annual rate of change measured at a one-year interval, which is given by $(p_n - p_{n-1})/p_{n-1}$.

Geometric growth rate. The geometric growth rate is applicable to compound growth over discrete periods, such as the payment and reinvestment of interest or dividends. Although continuous growth, as modeled by the exponential growth rate, may be more realistic, most economic phenomena are measured only at intervals, in which case the compound growth model is appropriate. The average growth rate over n periods is calculated as

$$r = \exp[\ln(p_n/p_0)/n] - 1.$$

World Bank Atlas method

In calculating GNI and GNI per capita in U.S. dollars for certain operational and analytical purposes, the World Bank uses the *Atlas* conversion factor instead of simple exchange rates. The purpose of the *Atlas* conversion factor is to reduce the impact of exchange rate fluctuations in the cross-country comparison of national incomes.

The *Atlas* conversion factor for any year is the average of a country's exchange rate (or alternative conversion factor) for that year and its exchange rates for the two preceding years, adjusted for the difference between the rate of inflation in the country and the rate of international inflation.

The objective of the adjustment is to reduce any changes to the exchange rate caused by inflation.

 Economy | States and markets | Global links | Back

Statistical methods

A country's inflation rate between year t and year $t-n$ (r_{t-n}) is measured by the change in its GDP deflator (p_t):

$$r_{t-n} = \frac{p_t}{p_{t-n}}$$

International inflation between year t and year $t-n$ ($r_{t-n}^{SDR\$}$) is measured using the change in a deflator based on the International Monetary Fund's unit of account, special drawing rights (or SDRs). Known as the "SDR deflator," it is a weighted average of the GDP deflators (in SDR terms) of Japan, the United Kingdom, the United States, and the euro area, converted to U.S. dollar terms; weights are the amount of each currency in one SDR unit.

$$r_{t-n}^{SDR\$} = \frac{p_t^{SDR\$}}{p_{t-n}^{SDR\$}}$$

The *Atlas* conversion factor (local currency to the U.S. dollar) for year t (e_t^{atlas}) is given by:

$$e_t^{atlas} = \frac{1}{3}\left[e_t + e_{t-1}\left(\frac{r_{t-1}}{r_{t-1}^{SDR\$}}\right) + e_{t-2}\left(\frac{r_{t-2}}{r_{t-2}^{SDR\$}}\right)\right]$$

where e_t is the average annual exchange rate (local currency to the U.S. dollar) for year t.

GNI in U.S. dollars (*Atlas* method) for year t ($Y_t^{atlas\$}$) is calculated by applying the *Atlas* conversion factor to a country's GNI in current prices (local currency) (Y_t) as follows:

$$Y_t^{atlas\$} = Y_t / e_t^{atlas}$$

The resulting *Atlas* GNI in U.S. dollars can then be divided by a country's midyear population to yield its GNI per capita (*Atlas* method).

Alternative conversion factors

The World Bank systematically assesses the appropriateness of official exchange rates as conversion factors. An alternative conversion factor is used when the official exchange rate is deemed to be unreliable or unrepresentative of the rate effectively applied to domestic transactions of foreign currencies and traded products. This applies to only a small number of countries, as shown in *Primary data documentation*. Alternative conversion factors are used in the *Atlas* methodology and elsewhere in *World Development Indicators* as single-year conversion factors.

 Front  User guide World view People Environment

Credits

1. World view

Section 1 was prepared by a team led by Neil Fantom. Neil Fantom wrote the introduction, and the Millennium Development Goal spreads were produced by Mahyar Eshragh-Tabary, Juan Feng, Masako Hiraga, Wendy Huang, Buyant Erdene Khaltarkhuu, Hiroko Maeda, Johan Mistiaen, Malvina Pollock, and Emi Suzuki. Tables were produced by Mahyar Eshragh-Tabary, Juan Feng, Masako Hiraga, Wendy Huang, Bala Bhaskar Naidu Kalimili, Haruna Kashiwase, Buyant Erdene Khaltarkhuu, Hiroko Maeda, and Emi Suzuki. Signe Zeikate of the World Bank's Economic Policy and Debt Department provided the estimates of debt relief for the Heavily Indebted Poor Countries Debt Initiative and Multilateral Debt Relief Initiative.

2. People

Section 2 was prepared by Juan Feng, Masako Hiraga, Haruna Kashiwase, Hiroko Maeda, and Emi Suzuki in partnership with the World Bank's Human Development Network and the Development Research Group in the Development Economics Vice Presidency. Emi Suzuki prepared the demographic estimates and projections. The poverty estimates at national poverty lines were compiled by the Global Poverty Working Group, a team of poverty experts from the Poverty Reduction and Equality Network, the Development Research Group, and the Development Data Group. Shaohua Chen and Prem Sangraula of the World Bank's Development Research Group prepared the poverty estimates at international poverty lines. Lorenzo Guarcello and Furio Rosati of the Understanding Children's Work project prepared the data on children at work. Other contributions were provided by Samuel Mills (health); Salwa Haidar, Maddalena Honorati, Theodoor Sparreboom, and Alan Wittrup of the International Labour Organization (labor force); Amélie Gagnon, Friedrich Huebler, and Weixin Lu of the United Nations Educational, Scientific and Cultural Organization Institute for Statistics (education and literacy); Chandika Indikadahena (health expenditure), Monika Bloessner, Elaine Borghi, and Mercedes de Onis (malnutrition and overweight), Teena Kunjumen (health workers), Jessica Ho (hospital beds), Rifat Hossain (water and sanitation), Luz Maria de Regil (anemia), Hazim Timimi (tuberculosis), Colin Mathers and Wahyu Mahanani (cause of death), and Lori Marie Newman (syphilis), all of the World Health Organization; Leonor Guariguata of the International Diabetes Federation (diabetes); Mary Mahy of the Joint United Nations Programme on HIV/AIDS (HIV/AIDS); and Colleen Murray (health) and Rolf Luyendijk (water and sanitation) of the United Nations Children's Fund.

3. Environment

Section 3 was prepared by Mahyar Eshragh-Tabary in partnership with the Agriculture and Environmental Services Department of the Sustainable Development Network Vice Presidency of the World Bank. Mahyar Eshragh-Tabary wrote the introduction and the highlights stories with invaluable comments and editorial help from Tariq Khokhar. Sonu Jain helped prepare the highlight story on wealth accounting. Esther G. Naikal and Chris Sall prepared the data on particulate matter concentration and natural resources rents. Ramgopal Erabelly provided technical assistance in calculating the population data for largest city and urban agglomerations. Neil Fantom and William Prince provided instrumental comments, suggestions, and support at all stages of production. Other contributors include Sharon Burghgraeve and Karen Tréanto of the International Energy Agency, Gerhard Metchies and Armin Wagner of German International Cooperation, Craig Hilton-Taylor and Caroline Pollock of the International Union for Conservation of Nature, and Cristian Gonzalez of the International Road Federation. The team is grateful to the United Nations Food and Agriculture Organization, the United Nations Environment Programme and World Conservation Monitoring Centre, the International Union for Conservation of Nature, the U.S. Department of Energy's Carbon Dioxide Information Analysis Center, the International Energy Agency, and the U.S. Agency for International Development's Office of Foreign Disaster Assistance for access to their online databases. The World Bank's Agriculture and Environmental Services Department devoted generous staff resources.

Credits

4. Economy

Section 4 was prepared by Bala Bhaskar Naidu Kalimili in close collaboration with the Sustainable Development and Economic Data Team of the World Bank's Development Data Group and with suggestions from Liu Cui and William Prince. Bala Bhaskar Naidu Kalimili wrote the introduction with suggestions from Tariq Khokhar. The highlights section was prepared by Bala Bhaskar Naidu Kalimili and Maurice Nsabimana. The national accounts data for low- and middle-income economies were gathered by the World Bank's regional staff through the annual Unified Survey. Maja Bresslauer, Liu Cui, Federico Escaler, Mahyar Eshragh-Tabary, Bala Bhaskar Naidu Kalimili, Buyant Erdene Khaltarkhuu, and Maurice Nsabimana updated, estimated, and validated the databases for national accounts. Esther G. Naikal and Chris Sall prepared the data on adjusted savings and adjusted income. Azita Amjadi contributed data on trade from the World Integrated Trade Solution. The team is grateful to Eurostat, the International Monetary Fund, the Organisation for Economic Co-operation and Development, the United Nations Industrial Development Organization, and the World Trade Organization for access to their databases.

5. States and markets

Section 5 was prepared by Federico Escaler and Buyant Erdene Khaltarkhuu in partnership with the World Bank's Financial and Private Sector Development Network, Poverty Reduction and Economic Management Network, and Sustainable Development Network; the International Finance Corporation; and external partners. Buyant Erdene Khaltarkhuu wrote the introduction with input from Neil Fantom, Tariq Khokhar, and William Prince. Other contributors include Alexander Nicholas Jett (privatization and infrastructure projects); Leora Klapper and Frederic Meunier (business registration); Jorge Luis Rodriguez Meza, Valeria Perotti, and Joshua Wimpey (Enterprise Surveys); Frederic Meunier and Rita Ramalho (Doing Business); Alka Banerjee, Trisha Malinky, and Michael Orzano (Standard & Poor's global stock market indexes); Kenneth Anye (fragile situations); James Hackett of the International Institute for Strategic Studies (military personnel); Sam Perlo-Freeman of the Stockholm International Peace Research Institute (military expenditures and arms transfers); Therese Petterson (battle-related deaths); Cristian Gonzalez of the International Road Federation, Narjess Teyssier of the International Civil Aviation Organization, and Marc Juhel and Hélène Stephan (transport); Vincent Valentine of the United Nations Conference on Trade and Development (ports); Azita Amjadi (high-tech exports); Vanessa Grey, Esperanza Magpantay, Susan Teltscher, and Ivan Vallejo Vall of the International Telecommunication Union and Torbjörn Fredriksson, Scarlett Fondeur Gil, and Diana Korka of the United Nations Conference on Trade and Development (information and communication technology goods trade); Martin Schaaper of the United Nations Educational, Scientific and Cultural Organization Institute for Statistics (research and development, researchers, and technicians); and Ryan Lamb of the World Intellectual Property Organization (patents and trademarks).

6. Global links

Section 6 was prepared by Wendy Huang with substantial input from Evis Rucaj and Rubena Sukaj and in partnership with the Financial Data Team of the World Bank's Development Data Group, Development Research Group (trade), Development Prospects Group (commodity prices and remittances), International Trade Department (trade facilitation), and external partners. Evis Rucaj wrote the introduction. Azita Amjadi (trade and tariffs) and Rubena Sukaj (external debt and financial data) provided input on the data and tables. Other contributors include Frédéric Docquier (emigration rates); Flavine Creppy and Yumiko Mochizuki of the United Nations Conference on Trade and Development and Mondher Mimouni of the International Trade Centre (trade); Cristina Savescu (commodity prices); Jeff Reynolds and Joseph Siegel of DHL (freight costs); Yasmin Ahmad and Elena Bernaldo of the Organisation for Economic Co-operation and Development (aid); Ibrahim Levent and Maryna Taran (external debt); Tarek Abou Chabake of the Office of the UN High Commissioner for Refugees (refugees); and Teresa Ciller of the World Tourism

 Front | User guide | World view | People | Environment

Organization (tourism). Ramgopal Erabelly, Shelley Fu, and William Prince provided technical assistance.

Other parts of the book

Jeff Lecksell of the World Bank's Map Design Unit coordinated preparation of the maps on the inside covers. William Prince prepared *User guide* and the lists of online tables and indicators for each section and wrote *Statistical methods*, with input from Neil Fantom. Liu Cui and Federico Escaler prepared *Primary data documentation*. Leila Rafei prepared *Partners*.

Database management

William Prince coordinated management of the World Development Indicators database, with assistance from Liu Cui and Shelley Fu in the Data Administration and Quality Team. Operation of the database management system was made possible by Ramgopal Erabelly in the Data and Information Systems Team under the leadership of Soong Sup Lee.

Design, production, and editing

Azita Amjadi and Leila Rafei coordinated all stages of production with Communications Development Incorporated, which provided overall design direction, editing, and layout, led by Jack Harlow, Bruce Ross-Larson, and Christopher Trott. Elaine Wilson created the cover and graphics and typeset the book. Peter Grundy, of Peter Grundy Art & Design, and Diane Broadley, of Broadley Design, designed the report.

Administrative assistance, office technology, and systems development support

Elysee Kiti provided administrative assistance. Jean-Pierre Djomalieu, Gytis Kanchas, and Nacer Megherbi provided information technology support. Ugendran Machakkalai, Shanmugam Natarajan, Atsushi Shimo, and Malarvizhi Veerappan provided software support on the DataBank application.

Publishing and dissemination

The World Bank's Publishing and Knowledge Division, under the direction of Carlos Rossel, provided assistance throughout the production process. Denise Bergeron, Stephen McGroarty, Nora Ridolfi, Paola Scalabrin, and Janice Tuten coordinated printing, marketing, and distribution. Merrell Tuck-Primdahl of the Development Economics Vice President's Office managed the communications strategy.

World Development Indicators mobile applications

Software preparation and testing were managed by Shelley Fu with assistance from Prashant Chaudhari, Neil Fantom, Mohammed Omar Hadi, Soong Sup Lee, Parastoo Oloumi, William Prince, Virginia Romand, Jomo Tariku, and Malarvizhi Veerappan. Systems development was undertaken in the Data and Information Systems Team led by Soong Sup Lee. Liu Cui and William Prince provided data quality assurance.

Online access

Coordination of the presentation of the WDI online, through the Open Data website, the DataBank application, the table browser application, and the Application Programming Interface, was provided by Neil Fantom and Soong Sup Lee. Development and maintenance of the website were managed by a team led by Azita Amjadi and comprising George Gongadze, Timothy Herzog, Meri Jebirashvili, Jeffrey McCoy, Leila Rafei, and Jomo Tariku. Systems development was managed by a team led by Soong Sup Lee, with project management provided by Malarvizhi Veerappan. Design, programming, and testing were carried out by Ying Chi, Shelley Fu, Siddhesh Kaushik, Ugendran Machakkalai, Nacer Megherbi, Shanmugam Natarajan, Parastoo Oloumi, Manish Rathore, Ashish B. Shah, Atsushi Shimo, Maryna Taran, and Jomo Tariku. Liu Cui and William Prince coordinated production and provided data quality assurance. Multilingual translations of online content were provided by a team in the General Services Department.

Client feedback

The team is grateful to the many people who have taken the time to provide feedback and suggestions, which have helped improve this year's edition. Please contact us at data@worldbank.org.